STUDIES IN ECONOMICS
Edited by Sir Charles Carter

Policy Studies Institute

18
International Institutions in Trade and Finance

STUDIES IN ECONOMICS

International Institutions in Trade and Finance

A. I. MACBEAN
&
P. N. SNOWDEN

Department of Economics
University of Lancaster

London
UNWIN HYMAN
Boston   Sydney   Wellington

Published by the Academic Division of
Unwin Hyman Ltd
15/17 Broadwick Street, London W1V 1FP, UK

Unwin Hyman Inc.,
8 Winchester Place, Winchester, Mass. 01890, USA

Allen & Unwin (Australia) Ltd,
8 Napier Street, North Sydney, NSW 2060, Australia

Allen & Unwin (New Zealand) Ltd in association with the
Port Nicholson Press Ltd,
Compusales Building, 75 Ghuznee Street, Wellington 1, New Zealand

First published in 1981
Third impression 1990

British Library Cataloguing in Publication Data

MacBean, A. I.
    International institutions in trade and finance.
    – (Studies in economics; 18)
    1. Economic policy
    2. Economics – History – 20th century
    3. Financial institutions
    I. Title   II. Snowden, P. N.
    330.9181′2   HD82

    ISBN 0-04-382032-8
    ISBN 0-04-382033-6 Pbk

Typeset in 10 on 11 point Times and printed in Great Britain by
Billing & Sons Ltd, London & Worcester

To our long-suffering wives
Marion MacBean
and
Anne Snowden

CONTENTS

PREFACE

What we have set out to do in this book is to examine the main institutions which influence international economic relations as continually evolving instruments of economic policy. We have tried to be critical, but constructive, by examining various ways in which they could be reformed so as to do their tasks better. The rules of the GATT, the IMF and the EEC constrain governments in various ways. The whole system is under a constant tension because of the trade-off between the short-term interests of governments in solving domestic problems at the expense of their neighbours and the long-term interest of nations in general in the preservation of an open world trading system.

The balancing act between the interests of particular nations, groups within nations and the broader interests of the international community has become still more precarious in recent years. The diminution of US hegemony and the emergence of increasingly assertive independent centres of economic power in the form of the European Economic Community, the OPEC nations and the concerted voice of the developing nations through the Group of 77 and UNCTAD have changed the international scene since the days of Bretton Woods. In these circumstances the ability of institutions to respond to new requirements is a necessary condition for preventing short-term national self-interest from dictating the course of international intercourse.

In our experience many students on courses in international economics are deeply interested in these institutions. Some knowledge of their purposes, of the economic and political theories which have influenced them, and of the events to which they have responded can greatly enrich students' appreciation of the relevance of at least some academic theories to the world in which we live. We hope that this book can make a useful contribution to courses on international economics and politics as well as be of interest to anyone who wishes to gain some insight into the roles of the institutions whose acronyms are sprinkled liberally in the press.

We are grateful for comments and suggestions from Professor Sir Charles Carter on the whole of an earlier version of this book and from Professors Max Corden, Edward Mason, Robert Stern, Wolfgang Stolper and Harry Townsend on parts of it. None of them, however, can be held responsible for the views expressed here, nor for any errors which remain in the book. We are also glad to have this opportunity to express our thanks to Stephanie Arkwright, Adele Anscombe and Stephanie Brown for their patient and efficient typing of successive drafts.

xi

PREFACE

We acknowledge permission from the British–North American Research Association to reproduce passages from *A Positive Approach to the International Economic Order Part I: Trade and Structural Adjustment* by Alasdair MacBean.

Lancaster, 1980   A. I. MACBEAN
                                                              P. N. SNOWDEN

LIST OF ABBREVIATIONS

ACP	African, Caribbean and Pacific (Countries associated with the EEC under the Lomé Convention)
Benelux	Belgium, Netherlands, Luxembourg Economic Union
BIS	Bank for International Settlements (Basle)
CACM	Central American Common Market
CAP	Common Agricultural Policy of the EEC
CF	Common Fund
CFF	Compensatory Financing Facility of IMF
CMEA	The Council for Mutual Economic Assistance (also known in the West as Comecon)
DAC	Development Assistance Committee of OECD
DC	Developed Country
EAC	East African Community
ECLA	Economic Commission for Latin America
ECSC	European Coal and Steel Community
ECOSOC	Economic and Social Council of the UN
EDF	European Development Fund
EEC	European Economic Community
EFTA	European Free Trade Area
EIB	European Investment Bank of EEC
EMS	European Monetary System
FAO	Food and Agriculture Organisation of the UN
GAB	General Arrangements to Borrow
GATT	General Agreement on Tariffs and Trade
GNP	Gross National Product
G1O	Group of Ten (Industrialised Nations)
GSP	Generalised System of Preferences
IBEC	International Bank for Economic Co-operation
IBRD	International Bank for Reconstruction and Development (The World Bank)
ICA	International Commodity Agreement
IDA	International Development Association
IEA	International Energy Agency
IFC	International Finance Corporation
IMF	International Monetary Fund
ISA	International Sugar Agreement
ITA	International Tin Agreement
ITO	International Trade Organisation
IWA	International Wheat Agreement
LAFTA	Latin American Free Trade Area
LDC	Less Developed Country
NIEO	New International Economic Order

NOLDC	Non-oil Less Developed Countries
OECD	Organisation for Economic Co-operation and Development
OEEC	Organisation for European Economic Co-operation
OMA	Orderly Marketing Arrangement
OPEC	Organisation of Petroleum Exporting Countries
SDR	Special Drawing Rights (IMF)
STABEX	Stabilisation Fund for Exports from ACP countries to EEC
UN	United Nations
UNCTAD	United Nations Conference on Trade and Development
VER	Voluntary Export Restrictions

CHAPTER 1

Introduction: The Main Institutions

Attitudes to the development of new institutions in the field of international trade in the aftermath of the Second World War were characterised by anxiety to avoid the chaos of the interwar period and by the need to reconstruct Europe. These were reflected in the negotiations at Bretton Woods to set up: (1) an institution to provide short-term finance to relieve countries of the necessity to deflate or restrict imports unduly when faced by temporary balance of payments deficits; (2) an organisation to promote freer trade and to help regulate trade policies, and (3) a bank to provide long-term capital assistance to support policies of recovery and growth.

The outcome of the negotiations differed somewhat from the intentions of the more ambitious reformers in this field. The International Monetary Fund (IMF), to some extent the brainchild of Keynes, fell far short of his ideal. The negotiations for the creation of an International Trade Organisation (ITO) never reached fruition, though the interim General Agreement on Tariffs and Trade (GATT) in fact survived and partially fulfilled some of the objectives of the planned ITO. The International Bank for Reconstruction and Development (IBRD) (World Bank), the third institution negotiated at Bretton Woods, gave relatively little assistance to reconstruction, and seemed to many to be too conservative in its early years to do much for the less developed countries. Since then it has grown in stature and with its associate body the International Development Association has become a major factor in the field of international aid to the developing countries.

THE CREATION OF THE IMF

Thinking on the subject of reform of the international monetary system began quite early in the Second World War. By 1943 two fully fledged drafts of plans for the setting up of an international monetary institution had been devised. These were the proposals for an *International Clearing Union*, a British Government Official Paper which was mainly the work of Keynes, and a United States draft for an *International Stabilisation Fund*, usually known as the 'White Plan' after its main author Harry Dexter White, then Assistant Secretary of the US Treasury. The declared

1

objectives of both these plans were liberal and progressive. Their basic philosophies were similar. Both believed in the advantages of free trade in promoting efficiency but were at least as concerned with the need to maintain high levels of demand and employment within national economies. They aimed at the creation of a system of generally stable exchange rates with adjustment from disequilibrium in the balance of payments smoothed and facilitated by the provision of credit and avoidance of recourse to foreign exchange restrictions, discrimination in trade or deflation and domestic unemployment.

Trade in the interwar era had been bedevilled by the adoption of just such restrictive measures. Between 1931 and 1936 a series of competitive currency devaluations disrupted trade and stimulated wild flights of hot money which in turn forced still further fluctuations in exchange rates. The principal trading nations of the world abandoned free trade. Australia, the USA, Britain and Nazi Germany, one after another adopted tariffs and discrimination in trade as economic policy. While each initiating country or trading bloc could temporarily improve its balance of payments or domestic employment by such measures it could do so only at the expense of the exports and employment of other countries. Such policies were self-defeating in the long run. It was to combat the risks of the recurrence of similar international anarchy in the economic relationships of nations in the aftermath of the Second World War that these two sets of draft proposals were put forward. They formed the basis of discussions which took place at Bretton Woods in New Hampshire in 1943. Both stressed a multilateral approach to the solution of international monetary problems. Yet for a long time, according to Sir Roy Harrod, Keynes wavered between this and a belief that Britain and the other European countries would only be able to pursue policies of full employment and reconstruct their war-torn economies if they could maintain strict controls on trade and capital flows. This was a view shared by many British Treasury officials and members of the government.[1]

Britain's more acute concern with employment and reconstruction difficulties accounts for the differences in emphasis in the British and American proposals. The Americans laid more stress on the need for multilateralism and non-discrimination and rather less on safeguarding the freedom of action of national governments to maintain domestic employment in the face of balance of payments deficits. As a large creditor nation the Americans were inclined to stress the obligations of debtor countries to adjust their economies so as to eliminate deficits while the British proposals laid equal emphasis on the need for creditors to take action to reduce their balance of payments surpluses.

These differences in attitudes were reflected in the two sets of proposals, in the Bretton Woods discussions, in the subsequent debates in the legislatures, and in the different interpretations which the two nations placed on the terms of the agreement.

THE PROPOSALS FOR AN INTERNATIONAL CLEARING UNION

The full text of these proposals is available in the British government publication, *Proposals for an International Clearing Union* (HMG, 1943) and has been reprinted in full in chapter 2 of *International Monetary Reform* (Grubel, 1963). Summaries are available in works by Gardner and Harrod which are listed in the Bibliography.

THE OBJECTS OF THE PLAN

The Plan itself gives lucid expression to its objectives summarised in the list of requirements below[2]:

(1) We need an instrument of international currency having general acceptability between nations, so that blocked balances and bilateral clearings are unnecessary . . .

(2) We need an orderly and agreed method of determining the relative exchange values of national currency units, so that unilateral action and competitive exchange depreciations are prevented.

(3) We need a 'quantum' of international currency, which is neither determined in an unpredictable and irrelevant manner as, for example, by the technical progress of the gold industry, nor subject to large variations depending on the gold reserve policies of individual countries; but is governed by the actual current requirements of world commerce, and is also capable of deliberate expansion and contraction to offset deflationary and inflationary tendencies in effective world demand.

(4) We need a system possessed of an internal stabilising mechanism, by which pressure is exercised on any country whose balance of payments with the rest of the world is departing from equilibrium *in either direction*, so as to prevent movements which must create for its neighbours an equal but opposite want of balance.

(5) We need an agreed plan for starting off every country after the war with a stock of reserves appropriate to its importance in world commerce, so that without undue anxiety it can set its house in order during the transitional period to full peace-time conditions.

(6) We need a central institution, of a purely technical and non-political character, to aid and support other international institutions concerned with the planning and regulation of the world's economic life.

(7) More generally, we need a means of reassurance to a troubled

3

world, by which any country whose own affairs are conducted with due prudence is relieved of anxiety for causes which are not of its own making, concerning its ability to meet its international liabilities; and which will, therefore, make unnecessary those methods of restriction and discrimination which countries have adopted hitherto, not on their merits, but as measures of self-protection from disruptive outside forces.

To achieve these objectives Keynes proposed an International Clearing Union which would operate with a new currency for which he suggested the name 'bancor'. This would be pegged to gold (though not at an irrevocable rate) and accepted as equivalent to gold by all members for the purpose of settling international debts. Each member would be allocated an initial quota, whose value might be, say, 75 per cent of the sum of its exports and imports on the average of the three prewar years with provision for annual revision after the elapse of the transitional period. National central banks would hold accounts with the Clearing Union. Countries which had balance of payments surpluses would run up credits with the Union, those with deficits would go into debt. If all payments were made in 'bancor' the debits and credits would be exactly equal and the total of bancor would remain the same. Of course restraints would have to be placed on countries' use of bancor to prevent their exploiting the fund to support higher consumption and investment at the expense of creditor countries.

These checks were[3]:

(1)   A member state shall pay to the Reserve Fund of the Clearing Union a charge of 1 per cent per annum on the amount of its average balance in bancor, whether it is a credit or debit balance, in excess of a quarter of its quota, and a further charge of 1 per cent on its average balance, whether credit or debit, in excess of half its quota.

This was a slight inducement to maintain a level balance.

(2)   Any member was also required to obtain the permission of the Governing Board before increasing a debit balance by more than a quarter of its quota in a given year. If a debit were to be allowed to reach half the quota the Governing Board could permit or require certain actions from the member country, e.g. devaluation of the currency, deposit of suitable collateral (gold, foreign or domestic currency, or government bonds), controls on capital movements, surrender of gold or other liquid reserves, appropriate internal measures to restore equilibrium in its international balance. If a member's debit balance exceeded three quarters of its quota on the average of at least a year it could be asked by the Board to take

measures to improve its position and if it failed to improve its position in two years the Board could declare that member in default. The member could then no longer draw on its account except with the permission of the Board.

The novel feature in all this was, of course, not the checks on the debtor but the interest penalty imposed on the creditor member. It was an attempt to induce nations with balance-of-payments surpluses to take action to restore equilibrium. Under the traditional gold standard system when countries followed 'the rules of the game' the burden of adjustment was shared. Surplus countries were forced to inflate at the same time as deficit countries had to deflate their economies. The British proposal aimed to restore this responsibility of surplus countries to assist the restoration of international equilibrium. Clause (9) of the Proposals took this even further[4]:

A member state whose credit balance has exceeded a half of its quota on the average of at least a year shall discuss with the governing board (but shall retain the ultimate decision in its own hands) what measures would be appropriate to restore the equilibrium of its international balances, including –

(1) Measures for the expansion of domestic credit and domestic demand.
(2) The appreciation of its local currency in terms of bancor, or, alternatively, the encouragement of an increase in money rates of earnings.
(3) The reduction of tariffs and other discouragements against imports.
(4) International development loans.

It is also clear that the British thought that the Clearing Union should have sufficient resources to assist the adjustment of the European economies from their war effort back to the operation of normal peacetime economies. 'The facilities offered will be of particular importance in the transitional period after the war, as soon as the initial shortages of supply have been overcome' (para. 15).

The scheme was also intended to enable expansion or contraction of international liquidity so as to control the aggregate of world purchasing power should there be worldwide deflationary or inflationary pressure. This could be effected through empowering the governing board to expand or reduce the quotas of all members. Moreover as trade expanded it was envisaged that quotas would be revised upwards fairly automatically. Other ideas mentioned, but not developed, were for accounts to be established in the Union on behalf of relief agencies and for a Commodity Control Authority which was to assist stabilisation policies.

THE AMERICAN PROPOSALS

The scheme put forward by the Americans was much less radical than the Keynes Plan. Their International Stabilisation Fund was to be composed of gold and currencies to be deposited by members in amounts fixed according to the size of their quotas. Members who ran into deficit on their balance of payments would draw upon their quotas with the Fund within prescribed limits. The quotas were to be fixed on a mixture of criteria including the size of the member's foreign trade, gold reserves and national income. One effect of this was to give America a much larger quota than Britain whereas the Keynes Plan criterion would have meant approximately equal quotas for Britain and the USA.

On the basis of the American plan the financial resources of the Fund would have been $5 billion. The British proposal of a Clearing Union would have given a total credit creating capacity of about $25 billion. The American plan was designed to give merely 'an iron ration to tide over temporary emergencies of one kind or another'.[5] While it was Keynes' hope that the British scheme would provide resources large enough to generate in governments sufficient confidence to both relax trade controls and pursue policies of full employment.

THE OUTCOME

Ultimately, the International Monetary Fund which emerged from the negotiations was based almost entirely on the American proposals. However, its resources were a little larger, $8.8 billion, and it incorporated a provision which appeared to meet the British and European countries' desire to have some incentive for creditor countries to adjust. This was the 'scarce currency clause'. The Americans agreed to the insertion of a clause which enabled member countries to impose discriminatory exchange controls against a country whose currency had been declared scarce in the Fund. Sir Roy Harrod relates how he first read the vital paragraph huddled in the corner of a wartime train packed with sprawling, sleeping soldiery. He was so excited by this American proposal that he felt like arousing the soldiers to exclaim to them[6]:

> Here, boys, is great news. Here is an offer, which can make things very different for you when the war is over; your lords and masters

6

do not seem to have realised it yet; but they soon will; see for yourselves this paragraph 7; read what it says. I know that you set great store by the Beveridge scheme; but that is only written on a bit of paper; it will all fall to pieces, if this country has a bad slump and trade difficulties. Here is the real thing, because it will save us from a slump and make all these Beveridge plans lastingly possible.

The later history of the IMF probably supports Keynes' original scepticism about the 'scarce currency clause' rather more than Harrod's enthusiasm. Up to the present the clause has never been invoked, though it could be argued that the threat of it has influenced the behaviour of persistent creditor nations.

THE INTERNATIONAL MONETARY FUND

The main characteristics of the monetary system which emerged from Bretton Woods were: relative stability of exchange rates with provision for orderly adjustment when necessary; some increase in international liquidity through the $8.8 billion of quotas with the IMF, the establishment of a body in which discussions on international trade and finance could be held. Members of the IMF were required to satisfy the Fund of their exchange rate parities and to keep their actual values within 1 per cent on either side of the declared parity. Members were permitted to alter their parities only if they were in 'fundamental disequilibrium' – a concept that was deliberately left undefined – and the Fund's consent had been obtained. If the proposed change together with any previous changes were less than 10 per cent of their original par value they did not require the Fund's permission. If the change did not exceed an additional 10 per cent of the initial par value the IMF could either concur or object, but must declare its attitude within seventy-two hours at the request of the member. If the change were larger then the IMF could either concur or object but could insist on a longer period in which to declare its attitude (IMF Charter, Article IV, Sec. 5, C).

The IMF resources are available to members for use to meet short-term balance-of-payments deficits. These resources resulted from the quotas assigned to members. Members were allotted quotas with the Fund on criteria mainly related to fluctuations in their trade and payments, their current holdings of gold and the size of their national income but political bargaining power also played some part. To become a member and obtain access to the Fund's facilities a country had to subscribe in gold as a minimum the smaller of either (1) 25 per cent of its quota or (2) 10 per cent of its net official holdings of gold and US dollars. The balance had to be paid in its own currency. Voting power in the governing body of the IMF is based on the size of the quota.

The problem of the persistent creditor was recognised in the agreement. The 'scarce currency clause' allowed the Fund to declare a particular surplus country's currency to be a scarce currency. This would permit other countries to discriminate against imports from that country. However, before implementing this the IMF could make use of provisions which entitled it to either buy with gold or borrow the currency from the creditor country so preventing the currency from becoming scarce in the Fund. Clearly the pressures to make creditors adjust were not very strong. The proposals of both the Keynes and the White Plans to do this had been largely dropped from the final scheme.

These represent the main features of the IMF as it emerged from Bretton Woods, and it is clear that it was much closer to the American than to the British proposals. It had none of the features of an international central bank able to create money at the stroke of a pen which Keynes had wanted. A good deal of the criticism of the IMF and the suggestions for its reform which have been put forward in the 1960s represent a revival of this basic conflict between the radical and expansionist proposals put forward by Keynes and the much more conservative plan drafted by the US Treasury. We shall return to the subject of the operations of the IMF and of the proposals for the reform of the Fund in Chapter 3.

THE WORLD BANK

The other Bretton Woods institution was the International Bank for Reconstruction and Development (IBRD) commonly known as the World Bank. This was an American idea and one for which the British showed little enthusiasm until a few weeks before the conclusion of the negotiations. Britain did not expect to gain much from it and did not view with much favour the necessity to contribute to its funds. Most of the efforts of the British negotiators were devoted to keeping down the size of the contributions to be made by members and stressing its role as a mechanism for raising private capital for investment through Bank loans.

As its name implied the IBRD was partly intended to assist the reconstruction of Europe by means of long-term loans. In the event the creation of Marshall Aid made this aspect largely redundant. Few countries would wish to borrow at the rates of interest charged by the Bank when the USA was making funds directly available on much more advantageous terms. Consequently the Bank sought and found another role — that of promoting the economic development of the poor countries.

In this, together with its affiliates the International Finance Corporation (IFC) and the International Development Association (IDA), the Bank has proved an extremely important institution, one that has moved from strength to strength. Now under the leadership of the dynamic McNamara the Bank bids fair to become the spearhead for the promotion of aid to the developing countries. Already through the consortia arrangements the Bank has done much to increase the quantity and effectiveness of bilateral aid as well as to channel resources directly into Less Developed Countries (LDCs). We shall discuss in Chapter 10 the aims and policies of the Bank Group and how far these have been successful in promoting economic and social development.

THE INTERNATIONAL TRADE ORGANISATION (ITO) AND THE GENERAL AGREEMENT ON TARIFFS AND TRADE (GATT)

At the same time as the discussions were going forward on the international monetary issues, proposals for an organisation to look after matters of trade and commercial policy were being considered by the United Nations. There was a good deal of agreement on the need to reduce barriers to trade but it was not until 1946 that the UN Economic and Social Council (UNECOSOC) appointed a Preparatory Committee of nineteen countries to draft a convention for the consideration of an 'International Conference on Trade and Employment'. Discussions in London and Geneva from October 1946 to August 1947 produced the charter for an International Trade Organisation. But throughout all the discussions there was a basic conflict between those who cared most for free trade and those who were most concerned with the need to preserve national discretion in relation to policies to maintain full employment. The ITO charter which emerged at the Havana Conference was inevitably a compromise. The charter was never ratified. As one commentator put it, 'There was head-on collision between those who were wedded to the idea of a free multilateral trading system on the one hand, and those who placed the whole emphasis on full employment policies on a national basis.'[7]

However, the collapse of the ITO did not spell the end of all attempts at multilateral commercial negotiations. Fortunately en route to ITO the Americans had put together in 1946 a draft charter for a general agreement on tariffs and trade and proposed that the provisional rules intended for ITO be incorporated in this. A number of nations signed it and so initiated GATT. Intended only as a stopgap, it had no formal organisation and no elaborate secretariat. As Gardner says, 'The

9

GATT was a slender reed on which to base progress towards a multi-lateral regime . . . Its signatories were bound to give effect to most of its trade rules only to the extent not inconsistent with their existing legislation. GATT was permeated by an atmosphere of impermanence.'[8] But in the event it has shown extraordinary powers of survival. *De facto*, GATT became an ITO. Now about ninety-one countries are members or associates. Any country can apply for membership and benefit, through the most favoured nation clause, from all tariff concessions which have been made available to the existing members. Newcomers are, however, expected to enter into tariff negotiations and to make concessions to the contracting parties in return for these privileges. In effect they have to pay 'an entrance fee'.

THE GATT PRINCIPLES

The two outstanding features of GATT lie in the principle of non-discrimination and the principle of reciprocity. The former is embodied in the first clause of the Agreement which includes the statement that:

> Any advantage, favour, privilege or immunity granted by any contracting party to any product originating in or destined for any other country shall be accorded immediately and unconditionally to the like product originating in or destined for the territories of all other contracting parties.

Reciprocity is mentioned in the preamble which also sets out a list of all the desirable objectives such as full employment, raising standards of living and developing the full use of the resources of the world which tend to characterise preambles to all international institutions however diverse their functions. In practice the main activity within GATT has been the pursuit of freer trade by negotiated reciprocal reductions in tariffs between the members on the basis of the most favoured nation treatment principle. All the contracting parties (members and associate members of GATT) undertake to negotiate tariff reductions with each other and to extend to all other contracting parties any reductions made in favour of any participating country. If, for example, Japan were to negotiate with the USA a reduction in the US tariff on Japanese exports of electronic equipment to the USA in return for reducing the Japanese tariff on imports of trucks from the USA both countries would have to reduce their tariffs to the same extent on such imports from all contracting parties.

The contracting parties also agreed not to extend new preferences though preferential agreements which existed before the formation of GATT could be continued, for example, British Commonwealth preferences and similar arrangements between France, Belgium, the Netherlands and their respective dependent territories as well as the special arrangements which existed between the USA, Puerto Rico and the Philippines. The margin between these preferences and other tariffs could not be increased beyond that obtaining on 10 April 1947 (Article I.4).

The one major exception to the operation of the general principle of non-discrimination permitted by the GATT rules was the possibility of creating Customs Unions or Free Trade Areas. These were permitted on the grounds that they would in general increase freedom of trade, but certain provisions were stated in the General Agreement (Article XXIV):

(1) The duties and controls imposed by the members of the Customs Union or Free Trade Area upon non-members should be no higher or more restrictive than prior to the institution of the CU, FTA or interim agreement;

(2) any interim agreement must include a plan and schedule for the formation of the CU or FTA within a reasonable time limit;

(3) duties and controls must be eliminated with respect to substantially all the trade between the constituent territories.

But even if proposals for a CU or FTA do not strictly comply with these requirements the contracting parties may, nevertheless, by a two-thirds majority approve such proposals. Both the European Economic Community and the European Free Trade Association did in fact require such special waiver of conditions.

Balance-of-payments difficulties represent another case where contracting parties are permitted to breach the rules and to impose restrictions on imports. Such restrictions should however be temporary and should avoid inflicting unnecessary damage to the commercial or economic interests of any other GATT member (Article XII).

From its inception to date GATT has had a great deal of success in reducing the barriers to world trade in manufactured goods. Three major failures have been in the field of agricultural protection, in non-tariff barriers and in the special trade interests of the developing countries in both temperate zone agricultural products and in labour-intensive manufactures. Whether these failures are inherent in the nature of GATT or whether they are due to the short-sightedness and intransigence of the rich industrial countries is left for consideration in Chapter 4 where we attempt to evaluate GATT's role in promoting trade and welfare. Whatever the factors at work these failures have been major causes of the creation of another institution in the field of trade which in many ways appears to duplicate the activities of GATT. This is the United Nations Conference on Trade and Development (UNCTAD).

11

GATT, THE DEVELOPING COUNTRIES AND UNCTAD

In fact GATT as originally constructed was not unmindful of the special needs of the less developed countries. In particular it recognised the infant industry argument and balance of payments problems of developing countries as justifying special escape clauses in their favour. Countries whose economies are in the 'early stages of development' can be allowed to 'enjoy additional facilities to enable them (a) to maintain sufficient flexibility in their tariff structure to be able to grant the tariff protection required for the establishment of a particular industry, and (b) to apply quantitative restrictions for balance of payments purposes in a manner which takes full account of the continued high level of demand for imports likely to be generated by their programmes of economic development' (Article XVIII). They are permitted to give special government assistance to infant industries. Article XVIII of the GATT does seem to give a wide measure of discretion to developing countries in adapting their commercial policies to their specific development objectives.

Nevertheless GATT was attacked by the representatives of the less developed countries for failure to take sufficient account of their needs despite the fact that the developing countries have a clear majority of the contracting parties. The first UNCTAD met in Geneva in 1964 as an alternative forum for the discussion of the trade and aid problems of the developing countries. It failed in its principal objective of establishing a new international order to promote the trade interests of the developing countries, but it did succeed in rousing the rich countries to an awareness of their grievances.

The concrete results of the Geneva Conference were small:

(1) an agreement to hold periodical conferences to meet every three years open to all UN members and the specialised institutions;
(2) the creation of a Trade and Development Board as the permanent executive organ of the UNCTAD;
(3) the setting up of a Secretariat with Dr Raul Prebisch, the main organiser of the first UNCTAD, as its first head.

The Board held its first meeting in 1965.

The three institutions set up immediately after the war (IMF, GATT, IBRD) reflected concern with the major problems of the interwar era: unemployment at home and beggar my neighbour protectionism in international economic relations. They were designed to remove or reduce the influence of the factors which had produced these policy responses. The new institution, UNCTAD, contained in its title the new issue – concern with the lot of the Third World and concern with the problem of economic development. Its successes and failures to date are considered in Chapter 5.

INTERNATIONAL COMMODITY AGREEMENTS

One of the intentions for the abortive ITO was that it should be concerned with the organisation of multilateral agreements between exporting and importing countries in endeavours to moderate instability in trade in primary commodities. Certain general principles were laid down in the charter of the ITO to guide negotiators in setting up such international commodity agreements (ICAs). Their principles included: adequate representation of consumer as well as producer interests; full publicity for the terms of agreements; that 'control agreements', that is, imposition of quotas on production or trade, could only be introduced in the event of large surpluses, unemployment or inadequate employment opportunities; where a control agreement is set up there must be adequate supplies and generally increasing use was to be made of the most efficient producers and no serious disturbance should be caused to the economic and social organisation of any country.

In the event very few ICAs have been successfully concluded. The major ones, which have operated between 1947 and the present, are the International Wheat Agreement, the International Tin Agreement, the International Sugar Agreement and the International Coffee Agreement. There have also been international agreements in cocoa and olive oil but they have not intervened in international trade or on prices. The four main ICAs have aimed at reducing price fluctuations, supporting commodity prices above free market levels and ensuring supplies at reasonable prices. The techniques adopted have included impositions of quotas, multilateral contracts and operation of buffer stocks. The actual operations of commodity agreements and an evaluation of their relative success in attaining these objectives are discussed in Chapter 6.

ECONOMIC INTEGRATION

The other main institutional development of the postwar period has been the proliferation of customs unions and free trade areas. As noted above in the section dealing with GATT these represent an important exception to the GATT general principle of non-discrimination. The *raison d'être* of economic integration is discrimination. In the form of a customs union, discrimination is implemented by the abolition of all tariffs and controls on trade between the members while a common external tariff is established against the exports to the member nations from non-members. The European Economic Community (EEC) is the outstanding example of this arrangement, though its objectives of closer economic and political association have led it to adopt much more wide-ranging policies of freedom of movement of labour and capital and of harmonisation of taxation, monetary policies and social security arrangements, for example.

The Free Trade Area as exemplified by the European Free Trade Association (EFTA) is a much looser organisation. In it trade barriers have been dismantled over manufactures only. Agricultural trade remains as before. The individual tariffs of the members *vis à vis* non-members are also unaffected by EFTA. This gives rise to certain problems of intra-EFTA trade, requiring certificates of origin for goods into one member and re-exported to another member.

The historical origins of these major areas of economic integration lay mainly in the need to solve the problem of Franco-German relationships in the aftermath of two world wars, the need to assist the recovery of Western Europe and to restore its strength as a counterweight to the growing power of the Soviet bloc. EEC emerged as the last step in a series of institutional developments designed to achieve these aims. First, the Organisation for European Economic Co-operation (OEEC) was created in 1948 as an instrument for ensuring co-operation between the democracies of Western Europe in the European Recovery Programme. It supervised the use of foreign aid (mainly from the USA) and of national resources. It helped to co-ordinate economic policies, for example in exporting to non-members, and established criteria for the allocation of American aid under the Marshall Plan.

Another step was the formation of the European Coal and Steel Community. This was designed for political reasons to internationalise control over the Ruhr. In 1950 Mr R. Schuman, Foreign Minister of France, proposed that the coal and steel production of Germany and France should be placed under the control of a common authority that would include other European nations. It was a deliberate first step towards economic and political integration in Europe.

Over the same period negotiations had been going ahead for an economic union between the Netherlands, Belgium and Luxembourg. Indeed the first steps were taken as far back as 1943 when a monetary agreement was signed between the governments in exile. Various steps were taken in monetary arrangements, agricultural and industrial trade and in capital movements, culminating in 1957 in the Treaty of Economic Union which established the European Economic Community.

Out of the Benelux discussions came a memorandum in 1955 which formed the basis for the negotiations to create the EEC. This stressed the need for economic integration to precede political. The EEC Treaty signed in 1957 did not conflict in any way with the ECSC, Benelux or Euratom. The main objectives of the EEC (as stated in the Preamble to the Treaty of Rome) were:

> To establish the foundation of an ever closer union among the European peoples.
> To ensure the economic and social progress of their countries by common action in eliminating the barriers which divide Europe.
> To ensure their harmonious development by reducing the differences existing between the various regions and by mitigating the backwardness of the less forward.

Article 2 of the Treaty states that,

> It shall be the aim of the Community, by establishing a Common Market and progressively approximating the economic policies of the Member States, to promote throughout the Community a harmonious development of economic activities, a continuous and balanced expansion, an increased stability, an accelerated raising of the standard of living and closer relations between its Member States.

The original six founding members of the EEC were Belgium, France, Germany, Italy, Luxembourg and the Netherlands. Several European countries, for one reason or another, could not or preferred not to join EEC. Most of them supported the idea put forward by the UK for a wider European Free Trade Area embracing all EEC members and including EEC within it. This did not prove acceptable to the EEC countries so seven of the non-EEC countries decided to go ahead on their own, and set up the European Free Trade Association (EFTA). Subsequent developments include the entry of Britain, Ireland and Denmark into the EEC.

At the same time as OEEC was formed the Eastern European countries along with Russia formed a Council for Mutual Economic Assistance, COMECON – see Chapter 10.

The operation and the effects on trade and welfare of regional trade groupings will be further considered in Chapters 8 and 9.

NOTES: CHAPTER 1

1   R. F. Harrod, *The Life of John Maynard Keynes* (London: Macmillan, 1966), Ch. 13.
2   R. F. Harrod, op. cit. from the original *Proposals for an International Clearing Union*, Cmnd 6437 (London: HMSO, 1943), pp. 526–7.

3 Cmnd 6437, op. cit.
4 Ibid., Clause 9.
5 Robert Lekachman, *The Age of Keynes* (London: Allen Lane The Penguin Press, 1966), p. 157.
6 Harrod, op. cit., p. 545.
7 Eric Wyndham White, Address at Tufts University, Massachusetts, April 1949.
8 Richard N. Gardner, *Sterling Dollar Diplomacy*, 2nd edn (London: McGraw-Hill, 1969), pp. 379–80.

CHAPTER 2

Criteria for Evaluation of International Institutions in World Trade

To judge the value of existing institutions, to assess the effects of changes in them and to make recommendations for their improvement requires some guidelines or performance criteria. It is not enough to take the purposes declared by the founders and examine how far they have been achieved, for the basic aims may have been wrong from the outset or inconsistent with the achievement of other, perhaps more important aims; or with changing times and circumstances the original objectives may have become obsolete.

The existing institutions are the result of compromises between the political and economic objectives of their members. Some of their objectives are likely to be held in common, but often national objectives will conflict. The interests of poor nations in trade patterns and capital flows, in international monetary arrangements and in tariffs and controls on trade and capital and labour movements frequently differ and often conflict with the objectives of richer nations. The interests of countries with major agricultural exports frequently conflict with the more industrial nations. Given this state of affairs it is not surprising that international institutions' objectives, and even more so their behaviour, should reflect the relative political and economic strengths of the members rather than any abstract ideal of what would bring the greatest good to the greatest number. Nevertheless, while recognising these harsh realities it is worthwhile using some ideal standard against which the performance of the institutions may be measured as this may bring out inconsistencies and inefficiencies which a more *ad hoc* empiricism, examining each institution within its own framework and aims, might fail to detect.

If we accept the need for more general and objective criteria than the institutions' own aims what should these criteria be? What precisely should be the *raison d'être* of economic institutions in the field of international trade? What purposes should they fulfil? Should they seek to promote freer international commerce or more efficiently controlled trade, more flexible or more rigid exchange rates, more or fewer controls on the movement of capital, etc? Faced with a need for criteria

17

for judging economic policies the economist naturally turns to that branch of his subject which has made a special study of these matters – welfare economics.

Unhappily, the considerable volume of literature on welfare economics has not yielded much by way of a consensus on criteria for judging whether a given change will improve or worsen economic welfare. The main difficulty arises from the fact that most important changes do not benefit each and every member of the community. Invariably, some are better off, some worse off as a result of the change. Any judgement as to whether the new situation represents an improvement or worsening of welfare involves comparing the gains and the losses of two different sets of individuals. This runs up against the difficulty that one cannot assume that an extra unit of income, say an extra pound, represents the same utility or welfare to all individuals. There seems to be no objective calculus of the net gain or loss of economic welfare possible without that assumption.

Given this objection the nearest to a widely acceptable generalisation attainable would be that a given change represents an improvement in economic welfare if, as a result of it, some people are better off and none are made worse off. It would limit severely the number of policy changes for which there could be any valid, objective, value-judgement-free approval. But even this unambitious criterion is subject to the criticism that human satisfaction is probably influenced by relative as well as absolute standards. If one group in a community is made absolutely better off then another group may feel that their position has worsened even if the total value of the goods and services which they can afford has remained the same. The outcry raised by skilled workers whenever their differentials are eroded by wage increases for lower paid workers illustrates this aspect of human nature.

A brave attempt to extend the scope of an objective economics of welfare is the 'compensation principle' associated mainly with the names of Kaldor, Scitovsky and Hicks. This states that there is an unambiguous improvement in economic welfare if those who gain from the change could afford to compensate those in the community who lose from the change, and still be better off than they were before. Note that the principle does not insist upon the actual payment of the compensation, merely that the gains potentially could be redistributed in such a way that at least some people are better off and no one in the community is worse off. Another way of putting this is that one determines how much money would have to be paid to the losers from the change to make them feel just as well off as before, and then determine what sum of money could be taken away from the gainers without making them feel worse off than they were before the change. If the sum which could be taken away from the gainers exceeds the sum which would have to be given to the losers then the economic welfare of the community has increased.[1] The compensating sums are assumed to measure the gains and losses in welfare. The principle has a certain appeal as enabling economists to recommend some changes even when they know that some people will be made worse off by them. However, it does not really get round the difficulty of considering the effects of any economic change upon the distribution of income. The compensation criterion could be satisfied by a change which made the rich richer and the poor poorer and as such could hardly be expected to gain universal or even majority approval.

In the context of a nation equipped with an efficiently administered and highly progressive structure of taxes and transfers the distributional worries may be less important. The potential redistribution of gains may to a large extent become actual. Then in practice there may be some justification for advocating changes which increase output without devoting too much attention to how the gains from individual changes among a stream of them are distributed. Most cost-benefit analyses implicitly make this assumption. In the international context, however, any assumption that the distribution of the gains from changes will automatically be spread widely over the community would clearly be invalid. There are no arrangements for progressive taxation of the rich nations, and most of the poorer nations of the world have very inefficient systems of taxation which, even when they are apparently progressive in structure, usually fail to tax their richer citizens as heavily as do the rich nations. These facts of the international situation make it impossible to rely on the rough justice which may work within the richer nations, and force us into explicit recognition of the importance to world economic welfare of the way in which the world's output of goods and services is distributed between nations and individuals within nations.

If welfare economics cannot supply us with objective criteria for the evaluation of international economic institutions how can we proceed? At a minimum, welfare economics reminds applied economists that policy recommendations or normative statements on economic matters have implicit value premises. Even the most positive of economists, who seeks only to work out the implications of policies laid down by the government, has to some extent made the value judgement that the government's objectives are sufficiently acceptable to his moral code to permit his working for the government. Welfare economics has focused attention on the two main mechanisms by which an increase in static welfare may be brought about. These are reallocations of resource inputs so that the total output of goods and services may be increased in real terms, and redistribution of a given output so that consumables are switched from people whose loss of satisfaction will be less than the gain to those who receive them. Normally, it is assumed that this will be achieved by redistributing income from rich people to poor people. Most economists have followed Pigou in assuming that an extra pound yields more satisfaction to a poor man than to a rich man. The fact that most governments legislate for progressive systems of taxation and various forms of social security, which at least in intention should redistribute income from the better off to the poorer sections of their communities, suggests that the policy aim of reducing disparities in the distribution of income has wide support. This would indicate that we may judge international institutions' contribution to economic welfare in terms of their effect on, first, the *efficiency* with which the world's scarce resources are utilised to produce the output of goods and services available for consumption, and secondly, the manner in which this output is *distributed* among humanity.

Difficult enough as these two criteria of efficiency and distributional effects are to apply one cannot stop at these. There are other factors to be taken into account. Individuals and communities are normally concerned not merely with their own current standard of living but with the prospects for the future for themselves, for their children and to some extent for future generations. Policies which raise current standards of living by over-exploitation of natural resources or which damage the environment and hence the living standards of the future are commonly regarded as misguided. On the other hand, some governments have been criticised for placing undue burdens and suffering on present generations in order to raise savings and investment rates to promote faster rates of growth whose benefits can only be enjoyed by future generations. It is also possible that relative rates of progress, as between nations or groups, affect the welfare or happiness of society through the increase of social and political tensions. Indeed, at the present time the growing gap between the living standards of the rich nations and of the majority of the citizens of the Third World is regarded by some as a major cause of international tension and an important argument for a new international order.

Probably most commentators would agree that the factors listed above are the main points to be considered when evaluating the impact of international institutions on world economic welfare. However, it is more difficult to gain any consensus on the relative weights to be assigned to each aspect. Some would concentrate upon efficiency, regarding income redistribution as subsidiary or as something that can be postponed. Some would even regard greater income disparities within nations as acceptable on the grounds that powerful incentives to hard work and risk-taking are essential stimulants to increased productivity and growth. Others might well take the opposite view. It could be argued that within the rich nations of the West redistribution in favour of the poor, devotion of resources to the solution of certain social problems and the reduction of all forms of pollution and other harmful side effects of industrial society should take precedence over further increases in private consumption. It could also be argued that the poor nations should pay more attention to the huge income disparities contained within their borders and worry less about the disparities between their average per capita income and that of the USA or West European nations. It may be true that the conspicuous consumption of the local landowner or industrialist causes more grievance to the poor peasant or factory worker than the rather abstract information that the average American family has two cars, a refrigerator and TV.

Even if agreement could be reached on the proper economic targets there would be widespread disagreement on how they should be attained. Some would regard the proper concern of international institutions as stopping short of national boundaries. Nations are, after all, sovereign on all issues which have not been explicitly yielded to some supra-national authority. It could then be argued that internal income distribution was no business of international organisations. Others would take the view that this should be a matter of concern to the international community. If an international commodity agreement is advocated as a means of transferring resources from the rich to the poor it may be worth investigating to see that this is what will actually happen. If it is intended to raise the price of a commodity whose production is in the hands of a relatively few and extremely wealthy individuals in a poor country and is consumed as a staple item by a large part of the population in the industrial nations the transfer may be regressive in its effects on income distribution and this could well affect the support which democratic regimes would accord to such an agreement. Should the World Bank consider the impact of aid which it gives to development programmes upon the distribution of income within recipient countries? It could well be argued that it should, both because the supporters of aid are generally concerned about such matters and because the distributional effects of development programmes may affect the political stability and economic progress of the recipient nations. The tragic histories of Pakistan and Iran are awful reminders of the dangers which may flow from neglect of these interrelationships.

Even the limited objective of efficiency, interpreted as the attainment of the largest real value of output of goods and services with given resources, would attract diverse recommendations. These could range from advocacy of freely competitive market solutions with minimum state intervention to total state control with physical target planning over all major economic activity including international trade and capital flows.

The economists' search for widely applicable, objective criteria

21

shorn of interpersonal comparisons, and attempts to quantify utility and value judgements have largely been in vain.[2] Nevertheless, the practising economist has to make judgements about the effects of policies and institutions on economic welfare. What welfare economics should have taught us is the need to examine carefully our basic assumptions and value judgements. These should be clearly stated so that the reader can decide for himself whether judgements based upon such assumptions and values are acceptable to him. Where the economist uses assumptions which attract a wide measure of support he can state conclusions with a fair degree of confidence that they will (at least if his logic has been sound) be accepted as reasonable. Henceforth, in this book it will be assumed that a change which reduces income disparities *ceteris paribus* improves economic welfare. Clearly any change which increases the total social product of the world without sacrificing future incomes too much, causing harmful side effects or decreasing the income of people who are already relatively poor should also increase economic welfare. There is, however, the serious problem of how to identify policies which are most likely to accomplish this. Probably, for our purposes, the most important single issue here is whether general reductions in barriers to trade are likely to increase world product without resulting in worsening the distribution of income or damaging the growth prospects of the poorer nations. This is a highly relevant question just because important institutions such as the GATT, the IMF and the IBRD all seek freer multilateral trade. Similarly, the impact of customs unions and free trade areas may be to increase or decrease barriers to trade. In principle this boils down to the classic question of the respective merits of free trade and protection in promoting economic welfare.

WORLD ECONOMIC WELFARE: FREE TRADE AND PROTECTION

The case for free trade is based upon the allocative efficiency of the price mechanism and must abstract from the issue of income distribution, for example, by assuming that the effect of a movement towards free trade is random in its effects on income distribution, or that it has no effect, or that the compensation principle can be adopted and that it can be shown that the gainers potentially could compensate the losers.

Trade can affect: (1) the efficiency with which existing resources are used to produce output; (2) the allocation of final output among consumers; (3) the efficiency with which factors of production are used within a firm; (4) the rate of growth of output; (5) the distribution of income between and within nations. Since all of these influence world economic welfare, there is a case for examining how the reduction of trade barriers and progression towards freer multilateral trade would affect them all.

THE STATIC ALLOCATION EFFECTS OF TRADE

It is not difficult to establish that under the usual assumptions of perfect competition within each country free trade necessarily increases the potential economic welfare of all provided international price ratios differ from domestic pre-trade price ratios. For simplicity the argument is usually spelt out in terms of a two-commodity, two factors of production model. The resource endowment of the economy, that is, the quantities of the two factors, are assumed to be given. There are constant returns to scale in the production of each good and perfect competition in both commodity markets and factor markets. There are no external economies or diseconomies associated with the production of either good. On the basis of these assumptions a production possibility curve can be drawn showing all the possible combinations of the two goods, blankets and rice, which the economy is technically capable of producing when all of its two factors are fully employed. This is represented by pp' on Fig. 2.1. Increasing the output of rice by a small amount means giving up a certain amount of blankets. Indeed, the cost of an extra ton of rice can be measured in terms of the sacrificed opportunity of having some number of blankets. The slope of the production possibility curve at any point on it measures the domestic rate of transformation of rice into blankets, that is, how much the

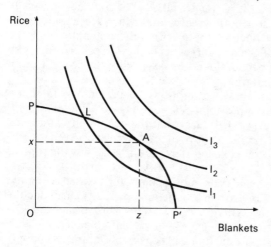

Figure 2.1   *Optimum resource allocation in a closed economy.*

23

community must give up of the one good to produce an extra unit of the other. The actual quantities of the two goods produced and the price at which they would exchange in an autarkic economy are determined by the interaction of these supply conditions with the community's demands.

The normal method of introducing demand into this analysis is through the medium of community indifference curves. This requires rather special assumptions which will be set out and discussed below. An individual's indifference curve is determined by his tastes, and by the relative amounts of satisfaction he obtains from the consumption of the two goods, rice and blankets. The curve represents different combinations of the two goods that would yield him the same amount of satisfaction so that he is indifferent to each collection of the two goods traced out by the indifference curve. Analogously with the production possibility curve, the slope of the indifference curve at any points shows the relevant marginal rate of substitution of one good for the other in consumption. The further away from the origin the curve is located the more of each good he can consume and the more satisfaction he is assumed to receive. It is possible to have a family of indifference curves showing different levels of satisfaction obtainable at various given income levels. However, to aggregate the consumption patterns of all the individuals to show a community indifference curve runs into the difficulty that individuals have different tastes and that increases in income may not be shared equally among them. An increase in income is then likely to alter not only the location but also the shape of a community indifference curve with the attendant risk that they may intersect. If this occurs it is no longer possible to state unequivocally that a particular increase in output represents an increase in welfare. To avoid this difficulty we have to employ either the assumption that the set of community indifference curves embodies a socially approved income distribution, or the Kaldor – Hicks – Scitovsky concept of an increase in potential welfare.

Making whichever of these assumptions we prefer we can superimpose on the production possibility curve in Figure 2.1 a set of community indifference curves. It is clear that the community attains its highest level of satisfaction at A the point of tangency between the PP' curve and the highest attainable indifference curve I_2. Any other point on the pp' frontier, say L, is on a lower indifference curve. At point A, the optimum production and consumption point for a closed economy, it can be seen that the slope of the production possibility curve and the slope of the indifference curve are the same. This means that the marginal rate of transformation (MRT) of rice into blankets and vice versa is the same in both production and consumption. In an economy with no international trade, A – the point at which the marginal rate of transformation in production is equal to the marginal rate of substitution (MRS) in consumption and is equal to the rate of exchange (or price) at which the two goods exchange – is the optimum, given all the restrictive assumptions made above. However, if rice can be exchanged for blankets at a different rate of exchange abroad then the possibility of gain from specialisation and trade emerges.

In Figure 2.2 AH represents the terms of exchange within the home country. If abroad the terms of exchange are such that blankets exchange for a great deal more rice than at home; for example, as indicated by the slope of CB. Then it will pay the home country to shift capital and labour from the production of rice to produce more blankets which can be exchanged for rice at the more favourable price.

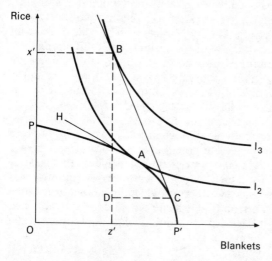

Figure 2.2   *Optimum resource allocation in an economy with international trade.*

In Figure 2.2 CD blankets can be exported in exchange for imports DB of rice. We are also assuming that the home country's entry into world trade does not influence the rest of the world's rate of exchange of rice for blankets. The home country now enjoys a higher national income and the community can attain the higher indifference curve I_3 (in Figure 2.2).

The slope of the line CB indicates the new equality of the MRT in production with the international rate of exchange, and with the new MRS in consumption. From the geometry it is easy to see that production or consumption at any point other than the one that satisfies these equalities will put the community on a lower indifference curve, indicating a lower level of satisfaction than the optimum.

It helps to have some intuitive understanding of these optimality rules. If the rate of exchange between blankets and rice is higher than the marginal rate of transformation of blankets into rice then the market is valuing blankets relative to rice higher than the costs of producing more blankets rather than rice. It will therefore lead to more potential welfare if resources are shifted out of rice into blankets giving up some of the lower valued rice in order to gain more of the higher valued blankets, up to the point where the increase in the marginal opportunity cost of producing extra blankets brings the MRT in production into equality with the rate of exchange of blankets for rice. The same argument applies to consumers' marginal rates of substitution.

From this it follows that any measure which prevents the achievement of these marginal equality rules will lower potential economic welfare. If a government imposes tariffs or quantitative controls on trade these will lead to a deviation of the prices paid by consumers from the prices paid in the rest of the world. Consumers will shift along their indifference curves until the MRS in consumption equals the domestic rate of exchange between the goods, but this will no longer equal the MRT through foreign trade nor the MRT in production in the rest of the world. Welfare will thus have been sacrificed.

This represents the basic case for free trade. Under the various assumptions stated free trade enables each participating country to achieve the highest possible level of potential economic welfare. Even if the assumption that individual countries cannot influence the terms of trade is relaxed it would still be true for the world as a community that free trade maximised potential welfare. Provided, then, that the income distribution that resulted from this was no worse than that obtained with barriers, free multilateral trade would yield the optimum static solution for the world community.

The main weakness of the case lies in the assumptions on which it is based. The internal economies of the nations of the world are not characterised by perfect competition. Oligopoly – competition among relatively few large firms – is the more characteristic market situation. Also external economies and diseconomies do exist.

The prices of factors of production are not always freely determined by supply and demand. Legislation, convention and relative trade union power influence wages and conditions of work. Full employment of all factors of production is not guaranteed by the existing system. Mobility of factors between occupations and regions is far from perfect. Prices are affected by taxes, subsidies and government controls. As a result of these distortions market prices do not reflect the true social marginal value of the community's output. The equalities of the social MRT in domestic production, the social MRS in consumption and the price ratio are not attainable in practice and so the efficiency optimum cannot be achieved through the free operation of the price mechanism. The impossibility of free trade achieving the ideal optimum clearly does not of itself justify autarky or even an increase in the general level of barriers to trade, but it does mean that even on grounds of efficiency, let alone equity, there may be a case for intervention.

Most of the economic arguments for protection stem from the existence of these domestic distortions. Protective measures in the form of tariffs or controls on imports, or subsidies to exports or import competing goods, are recommended as a means of correcting these distortions. The issue really boils down to whether intervention in a country's foreign trade is a better way of correcting the distortions than more direct measures of internal economic policy, for example, measures to control monopoly and cartels, subsidies or taxes on certain industries, readjustment of existing taxes and subsidies to reduce distortions, fiscal or monetary expansion to cure unemployment.

Based on our previous argument the optimum solution necessarily requires that for a given country the marginal social rate of transformation in the domestic economy ($MSRT_d$) should equal the marginal social rate of substitution in consumption in the domestic economy ($MSRS_d$) which should equal the marginal rate of transformation of the one good into the other through international exchange (MRTT), that is, the international price or terms of trade between the exportable and the importable good. In symbols

$$MSRT_d = MSRS_d = MRTT \qquad (1)$$

A domestic distortion in the presence of free trade means that the $MSRT_d$ will not be equal to the $MSRS_d$ but the $MSRS_d$ will equal the MRTT.[3]

$$MSRT_d \neq MSRS_d = MRTT \qquad (2)$$

If a tariff were now imposed domestic production of the importable good could be expanded so that $MSRT_d$ would equal the MRTT. But this would have been achieved at the expense of creating inequality between $MSRS_d$ and MRTT because the tariff raises the price of the importable good to domestic consumers.

$$MSRT_d = MRTT \neq MSRS_d \qquad (3)$$

There is no certainty that position (3) is superior to position (2). A superior policy would be a suitable subsidy and/or tax on domestic production of the two goods which could achieve position (1).

On the basis of a similar but much elaborated argument a leading international trade theorist, H. G. Johnson, concludes that[4]

> The only valid argument for protection as a means of maximising economic welfare is the optimum tariff argument; all other arguments for protection are in principle arguments for some form of government intervention in the domestic economy, and lead to the recommendation of protection only when supported both by practical considerations that render the appropriate form of intervention unfeasible, and empirical evidence that protection will in fact increase economic welfare.

This establishes a general case against measures which interfere with free multilateral trade while recognising that certain practical considerations may make protection justified as the only available method of correcting a domestic distortion. But the burden of proof is on the advocates of protection.

It should also be remembered that a frequent cause of domestic distortions is protection itself. Monopolies and cartels can be built up behind a tariff barrier secure in the knowledge that foreign competition is excluded or severely handicapped in their markets. Management may become oversecure and less enterprising as a result of protection and so use the resources at its disposal less than optimally.[5] From a world economic welfare viewpoint the optimum tariff argument cited by Johnson as a valid argument for protection is invalid. It cannot increase the potential economic welfare of the world by improving efficiency in production or consumption. Indeed it lowers efficiency by shifting production from a low cost to a higher cost producer. The only possible justification left for it is that of income distribution. If either country has the capacity to alter the terms of trade in its favour by means of a tariff, it may by a correct choice of tariff redistribute income from its trading partners to itself, but the total output of the world will be lower as a result. It is in any case likely to bring upon itself retaliation in the form of tariffs upon its own exports. While it is true, in principle, that even with retaliation the originator of the tariff war may achieve a higher level of economic welfare than with free trade it is rather unlikely in practice.[6] The major exception to this is where a group of countries such as the OPEC nations has a near monopoly of a vital resource. They can, of course, greatly improve their income by joining forces to limit exports and raise prices. The consensus of experts on minerals is that oil is almost unique in this possibility of successful cartelisation. From the viewpoint of the world community some other way of transferring income to a poor country while avoiding tariffs would clearly be more efficient, for example, by international aid or by reducing existing barriers to its exports.

28

THE INFANT INDUSTRY ARGUMENT FOR PROTECTION

One special and important case of domestic distortion, which has been widely used to justify protection and is accepted by GATT as an exception to its general rules, is the infant industry argument. Most of the developing countries and many of the rich countries have used this argument to justify tariffs or controls on imports. It is an argument based upon dynamic considerations. It recognises that a country may be able to alter its resource endowment and comparative cost structure by providing temporary protection to industries which are at present unable to compete with foreign firms. Eventually, with the aid of protection the industries may become competitive. The country would have changed a potential into an actual comparative advantage, the temporary protection could then be removed and world economic welfare would be increased (assuming distribution was no worse than before).

The free trader, however, may well suggest that *if* these future gains, properly discounted, were sufficient to recompense investors for current losses during the building up and training period so that returns on the investment would be higher than average, then surely private capitalists would undertake this task for themselves. After all, it is only worthwhile if the social rate of return on these industries is higher than the social rate of return on alternative investments. The answer lies in the possibility that the social rate of return may well be high enough to justify setting up the industry, but that the returns which private investors would gain for themselves may be inadequate to compensate them for the risks involved as they see them. A likely reason for such a divergence is that setting up the industry will generate external economies. The organisation of 'know-how' may benefit other industries in the economy. Skilled workers and managers trained for the infant industry may leave for other jobs. This benefits the economy as a whole, but private investors in the infant industry would be unable to capture for themselves any part of these benefits. Indeed, if trained workers and managers aid rival concerns to enter the industry and bid away the supra-normal profits which would be required in order to recoup their earlier losses the external benefits to the economy would act as a deterrent to private investors. This may be a realistic picture of some situations, but it does not necessarily justify either tariff protection or subsidies for setting up the industry. A superior policy would be to offer subsidies directly to labour and management of an appropriate kind so that these costs do not have to be borne by private investors.

Other reasons for a potentially successful infant venture failing to attract private enterprise investment may be unwillingness of local entrepreneurs to undertake the risk due to excessive pessimism or traditional attitudes or imperfections in capital markets. The appropriate policies here may be dissemination of better information and subsidies or guarantees on capital invested in the infant industry. Whatever the reasons for the domestic distortions which discriminate against the setting up of the infant industries, as Johnson argues,[7]

> The optimal policy entails some sort of subsidy to the infant industries rather than (tariff) protection ... The reason is that protection increases the social cost of the investment in the learning process of the infant industry by adding to the cost of a transitional subsidy the consumption cost of protection. The additional cost may be sufficient to reduce the social rate of return on the investment below the social rate of return on alternative investments.

To justify some form of assistance it has to be shown that the infant industry or industries satisfy certain criteria. The present value of the expected stream of direct and indirect benefits discounted at an appropriate rate must exceed the present value of the private and social costs involved in setting up and nurturing the infant. Passing this hurdle will almost always mean that in principle assistance should be in the form of a subsidy rather than a protective tariff. The tariff distorts consumption in a way that is avoided by subsidies which can maintain the equality of the domestic marginal rate of substitution with the foreign rate of transformation. Only if a subsidy is impractical for political or administrative reasons would a tariff be an acceptable policy. Taxes to raise the revenue for the subsidy can be designed to minimise any tax-induced distortions.

It can be seen that the efficiency case for relatively free international trade is fairly strong when the arguments for tariffs have been examined. In only one case can it be established logically that a tariff would be superior to either free trade or policies of domestic subsidies and taxes rather than a tariff or controls on trade. That one case rests on the theory of optimum tariffs, and applies only for a given country and not for the world as a whole. Even for that given country the assumptions that have to be fulfilled in order that it should actually be better off with an optimum tariff are so stringent as to make it totally unrealistic even if the optimum set of tariff rates for every import could be calculated.[8]

It should also be remembered that protection itself creates domestic distortions in both production and consumption. It stimulates monopoly and cartels, reducing domestic efficiency below potential, and it raises the prices of domestically purchased goods above the rates at which they can be obtained through trade.

TRADE AND THE DISTRIBUTION OF INCOME

Probably enough has been said here to demonstrate the likelihood that, in general, freer international trade is likely to lead to a higher level of efficiency in world production and consumption. There remains for consideration the question of income distribution. Would free international trade be likely to make for a more or less equitable distribution of income within and between nations? It would, of course, be sufficient for the free trader if its effects were neutral or perhaps even random, for if it led to higher world output and income distribution was no worse than before there would be a definite gain in economic welfare. However, it would be even better for that case if it could be shown that free trade was likely to reduce inequalities in income distribution.

C. P. Kindleberger, in his famous textbook *International Economics*, argues that there is at least as much likelihood that free trade will improve as that it will worsen the distribution of income. Indeed he suggests at least one *prima facie* reason for expecting the former result. Protection, he argues, is largely the outcome of political power within countries. In most countries the rich have more power than the poor; hence it is likely that removal of barriers to trade will transfer income from the rich to the poor.[9] However, he is the first to admit that this alone is insufficient to justify any general presumption that the distribution of income is likely to be superior with free trade than with tariffs.

There are two more general theories which bear upon this issue. One is the theory of factor price equalisation associated with Hecksher, Ohlin and Samuelson. The other is the theory of cumulative disequilibrium, mainly associated with Myrdal. The factor price equalisation theorem is logically derived from a theory of trade between nations which makes the basic determinant of their specialisation the relative factor endowments of nations. Thus if the ratio of capital to labour in country A is greater than in country B, A will export goods which utilise capital more intensively in their production and will import from B those goods which utilise relatively more labour. This will hold true as long as the taste pattern, and hence demand, is not such that the capital-intensive good's domestic price in A is raised or that the capital-intensive good becomes relatively as or more expensive than in B pre-trade. If tastes in both countries are identical, then the physical factor endowment will determine the relative prices of the final goods and the gains from trade will stem from the degree of difference in factor endowments. Before trade begins capital will be (relatively) the cheap factor in A while it will be relatively dearer in B. Opening up trade will, however, increase the demand for capital in A and reduce it in B. Interest rates will tend to rise in A and decline in B while wages will fall relatively in A

31

and rise in B. For our purpose it is not essential to pursue this argument to the point of demonstrating that free trade will lead to precisely equal factor returns in all nations. The tendency to do this is sufficient.[10] If the tendency exists, it implies that free international trade would tend to reduce the enormous differences which at present exist in the wage rates of comparable types of labour in one country as against another. The movement of goods would substitute for the movement of factors of production so that wages, rent and profit for factors of production in one country would tend towards equality with rates of return to similar factors in countries which trade freely with it.

It should be noted that the factor price equalisation argument is essentially static. Given the existing resource endowment of the countries and given all the other static, perfect competition and technology of production assumptions of the Hecksher-Ohlin-Samuelson model, factor price equalisation necessarily occurs when free trade is achieved. But if one country has higher savings rates so that it accumulates capital faster and also acquires technology faster than its trading partners its productivity and hence its per capita income may grow much faster than theirs.

A crucial assumption of the H-O-S model is that goods are produced with similar technical combinations of factor inputs in all countries. Clearly if in a labour-abundant country rice is produced by labour-intensive methods and exported to another country which is labour scarce and where foodgrains are produced by relatively capital-intensive methods trade will tend to cause factor price divergence instead of convergence. The empirical evidence on whether goods produced by relatively labour-intensive methods in one country will be produced by relatively labour-intensive methods in all countries is rather inconclusive.[11] The existence and importance of economies of scale, differences in the 'quality' of factors of production, particularly labour, and the existence of transport costs, all of which are assumed away by the theory, together with the likelihood of differences in the combinations of factor inputs through substitution in response to differences in factor prices, lead one to doubt the simple efficiency of free trade in substituting for factor mobility as a means of reducing disparities in per capita incomes between nations.

Other theories, associated mainly with Myrdal and Linder, argue that the operation of the price mechanism through free international trade would increase the existing gaps in standards of living between nations.

The effect of free trade, particularly when accompanied by relatively free movement of capital and technology, may result in the growth of inequality between rich and poor nations. The argument draws support from the historical experience of regional disparities in the rich countries. Sicily and the southern parts of Italy have lagged behind the growth of the industrial North. Despite government action to assist the South, capital and educated and skilled workers tend to flow from the backward South to the prosperous North. This adds to the advantages of the North by raising the productivity of labour there, increasing the size of markets and so allowing the achievement of economies of scale, and by creating an environment with considerable external economies which attracts more industry to move there. Conversely, it damages further the prospects for growth in the South.

Similar forces are seen at work in Northern Ireland, Wales, Scotland and the north of England *vis-à-vis* the South and Midlands. The Southern states of the USA appear also to have suffered from exposure through ties with the competition from the North. The argument gains support from recent partial theories of international specialisation. For example, it is argued that countries which export manufactures normally do so in industries for which they have a large internal market. This enables them to acquire the technology and economies of scale needed to lower production costs and enables them to compete effectively abroad. If so it bodes ill for newcomers to manufacturing in the Third World. Because their per capita incomes are low they do not possess/provide large domestic markets for modern manufacturers. Consequently they cannot achieve the volumes of production needed to lower costs sufficiently to break into export markets in any but the most unsophisticated goods.

Another interesting hypothesis suggests a technological cycle in the pattern of trade. [12] A country like the USA, because of its huge research and development capacity, pioneers new processes and products. It exports these to the rest of the world. There, after a period, the technology takes root, the goods are produced locally and then sometimes exported back at a cheaper price to the USA because of lower labour costs. By then the USA has moved on to other exports embodying still newer fruits of research and development. Always the USA leads and so reaps the rewards of the entrepreneur – the higher initial profits which reflect the short-term monopoly position and the returns to research and development. Not only this, the production of the goods abroad in itself brings substantial returns to the USA in the shape of royalties and/or repatriated profits from subsidiaries and joint ventures. The arguments of these modern partial theories of international trade lead to the conclusion that the rich countries possess enormous absolute advantages in the production of manufactured goods. These advantages are so great that the poor countries have little hope of establishing manufacturing industries in the face of foreign competition and practically none of breaking into export markets. If the establishment of manufacturing is a necessary step to the attainment of improving

33

standards of living the only way this can be achieved in most of the developing world is through deliberate intervention with the normal working of free markets. But this conclusion does not accord well with experience. Several LDCs with tiny internal markets have succeeded in achieving very rapid growth in exports of manufactures: Hong Kong, Singapore, Malaysia, Taiwan and S. Korea. Moreover, as was argued above, intervention need not necessarily mean tariffs or controls on trade. Infant industries would be more efficiently fostered by domestic subsidy/tax policies.

Another conclusion from such theories is that free trade will increase rather than decrease the gap in the standards of living between rich and poor countries. This stems from the dynamic 'growth poles' arguments described above. But these arguments have been used mainly in regional economics. How legitimate is their extension to the international field? One major difference lies in the difference in factor mobility within as compared with between nations. It is still true that factors of production move much more readily within nations. Most nations maintain firm controls on the migration of labour and some on capital. But the main part of the 'poles of growth' argument stems from the attraction to factors of production which the centre exerts upon the periphery. If factor mobility between nations is still small the argument loses much of its force. It is still of course generally true in the growth stakes that nothing succeeds like success. High rates of growth on top of an already high basic standard enables larger savings and investment in both capital and technological advances. These in turn contribute to faster growth: the gaps in standards of living between the richest nations and the poorest may continue to grow. But many LDCs (even excluding the oil exporters) have achieved faster growth than the developed industrial nations. Would it help the poor nations to cut themselves off from or greatly reduce their participation in international trade? Would this slow down the rate at which the gap continues to grow? It is difficult to see any important reason, apart from the infant industry argument, and its derivatives, why such autarkic policies should achieve such an end. Indeed any substantial withdrawal from trade would certainly reduce current standards of living for most poor countries. This is because the domestic opportunity cost for them of producing many types of manufactures is inordinately high compared with the cost of obtaining them by exchanging exports of raw materials, food products and elementary processed goods for such manufactured imports.

While it is clearly difficult to establish a cast iron case on the beneficial effects of trade on the distribution of world income it seems more likely that such effects as it has tend to make the poor better off than they would otherwise be.[13]

34

CONCLUSIONS

The upshot of this brief venture into the esoteric world of welfare economics and the pure theory of international trade is the following rather tentative conclusions:

(1) We may judge the contribution of our international institution to economic welfare in terms of:

(a) its effects on the efficiency with which the world's scarce resources of manpower, capital and natural resources are used. Our judgements of efficiency must take account of future as well as current outputs so as to allow for societies' evaluations of the respective merits of present versus future consumption both for themselves and for generations to come;

(b) the distribution of benefits and costs between the rich and the poor.

(2) We have a general presumption that freer rather than more restricted trade between nations will be conducive to more efficiency and possibly also to more tendency to equality in income distribution than would more barriers to trade.

NOTES: CHAPTER 2

1 T. Scitovsky, 'A note on welfare propositions in economics', *Review of Economic Studies* (1941) pointed out that the principle was not so unambiguous as it may appear. Because of the connection between the prices of goods and the pattern of their distribution a paradoxical situation can occur whereby it may pay the losers to bribe the potential gainers not to make the change even though the change would have satisfied the Kaldor criterion. In a world of many goods and many people this situation is unlikely to arise and is probably best left to the footnotes of a work on applied economics.

2 See I. M. D. Little, *A Critique of Welfare Economics*, 2nd edn (London: Oxford University Press, 1957); J. de V. Graaf, *Theoretical Welfare Economics* (Cambridge: Cambridge University Press, 1957).

3 The argument set out here is derived from a brilliant article by Professor Jagdish Bhagwati and the late V. K. Ramaswami, 'Domestic distortions, tariffs and the theory of optimum subsidy', *Journal of Political Economy* (February 1963).

4 H. G. Johnson, 'Optimal trade intervention in the presence of domestic distortions', in R. E. Caves, P. B. Kenen and H. G. Johnson (eds), *Trade, Growth and Balance of Payments* (Amsterdam: North Holland, 1965). Also reprinted in J. Bhagwati (ed.), *International Trade* (Harmondsworth: Penguin, 1969), p. 186.

5 This last argument should not be pushed too far. Reducing barriers makes life easier for exporters at the same time as it makes it tougher for import competing firms. *A priori* it is very difficult to say what the 'efficiency' stimulating effects of freer trade would be overall. cf W. M. Corden, 'The efficiency effects of trade and protection',

in I. A. McDougall and R. H. Snape (eds), *Studies in International Economics* (Amsterdam: North Holland, 1970).

6 H. G. J. Johnson, 'Optimum tariffs and retaliation', *Review of Economic Studies*, vol. 22 (1953/4).

7 Johnson in Bhagwati, op. cit., p. 211.

8 The case for joint action by a group of countries in concert is much stronger. They may well succeed in benefiting themselves where they have control over a major export such as oil, but of course they do so at high cost to the rest of the world. It is only if the resulting income transfers are socially desirable that such a policy can be justified on our welfare economics criteria.

9 C. P. Kindleberger, *International Economics* 3rd edn (Homewood, Ill.: Irwin, 1963), p. 316.

10 See P. A. Samuelson, 'International trade and the equalisation of factor prices', *Economic Journal* (June 1948), and a sequel in the *Economic Journal* (June 1949), for the full development of the equalisation argument.

11 See B. S. Minhas, *An International Comparison of Factor Costs and Factor Use* (Amsterdam: North Holland, 1963) and H. B. Lary, *Imports of Manufactures from Less Developed Countries* (New York and London: Columbia University Press, 1968).

12 R. Vernon, 'International investment and international trade in the product cycle', *Quarterly Journal of Economics* (May 1966).

13 In a brief chapter of a book on institutions it is not possible to deal with more than the main arguments on trade and protection. For a much fuller exposition see W. M. Corden, *Trade Policy and Economic Welfare* (London: Oxford University Press, 1974).

CHAPTER 3

The International Monetary Fund (IMF)

INTRODUCTION

The approach in Chapter 2 suggests that the IMF should be judged according to how far it has helped to provide international monetary conditions which have contributed to the free flow of trade between nations in the postwar world. As with other such institutions, however, limitations on this role have been imposed by the inevitable political compromises incorporated in its Articles.

Despite the preceding unique spirit of wartime collaboration, Keynes saw that a compromise had to be reached between the American desire for maximum freedom of trade, epitomised by Cordell Hull's utterances, and a Britain nervous of freer trade but needing American willingness to provide international liquidity.[1] Oversimplified though this was, the need for negotiation was clear from the divergent approaches of the Keynes and White Plans to the postwar international monetary order.

The Articles of Agreement of the IMF concluded in July 1944 at Bretton Woods were the outcome of those negotiations and were concerned in principle with two major issues: international liquidity and balance-of-payments adjustment. By the first was meant the provision of adequate foreign exchange reserves allowing nations to avoid restrictive trading practices in the face of temporary balance-of-payments difficulties. The second issue concerned the way in which countries would seek to remedy payments difficulties when they arose. The IMF's role in these two regards must form the focus of an assessment of that institution but we first provide a context for this task in the form of a brief outline of the Keynes Plan.

Although certainly not conceived from political naivete[2] it was a plan *not* arrived at by compromise. As such it had undoubted appeal to professional economists as an elegant means of achieving financial conditions conducive to the aims suggested by Chapter 2, namely, the maximisation of international economic intercourse. Proposals for reform emanating from academic as well as political circles have frequently echoed its insights[3] and we may therefore assess the institutional evolution of the IMF in the light of this widely acclaimed model.

In this way we hope not only to examine the impact of the IMF on events, but also its own achievements in becoming a more satisfactory[4] institution, a consideration particularly important in assessing the Fund's future role.

The technical aspects of the Keynes Plan are certainly clear in their intent. Based on the 'clearing bank' principle it recognised that for the world system one country's surplus had a counterpart deficit elsewhere. Thus, the surplus country (in postwar conditions the USA) could build up creditor positions with an international 'Clearing Union' and such deposits would be denominated in a new reserve currency unit, 'bancor'. Once relative exchange rates between currencies could be re-established (a difficult task, this, given the wartime destruction in Europe) the bancor credit balance would be exactly matched by the bancor 'overdrafts' of other nations. The credit being provided by the 'creditor' would be costless to it in the sense that they would be funds voluntarily left idle and could be 'spent' at any time (para. 5). The advantage as Keynes stressed was that such idle funds would automatically re-enter the system as 'overdrafts'. Indeed as he stressed (para. 4) the aim was to substitute 'expansionist' as opposed to 'contractionist' pressures on world trade. He was as much concerned with the depressed level of international demand preventing balance-of-payments adjustment as he was of overvalued exchange rates. Thus, he suggested that adjustment of excessive credit and debit balances should be the joint responsibility of creditors and debtors (para. 16). Each nation would have a trade weighted 'quota' indicating its maximum debit balance and interest would be chargeable on a debit or credit balance in excess of 25 per cent of that quota. The quotas would be increased at will as trade needs warranted.

There were to be restrictions on the *rate* at which a country could draw more than 25 per cent of its quota in any one year and devaluations of the nation's currency would be *permitted* and then *required* depending on the rate at which the quota was being exhausted.

The crucial point for the present analysis was that the Clearing Union would never be threatened with illiquidity and 'bancor' would take over the role of the dollar *and* sterling, except where the latter were held as reserves in *voluntary* sterling or dollar 'blocs' (para. 37). Contemporary discussion of a 'substitution account' reflects this scheme and other features such as commodity stabilisation and development overdrafts (paras. 54(1), (4), (5)) have to some degree been realised.

The Articles of Agreement that finally emerged after Bretton Woods, however, bore much less resemblance to the outline above than to the alternative White Plan. Partly, this was the result of the US fear, as Keynes put it, of becoming the 'milch cow of the world in general' but more important the anonymity of financial flows implicit in the Keynes

Plan was a positive disadvantage given the US desire for political hegemony.[5]

Thus, although the quotas agreed at Bretton Woods (trade weighted) were greater than those originally proposed by White, each country would cover its quota (as White had suggested) by supplying 25 per cent gold and 75 per cent *local* currency and denominated assets. This opened the possibility that the Fund could easily become illiquid if the borrowing countries sought to obtain dollars in excess of those which the USA had contributed to the Fund. Such a position was implicit in the quota totals. The important result was that drawings to finance payments deficits were made *conditional* and in no sense drawing *rights*. Republican 'milch cow' fears, voiced by Taft in particular, in fact caused the draft agreement to be made less liberal on this point.[6]

Finally, in connection with the Articles a 'par' value for each national currency was to be maintained (within a 1 per cent range either side of the declared value) and any country that freely bought or sold gold in international transactions was 'deemed' to be maintaining its rate within such margins. This clearly referred to the dollar with the effect that the USA did not need to intervene in foreign exchange markets. Other countries would have to maintain parity with the dollar and the world was thus placed on a dollar standard.[7] Related to this, the Articles required that each nation maintain its exchange rate except in cases of *fundamental* disequilibrium. As 'fundamental' has never been defined this reflected US preferences in that countries were told when they should *not* alter their exchange rate and not when they should.[8] A potential 'deflation bias' was therefore present contrary to Keynes' expansionist vision.

These politically imposed limitations were there, then, when the Fund was established. The question now concerns how the Fund has developed its role and to what effect, within the confines of its Articles.

EARLY EXPERIENCE TO 1960

From the point of view of liquidity, given its resources (the total of members quotas), and more particularly the conditional nature of withdrawals, it is perhaps not surprising that the Fund, in Triffin's words, was condemned to 'impotence for the post war decade'.[9] Unlike the Keynes Plan, where extended overdrafts would have been available, the fund was explicitly excluded from providing relief and reconstruction finance (Article XIV). This was to be provided by the IBRD, or, in practice, by bilateral (Marshall) aid. It became clear, however, after 1948 that drawings were particularly low and it was increasingly apparent that this was partly due to uncertainty over the conditionality of Fund resources. Not until 1952 was clarification provided on this – the 'Rooth Plan' which specified the importance of the 'gold tranche'.[10] On reading this account it is difficult to avoid the conclusion that political constraints on the Executive Board were present in this tortuous discussion, although the preference of recipient countries for Marshall Aid probably ensured that severe disruption did not result in practice. Nor did strictures in the Articles prevent the major European currency devaluations of 1949. These were seen by the Fund as a particular adjustment to the aftermath of war.

A potentially more serious criticism has been made, however, of the Fund's position at this time on the 'reserves adequacy' debate. During the period under review concern was building up over the nature of reserve expansion. In the initial postwar period the difficulty was the general shortage of gold and dollars in European reserves. But when, after 1958, the USA began to incur serious balance-of-payments deficits the problem was increasingly seen as one of the *nature* of reserve expansion. The US deficit meant a growth of dollar holdings adding to reserves worldwide, but with a continuing US deficit there was the likelihood of a gradual collapse of confidence in the official gold value of those reserves. After two somewhat complacent reports from the IMF Executive,[11] the Fund 'lost the initiative on the reserve question'.[12] The Group of Ten began to dominate monetary discussions, a situation only partially reversed in the late 1960s. Additionally, by 1958 the potential need for borrowing by deficit countries – now in principle, at least, including the USA – could easily outweigh the Fund's resources. The illiquidity risk implicit in the Fund articles became a potential reality as soon as something like normal operating circumstances were attained in 1958–60.

There were, however, some positive achievements during this early period in relaxing access to Fund resources. The Articles (V Sec. 8) provided for escalating interest charges as a member's drawings from the Fund rose in units of 25 per cent above its quota. When for any reason this process led to an interest charge of 4 per cent the member would have to negotiate with the Fund how the latter's holdings of that country's currency could be reduced. Persistent American pressure led to further restrictions, specifically, as in the 'Rooth Plan', that borrowings should usually be repaid in a three- to five-year period, and loans beyond the gold tranche would be subject to *increasing* conditions. In spite of this, however, borrowings of up to 25 per cent of quota (that is, borrowings not exceeding the members original gold contribution or gold tranche) were increasingly seen as a *right* and allowed automatically although this was formalised only in 1969.

Additionally there was the development of 'stand-by' agreements. These were arrangements whereby a member after negotiation would be permitted to withdraw an agreed amount (generally up to 25 per cent of quota) as and when balance of payments considerations dictated. Thus *assurance* of funds was provided, although increased *reserves* were not. Initially, US pressure insisted that these be repaid in six months, but on the basis of encouraging the 'convertibility' of member's currencies, loans of up to twelve months *with renewals* were gradually permitted.[13] This particular form of credit was of special importance to the UK and Italy, together with Third World countries in the later 1960s, and the development of the facility at this time was important. The stand-by principle has been expanded considerably in recent years.

Thus, as the 1960s approach, we see the IMF, on the one hand, failing to take a lead in the evolving discussion of monetary reform, major initiatives being instigated by the Group of Ten, and on the other, gradually developing its lending policy on more liberal lines. Some credit can also be claimed for the doubling of quotas, again despite some political opposition, from $7.1 billion to $14.6 billion[14] in 1959.

It has to be noted, however, that these early indications of independent evolution at the IMF were not strong enough to prevent major political pressure on France by conditions attached to stand-by agreements in 1956–58 subsequent to Suez.[15]

THE POSITION OF THE FUND IN A DECADE OF WORLD ECONOMIC EXPANSION 1960–1970

By 1958 the period of postwar reconstruction, financed massively by US Marshall Aid, had been brought effectively to a close. In that year the major European currencies had been declared convertible for current transactions and the dollar shortage which had characterised the postwar years up until that time was officially over. The IMF was describing the US balance-of-payments deficit as a 'problem', when American gold reserves began to decline, as they did in an unbroken run until 1969. The dollar outflows associated with overseas investment, government and military expenditures were leading some overseas holders to convert their dollars into gold at the official price at the end of the period. Additionally, by 1970, the cost competitiveness of American exports was being questioned. The latter is significant as an indicator of the fundamental change in the world economy witnessed by the 1960s. As we have said the postwar reconstruction of Europe was complete by 1958. By 1968 the European countries, together with Japan, were massively challenging American commercial dominance, a factor of some importance to the evolution of the IMF as will become apparent.

As the decade opened the dominating concern was with the nature of reserve expansion, the bulk of this expansion being provided by US dollars, with the USA acting as 'a world central bank, fulfilling a function left unspecified in the Bretton Woods agreement'.[16]

Thus without an easily reproducible asset in the 'bancor' mould, the IMF could do nothing to satisfy the reserve needs of rapidly expanding trading nations, 'conditional' liquidity being no substitute in the eyes of central bankers. It has to be stressed that this defect, far more than tardiness in identifying the problem, to which reference has been made, caused the Fund's eclipse at this time. Thus, in November 1961, for example, the USA had a potential right to borrow $5.8 billion from the IMF, but the Fund's holdings of the currencies of the major industrial countries other than the UK (which had itself just borrowed from the Fund) amounted to only about $1.6 billion.[17] More generally US gold reserves at the end of 1956 have been estimated at $22 billion[18] whereas between 1958 and 1960 they fell by $5.1 billion.[19] It was becoming increasingly apparent that the Bretton Woods system was leading inexorably to a 'dollar standard'. That is (as with a banking analogy), the ultimate right to convert dollars into gold (deposits into cash) could only be preserved providing that the right was not exercised.

As with deposit banking, confidence was again the crucial issue, and in this respect there was another deficiency in the Bretton Woods Articles. Specifically Article VI had assumed that capital movements – the vehicles by which the state of 'confidence' was expressed – would in fact be subject to strict controls. Measures to stabilise such flows were not a concern of the IMF from its inception.

The dollar as a reserve currency thus had to be supported by other means. President Kennedy's economic advisers, particularly Robert V. Roosa, produced two in 1961–62. 'Roosa Bonds' issued by the US Treasury to foreign central banks were denominated in the currency of the holder – for example, mark bonds with the German Federal Bank. Thus Germany's dollar reserves could be held in such bonds not only earning interest but with the guarantee that a dollar devaluation relative to the mark would not affect the redemption value. The next innovation with a similar intent was the negotiation of 'swap' facilities by the US Treasury with European central bankers, through the BIS at Basle. The Federal Reserve Bank of New York took over operation of this arrangement whereby the FRBNY would be granted a facility (account) at, say, the German Federal Bank, in marks, in exchange for an equivalent dollar facility at the FRBNY for a three-month period. When the FRBNY has supported the dollar its mark facility has been used to buy dollars from the German Bank, the latter having been acquired in support of the dollar/mark exchange rate. The advantage of this is that whereas the dollars so acquired in the market are subject to an exchange risk if the dollar were to be devalued, the dollars acquired in the swap were exchangeable after three months at the previously prevailing exchange rate. Again the value of dollar reserve holdings were being guaranteed by the US actions.[20] These arrangements, of course, were entirely separate from the Fund and were designed specifically to counter short-term capital flows.

Of more direct relevance to the Fund itself were the negotiations of the General Arrangements to Borrow (GAB). Following American membership of the OECD, regular meetings took place, particularly in 'working party three', made up exclusively of finance-ministry and central bank officials of the ten largest countries of the OECD. As Solomon points out[21] this became the principal forum for discussion of international monetary and balance of payments policies. After the original idea had been put forward by IMF staff,[22] it was from this forum that the GAB emerged. Ten countries would provide $6 billion credits to the Fund. In the negotiations that produced this arrangement the shift in relative power towards Europe was clear. The IMF would *not* be allowed to on-lend this money at its own discretion. The lenders would have to consult over a proposal from the Fund's managing director that a loan be made and the borrowing country would *not* be allowed to vote. The latter was presumed to be the USA although the first loan was made to the UK during the 1964 sterling crisis. In this sense the Group of Ten (G10) were put in 'a power position *vis-à-vis* the Fund ... which ... is in principle open to criticism'[23] and the Europeans began to impose 'conditionality' on the USA.

The criticism of G10 power *vis-à-vis* the Fund mentioned by Harrod was to become a practical reality in the later 1960s when negotiations got under way for the creation of a new international reserve asset, and the outcome will be dealt with shortly. The 1960s, however, produced, at the same time as the discussion about reserves, a major debate about the other aspect of international monetary matters – the adjustment mechanism. For present purposes it is the IMF position on this subject that is important as the failure of the Bretton Woods system at the beginning of the 1970s was far more a failure of that mechanism than of the problems of the growth of reserves. As we shall see, however, the two were associated, and, indeed, the European imposition of conditionality on the USA reflected the belief that reserve reform without agreement over adjustment to payments imbalances was of little value. The basis of the European position was that US payments deficits in the 1960s were an inflationary influence on the rest of the world. Inflows of dollars to European central banks tended to expand local money supply despite extensive controls. The Americans, on this thesis, were able to take a view of 'benign neglect' as these dollar accumulations abroad did not mean a reduction of US reserves. The Americans, on the other hand, regarded such accumulations as 'demand determined', that is, as dollars were the only source of reserve expansion, the demand by other countries for reserves *obliged* the USA to run a deficit to allow such accumulations. America had to be the '*n*th' country in the system. By this was implied that an American payments surplus would prevent other countries from acquiring reserves. A balanced retrospective view perhaps requires elements of both arguments. During the early 1960s reserve growth in European countries was *not* excessive relative to income growth,[24] and although monetarist economists might still argue that the USA exported inflation the Fund director did not believe so.[25] On the other hand, as Williamson pointed out in reference to later experience, after the arrival of alternative fiduciary reserve assets (SDRs) the US balance-of-payments deficit exploded, and perhaps with it the notion that that deficit was the result of world demand for dollars.[26] It seems reasonable to conclude from these opinions that, at the least, the mounting problems of the dollar were the result not of a shortage of other liquidity but an inability, under the Bretton Woods system, to adjust the US balance of payments.

How, then, was the IMF's position developing on this crucial issue of 'adjustment', and in particular the question of parity realignments by revaluation or devaluation? The IMF Annual Reports of 1964 and 1965 stated this position. In 1964 stress was laid on internal reflation or deflation to attain external balance as well as internal. Following Mundell, it was suggested that monetary policy might be aimed more explicitly at the foreign balance through the control of interest rates. As the Articles stated, exchange rate changes would be left for situations of fundamental disequilibrium which should not arise if fiscal and monetary policies were correctly followed. Likewise in 1965 exchange rate changes are the last on the list in terms of policy measures.

In these respects the Fund was voicing the conventional wisdom of the time. A dollar devaluation to cure the US payments deficit was seen as a blow to the heart of the entire system and thus was not entertained. European countries also, at this time, saw the main problem as being US capital outflows and not American uncompetitiveness *vis-à-vis* Europe. They would have objected to a dollar devaluation through its possible effects on their own competitiveness.

However, as with the reserves adequacy issue and the IMF report of the earlier period, the point has to be ventured that the Fund was excessively cautious. A contemporary report (August 1966) did include exchange rate changes as a possible policy for deficit *and* surplus countries and the notion of floating exchange rates was not new.[27] Given the importance of the issue for the correct functioning of the world economy could not the Fund have at least explored possible alternatives rather than confining itself so rigorously to its Articles on the exchange rate issue? After criticising the Fund for being 'strangely silent' on the liquidity issue to which we have referred, Gardner makes a comment about the US balance-of-payments policy which really applies to the adjustment problem[28]:

> The payments problem caused, or at least reinforced, policies of tight money and fiscal restraint in periods such as 1959–61 when the US economy needed expansionist measures, costing perhaps tens of billions in lost growth. There was increasing resort to devices such as tied aid, the Interest Equalisation Tax, and 'voluntary' (later mandatory) controls on capital export.

A similar catalogue could be made up for the futile British defence of sterling's parity between 1964 and 1967. Although the credit squeezes imposed were more justifiable in the context of domestic overheating than the US case cited above, the persistent need for macroeconomic policy to move erratically as a result of balance of payments and, particularly, capital account transactions, has been a relevant factor in the poor UK growth performance in recent years. Curiously, the temporary import surcharge of 1964 was contemporary with the first mobilisation of GAB funds through the IMF in support of sterling's parity. The direct responsibility for making funds available in this endeavour was of course not with the Fund but with that 'conservative forum weighted ... in ... surplus country interests'[29] – the Group of Ten.

In fact the involvement of the G10 in these loans indicates the conventional wisdom of the time, but, it may be argued, it is precisely this conventional wisdom that the IMF, on however confidential a level (the Articles permit the Fund to give confidential unsolicited advice to a member), should have been challenging.

That the Fund has been able to take a more activist, innovative role is illustrated by the course of negotiations over the creation of a new international reserve asset, the SDR, designed to allow world reserves to respond without the need for an American deficit. This is not to say, however, that the IMF took a leading role; talk of reform had emanated originally from the Kennedy administration and American pressure led to an initial study by the G10 deputies which produced its report in June 1964. Observers from the IMF were allowed but not directly involved and European suspicions of that institution were epitomised by the French proposal for a 'collective reserve unit' to be used *outside* the IMF by members of the G10.

The Fund, however, under its new managing director, Pierre Paul Schweitzer, had initiated its own studies and, more important, Schweitzer actively canvassed for the reserve negotiations to be conducted within the Fund and not the G10. Significantly, but not surprisingly, given the foregoing the USA favoured this proposal. The Americans wished in doing so to obtain a less favourable forum for the ascendant surplus European countries and found strong support from the LDCs who felt excluded from negotiations in the G10 which were of considerable importance to them. European suspicions of an American/LDC coalition continued to grow through the various deliberations of the G10. None the less, following public declarations from Schweitzer over the desirability of a universal approach to reserve asset creation, a series of joint meetings was arranged between the G10 deputies and the IMF Executive Board. This fundamental decision was taken at the G10 Ministerial meeting in the Hague in July 1966. Four joint meetings were arranged in 1966–67, the main discussion being between the Ten and ten of the Fund Directors who were not representatives of the countries which comprised the Ten.

Whereas the first two meetings were marked by considerable dissent between France and the others over whether or not there was in fact a need for a new asset, and the second two by debate over direct transferability between Fund members and the question of reconstitution, an outline agreed plan was produced during the fourth meeting.

There were, however, a number of unresolved issues which had to be decided politically at the Ministerial meetings of the G10. 'When the latter had made a firm decision, the Fund could be nothing more than a rubber stamp.'[30] This particular observer goes on to say about the four meetings, however[31]:

> Despite this fact, the universal participation in these meetings materially affected the final form of the monetary reform agreement. In particular the plan probably would have been less universal in character, at best giving only a limited participation of junior status to the non-ten countries ...
>
> The joint meetings also extended the opportunity for the IMF's uniquely qualified staff of international civil servants to supplement the efforts of the Group of Ten Deputies. The Fund staff was a 'neutral secretariat' which outdid itself in accomplishing something which the deputies never could: the actual drafting a paper of the outlines of a single reform plan. The large and thoroughly experienced Fund staff, unlike the deputies, could work continuously together for extended periods of time on the wording of specific provisions. They also could advance a plan without its having the connotation of being the work of a particular country. The IMF's expertise and pragmatism helped to convert the liquidity talks from a repetition of old arguments to a discussion of specifics.

The document to emerge from this process was the 'Outline of a

Facility Based on Special Drawing Rights in the Fund' (released 11 September 1967). Further political negotiation within the G10 (at Stockholm in early 1968) was necessary before support could be provided for the main provisions. Some allowances had to be made for French reservations regarding the creation of a reserve asset other than gold. In particular, the SDR would *not* be allowable in payment for quota increases at the Fund and a member was to be allowed to refuse an allocation of SDRs when those already allocated were equal to one half of its IMF quota. None the less, the desire to maintain EEC unity, and the political violence in France in May 1968 which forced that country to seek international financial support, provided sufficient agreement to allow the Fund articles to be amended to include the SDR provisions and for the first issue to be activated in June 1969 – $9.5 billion worth to be issued in three annual instalments.

It was in the process of the creation of the SDR that we see the IMF at its most active and in its most central role since its foundation. Moreover, in the creation of this fiduciary instrument the IMF was provided with something like the 'bancor' balance suggested by Keynes twenty-five years previously. We can illustrate this by the following outline of the SDR as originally constituted. It was available for use in balance-of-payments or reserve needs without prior consultation with the Fund. Repayment was not required to any fixed schedule (as were tranche drawings) although French pressure did lead to a mild 'reconstitution' provision being built in.

Members of the Fund were required to accept the SDR in exchange for a national currency, up to the limit that no country be required to hold more than three times its 'net cumulative allocation' of SDRs as issued over time by Fund decision. In terms of this net cumulative allocation the reconstitution provision mentioned above required that a country's average holdings of SDRs be not less than 30 per cent of the average of its net cumulative allocation over the same period. Reconstitution was required if the average fell below this amount.

Two types of transaction in SDRs were permitted. First a country could buy back its own currency from a country; thus central banks would deal directly in SDRs. Secondly, the country could release its SDRs through the Fund (e.g. when in overall deficit) and the Fund would designate other countries to whom the SDRs were to be transferred. These, again, must be accepted up to the ceilings mentioned.

The initial valuation of the SDR was one thirty-fifth of an ounce of gold equal to $1 in the exchange rates then prevailing. The change in this procedure following 1974 will be noted presently.

In one major respect, however, the SDR fell short of the 'bancor' scheme, and this was in the question of interest payable on SDR holdings. Under Section 20 of the proposed amendment to the Articles of

Agreement[32] a small interest rate would be payable on the *excess* of holdings of SDRs by a country over its net cumulative allocation. Likewise, interest would be paid by a country on the *shortfall* of its holdings below the net cumulative allocation. The interest rate would be 1.5 per cent.

This rate was unattractive relative to other means of holding reserves, particularly the holding of dollar denominated assets, and while this would be good for developing countries who would expect to be net users it did mean that the SDR would be unlikely to take over from the dollar as the major reserve asset. As one suspects the Americans may have wished, the world ended the decade of the 1960s on a dollar standard despite the advent of the first entirely fiduciary (non-exchangeable for gold) reserve asset. However, the years after the sterling devaluation in 1967 were years of increasing crisis, with the French troubles of 1968 and their monetary aftermath, culminating in persistent pressure for a revaluation of the German mark.

Clearly, while the world had been discussing the need for new reserve assets the emerging main issue was not reserves but the inflexibility of the adjustment mechanism. Where the SDR could in principle have helped, by taking the world off a dollar standard, thus allowing that currency to play its part in adjustment, political factors had guaranteed frustration. The SDR scheme was too late to save Bretton Woods, although, as discussed in the concluding section, it continues to evolve and may yet have a major role to play in international monetary reform.

As we turn to the 1970s, when the role of the Fund with respect to the LDCs becomes of increasing relevance and interest from our present point of view, it is worth noting the development in 1963 of a Compensatory Financing Facility in the Fund. This was aimed primarily at primary producers, to compensate them for temporary shortfalls in export receipts that were primarily attributable to circumstances beyond their control. Compensation was limited generally to 25 per cent of quota and was in addition to amounts that a member could purchase under the tranche policies. Special criteria were prescribed that were less severe than those that applied at least for the higher credit tranches. By 1966 this was fully separated from the tranches in that purchases from the facility would not affect tranche drawings. This provision was placed in the Amended Articles in 1969.

Of some importance in this context also was the tendency to provide balance-of-payments assistance, following a legal clarification of the Articles,[33] for countries suffering a *capital* outflow provided this was deemed to be of a temporary nature. Strength was given to this position by the activation of the GAB for such circumstances.

As essentially a commodity related scheme the Compensatory Financing Facility, as well as the Buffer Stock Scheme, is examined in

Chapter 6. In the following section, however, IMF financial arrangements relevant to the LDCs are considered.

THE IMF FROM THE COLLAPSE OF BRETTON WOODS TO THE AFTERMATH OF THE OIL CRISIS 1971–80

The growing crisis of adjustment noted at the end of the preceding section culminated in the August 1971 measures announced by the US Government. Following continuing pressure on the dollar in world money markets the convertibility of dollars into gold was suspended. This central feature was supplemented by a 'temporary' 10 per cent import duty required, it was alleged, because of 'unfair exchange rates'. 'The time has come for exchange rates to be set straight and for the major nations to compete as equals'.[34] Here, then, was a striking realisation that the adjustment mechanism had failed and reform was to be achieved.

At this stage the response, including that from the IMF, was to seek a reform of exchange rates within a regime of fixed parities, notwithstanding that the German and Dutch currencies had been floating since May 1971 following excessive dollar inflows to their central banks. The initial US position had been that there should be a concerted upward float of European currencies against the dollar, with the dollar price of gold unchanged. However, politically, the need for an American 'contribution' to what was clearly a crisis of confidence in the dollar became imperative.

The Smithsonian agreements of December 1971 among the G10 brought about this result: the realignment of parities with wider margins of fluctuations and a symbolic devaluation of the dollar against gold. The realignments, however, were not sufficient to give the USA a sustainable foreign payments position especially as in 1972 the US economy grew more strongly than anticipated.

The USA, with support from the LDCs who had continued to voice their complaints over being excluded from the process of negotiations which had led up to the Smithsonian Agreements, pressed for a forum based on the twenty nations which formed the constituents of the IMF Executive Board. The aim was to formulate a thoroughgoing reform of the international monetary system. This broader forum, including the LDCs, was necessary, as Williamson points out,[35] if for no other reason than that an agreed reform would require amendment to the IMF Articles and the LDCs had more than enough votes *en bloc* to prevent ratification. The interesting feature from the point of view of our own narrative, however, is that the decline in the power of the USA relative to Europe and Japan, together with the degree of solidarity being achieved by the LDCs in international negotiations, had thrust the IMF to the centre of the stage.

The vehicle for negotiation within the IMF was to be a specially formed *ad hoc* committee which became known as the 'Committee of Twenty' (C20). Each of the twenty IMF 'constituencies' was represented by a 'member', the latter generally being the Minister of Finance of the largest country in the constituency. Each such member had two associates, generally a central bank governor and the finance minister's deputy. Directly below the committee were the deputies (generally senior officials from finance ministries and central banks), two from each constituency, accompanied by their IMF Executive Directors and by advisers.

This body of deputies, presided over by a bureau drawn from themselves, did much of the preliminary work in narrowing areas of disagreement over international monetary reform. Major questions of choice on the political level were to be dealt with by the ministers on the committee. The issues discussed were essentially four: (1) adjustment to payments imbalances; (2) financial settlement of these imbalances; (3) the volume and composition of international reserves; (4) requirements of the LDCs.

It is perhaps fair to say that most of the discussion centred around the first two issues and it was the difficulty in finding an agreed approach that caused negotiations to take so much time that they were ultimately overtaken by events. Thus, on the question of payments adjustment the US position became, as Solomon notes,[36] strikingly similar to the Keynes proposals discussed at the outset. 'Graduated pressures' were to be exerted on surplus and deficit countries through the IMF based on the rate of *reserve* growth or decline of the country concerned. For obvious reasons, as a result of the change in their own circumstances, the Americans were seeking to put into the system a provision that surplus countries would take full part in adjusting their payments positions. Notwithstanding the (never activated) scarce currency clause in the original Articles, the system had tended to presume that it was the deficit country that would adjust through domestic deflation. After all, reserve growth is far easier to live with than reserve decline if there are no external sanctions on the former.

Coming to the question of settlement of payments imbalances, we see the European interest in reducing the role of the dollar, resulting from increasing vulnerability to speculative pressure. An Italian proposal combined 'asset settlement' – that is, the USA providing gold and SDRs to cover further dollar outflows due to payments deficits – with consolidation of outstanding dollar reserves on a voluntary basis, with countries exchanging dollars for SDRs through a substitution account at the Fund. There was some measure of advance on both of these major reform issues but continued American unwillingness to see a competitive interest rate on SDR holdings ensured that progress towards a major reduction in the reserve role of the dollar was prevented.

Further major progress in these discussions, however, was interrupted by a crisis in foreign exchange markets during 1973. At the beginning of the year, US wage-price controls were relaxed causing fears for the dollar, and an outflow of Italian capital into Switzerland led to the floating of the Swiss franc. Subsequently speculation mounted that the deutschmark would be allowed to float and finally in February the dollar was devalued by 10 per cent. The response to this did not take long and by March the major European currencies were jointly floating. Although the C20 pressed on with its negotiations under increasing doubts about its own relevance the final blow was struck by the major oil price rises commencing in October 1974. In the face of the payments disruptions implied, the committee had to agree to let the reforms over which they had been deliberating emerge out of new experience.

Ultimately the C20 had achieved very little. The final product called 'Outline of Reform' drafted in the broadest terms a new international monetary system characterised by a 'symmetrical' adjustment process with generally a 'stable' but 'adjustable' exchange rate regime. There was to be an 'appropriate' form of convertibility for settlement of imbalances and SDRs would become the main global reserve asset. Finally, the net flow of real resources to developing countries needed to be enhanced. Thus, although the ends at this level could be seen as common to participants in the negotiations, the precise means could not be agreed.

While the main aims of this new IMF-based forum were clearly not achieved, some progress was made with regard to the committee's proposed 'immediate steps'. First, the basis of valuation of the SDR was changed to be valued according to a trade weighted basket of major currencies. While this was a response to the presence of floating currencies it was also a step of some significance as the SDR was no longer valued in terms of gold. It was now fiduciary both in regard to its 'backing' and in its valuation, and its 'bancor' potential was now apparent. Secondly, although currencies were now floating, the IMF was to produce 'guidelines' which would emphasise the need to avoid competitive 'dirty' floating.

Two measures were also of direct relevance to LDCs. Early on in the C20 negotiations it had been decided to create an 'Extended Fund Facility' which would provide longer-term assistance to developing countries whose balance-of-payments problems were regarded as being of a longer-term structural nature. By this means, although there was no agreement at this stage to increase international reserves the 'conditional' liquidity of the Fund was increased in a potentially significant direction. It will be remembered that Article XIV explicitly excluded the Fund from providing 'reconstruction' finance. This new facility, however, was tending in the direction of longer period provision.

The second measure of real significance for the LDCs was the agreement in principle at the end of C20 deliberations to create an oil facility within the Fund to assist those countries particularly hard hit by the contemporary rise in oil prices.

Of less direct significance to the LDCs, but of considerable potential significance, was the decision to perpetuate the C20 as an 'Interim Committee' and then permanently as a Council within the Fund. On this committee the LDCs have about half the representation and non-industrial countries, as a whole (e.g. including Australia), have more than half. As Hirsch concludes:

> Since voting on the IMF and the World Bank is on a weighted basis, the industrial countries have kept their formal control. But undoubtedly there has been a drift of influence. The solidarity of the Group of 77 [based on UNCTAD, see Chapter 5] has generally held *vis-à-vis* the industrial countries; the oil and non-oil developing countries have established a common front. As a result, the developing countries as a whole were able in 1975–76 to exercise an unprecedented degree of influence over international economic and political decisions.

The new committee may act as a vehicle to enhance that representation with possibly considerable effect. Its first task was to consider the amendment of the Fund's Articles to, among other things, legalise floating. It was also to supervise the management of the international monetary system until the Amended Articles formally instated the permanent Council in the Fund at ministerial level. This Interim Committee (and later the Council) would then be in a supervising position with regard to the Executive Board of the Fund.

Between 1974 and 1976 the Committee and the Executive considered matters of immediate concern, especially the recycling of oil revenues and an increase in IMF quotas.

The first oil facility commenced operations in June 1974 and was somewhat enlarged in January 1975. Although recognised to be only a partial measure, particularly for Third World countries 'in view of the nature and magnitude of the balance of payments problems created', such assistance was to be supplementary to any assistance that members could obtain under other policies on the use of the Fund's resources. It was to be a separate facility because of the particular nature of the problem which was in *addition* to other problems of adjustment faced by some members.

Partly to avoid excessive calls on the Fund's own liquidity, but mainly because surpluses were concentrated in the hands of the oil producing countries, it was decided that the facility should be financed by borrowings, particularly from the oil producers. Interest paid on these borrowings by the Fund was 7 per cent in 1974 and 7.25 per cent in 1975. Charges to drawings on the facility were 7.5 per cent and 7.75 per cent, respectively, covering only a 'handling charge' for the Fund. An innovation here was that in 1975 an interest subsidy account was opened, subscribed by voluntary contributions from members to assist the 'most seriously affected' members – the poorest countries.

Unlike under the otherwise rather similar GAB previously discussed, loans for the oil facility were actual commitments to pay to the Fund up to the agreed amounts as and when the Fund required them for loans under the facility – the Fund did not hold the borrowed currencies in its own accounts, but could call upon them when it required to do so.

The loans are denominated in SDRs and can be outstanding for between three and seven years, repayments to be made in eight semi-annual instalments starting after three years. Lenders who have already made a commitment to the facility are permitted to transfer their claim provided the new lender's conditions are acceptable to the Fund. Seventeen lenders are involved, contributing SDR 7 billion and loans have been made to fifty-five countries.

Perhaps the most interesting feature of the oil facility, even more than the GAB with the latter's external control of the borrowed funds, is that it has great similarities to Keynes' original idea of debit and credit balances within the Clearing Union. Thus, structural surplus countries were lending short term since they could request repayment for balance-of-payments reasons and the Fund was committed to meeting this, giving overwhelming benefit of interpretation of those reasons to the country in question. The 'clearing' function of the Fund (or more aptly 'intermediation' function) converted these short-term deposits into medium-term loans to the deficit nations, permitting a more gradual adjustment of their payments deficits.[37] The fact that the loans could be outstanding for seven years underlines this point.

The negotiations of the 'Interim Committee' were completed at their meeting in Jamaica in January 1976. In view of the oil price dislocation, and its severity in the non-oil producing LDCs, it was agreed that until the sixth round of quota increase had been ratified a 45 per cent expansion of countries' potential borrowing right at the IMF would be allowed. This, in fact, only partly compensated for the decline in the relative size of Fund resources which was by then apparent. Thus, quotas in 1976 in terms of world trade were only between one-third and one-half of what they had been during the 1950s.[38] The sixth review of quotas, since ratified, is in this context to be seen as 'modest'.[39]

A further advance at Jamaica was the agreement to liberalise the operation of the Compensatory Financing Scheme already mentioned. In regard to this, however, there was no doubting the scheme's growing unpopularity among the larger members of the IMF.[40] The Amended Articles which had been the subject of the Fund Executive Board's deliberations were also agreed.

As a footnote to Jamaica it should be added that no further progress was made on the major questions of reserves and adjustment. In supervising exchange rate arrangements, as envisaged in the Amended Articles, the Fund was clearly going to have to work out its own case law. Hirsch summarises matters by stating that the Amended Articles 'involve nothing less than abandonment of a specified monetary order'.[41]

Paradoxically, however, the single major event which led to this abandonment, the oil price increase, also contributed to a significant new phase in the evolution of the Fund. The need to finance the resulting payments deficits prompted the first 'oil facility' and during 1977 a new expanded facility, of similar nature, was successfully negotiated by the IMF Managing Director, Mr Witteveen. The new arrangements permitted $10 billion to be raised with $4 billion of this coming from the OPEC countries. At the insistence of these OPEC contributors interest rates on the loans were to be linked to commercial rates, in this case the US Treasury Bill rate, with provision for adjustment every six months.[42]

The intention was that the loans should be made to countries whose balance-of-payments problems were large in relation to the size of their economies. Such eligible countries were able to almost double the Fund resources normally available to them under the credit tranche procedures. Contributors and potential contributions under the 'Witteveen facility' are shown in Table 3.1.

Having brought the development of IMF facilities up to date in this way, it would perhaps be illuminating to compare the cumulative use actually made of the various sources of funds to the present time. Table 3.2 summarises progress made in utilising the facilities discussed so far.

Drawings under the four credit tranches have been quantitatively the most significant source for both developed and less developed countries and this fundamental importance is underlined by the fact that it is this source which is available to underscore general balance-of-payments adjustment policies. The other sources by their nature are more restrictive. None the less the compensatory drawings and oil facility drawings have been highly significant, the former particularly for the LDCs, the

Table 3.1   *Contributions to Witteveen (in SDRm.)*

Industrial Countries		OPEC Contributors	
USA	1450	Saudi Arabia	1934
W. Germany	1050	Venezuela	500
Japan	900	UAE	150
Switzerland	650	Kuwait	400
Canada	200	Nigeria	220
Belgium	150		
Holland	100		
Austria	50		
	4550		3204

Source: IMF International Financial Statistics (June 1980).

latter being evenly split between the developed and less developed world.

However, the actual drawings under the supplementary financing facility (the 'Witteveen facility') as evidenced by columns (c) and (g) are disappointing, given the potential 7.7 billion SDRs made available, and the fact that the halfway stage has been reached in the scheme's projected life. There have been no major borrowers from the industrialised countries and even LDCs are steering clear. The problem seems to be that the Witteveen money is essentially an adjunct to other IMF loan finance and, as such, is available on condition that policies approved by the IMF are followed. In addition to this, of course, the loans are at a commercial rate reducing the attractiveness of the facility in comparison with borrowing on international capital markets.

Indeed, international capital markets and their rapid emergence during the 1960s and 1970s (contrary to expectations of continued restraints on capital flows when the IMF was established) are of considerable importance when we come to consider the institution's future role.

PROSPECTS: THE 'ADJUSTMENT' AND 'RESERVE' ISSUES IN THE 1980s

In principle, with the establishment of floating exchange rates much of the force of the 'adjustment' and 'reserve' difficulties which have previously concerned the IMF should have been dissipated. Flexible rates should maintain all countries' payments balances without the need for intervention and, therefore, without the need for foreign exchange reserves.

Table 3.2: Total Drawings to Date: Fund Accounts (end April 1980: SDRm.)[a]

| | SDR Accounts | | Drawings | | | | | | | |
	(1) Allocations	(2) Net Acquisition or Net Use	(a) Reserve Tranche	(b) Credit Tranche	(c) Credit Tranche SFF	(d) Compensatory Drawings	(e) Buffer Stock Drawings	(f) Extended Facility Drawings	(g) Extended Facility Drawings SSF	(1) Oil Facility Drawings
All countries	17,380.8	-1407	16,654.4	21,058.7	383.5	5,270.8	103.8	628.0	119.0	6,902.5
Industrial countries	11,894.5	-283.3	13,383.5	11,752.3	—	631.0	23.8	—	—	3,491.6
Oil Exporting countries	1,112.8	386.8	339.8	313.5	—	17.5	7.1	—	—	—
Non-oil producing developing countries	4,373.8	-1.510.5	2,712.6	8,953.4	383.5	4,622.3	72.9	628.0	119.0	3,410.9

[a]Apart from the first two columns these are *total* drawings to date and *not* the net position in each account.

Source: IMF International Financial Statistics (June 1980).

In practice, this has not happened. Countries have felt obliged to intervene in foreign exchange markets as exchange rates have tended to 'overshoot' (or oscillate around) their long-run purchasing power parities. Speculation it seems has not been stabilising, with international capital markets adjusting at a faster rate to new circumstances than goods markets. For example, an initial loss of competitiveness by one country would tend to lead to a financial outflow induced depreciation of the currency in excess of that required when import and export markets fully adjust to new circumstances. Moreover forward exchange markets have proved too myopic to cater for this lagged process. As excessive movements, either way, of a currency lead to substantial social costs being incurred in the 'real' economy, government intervention continues to be necessary. The corollary, of course, is that centrally held international reserves also continue to be necessary.

Clearly, however, the advent of floating rates has removed much of what was previously difficult in the adjustment process, with national prestige no longer tied up in maintaining an unrealistic exchange rate. The adjustment problem of the 1980s seems instead to be concerned with the structural imbalances which substantially result from the oil crisis, but which at least for the non-oil developing countries probably have deeper roots.

The flexible exchange rate model where excess demand for the goods of another country would lead to a rise in the domestic price of that currency (and thus maintain payments equilibrium on a continuous basis) is not entirely appropriate to the world oil market. As most transactions between the OPEC producers and the rest of the world are conducted in US dollars (and not, for example, in Saudi Riyals) the equilibrating mechanism cannot work exactly as specified. Instead of the consumers' price of oil rising continuously as the dollar depreciates against the Riyal, the price of oil is set by the OPEC producers in dollars, somewhat *increasing* the underlying demand for that currency. The OPEC producers have tended, therefore, to accumulate dollar balances even more than they would have done if Western goods had been appearing on their markets at declining domestic prices (resulting from a rising Riyal/$ rate). Western industrialised countries have been able to attract these funds, financing trade deficits by the associated capital inflows.

Two important problems result from this situation, however. First, confidence in the US dollar as a reserve currency has to be maintained if foreign (especially OPEC) holders are not to cause massive destabilisation of foreign exchange rates as they seek a more secure asset. One condition for this may well be a strengthening of the underlying US balance of payments. This observation, despite the current German and Japanese deficits, leads to the second problem – the distribution of the payments deficits which must, at the world level, balance the OPEC surpluses. Current estimates suggest that following the latest (1979–80) round of oil price rises, the OPEC joint surplus for 1980 may well reach $100 billion. The counterpart deficit is expected to be shared roughly equally between the OECD nations and the non-oil developing countries[43] with the outturn probably being less favourable to the latter. These deficits are to be visited upon the poor countries at a time when, for many, indebtedness on world capital markets is at record heights. This, in turn, dates from previous terms of trade losses induced by rising oil prices and the associated recession in OECD export markets. It is not yet clear whether the level of borrowing achieved on Euro-currency and Euro-bond markets by these nations will be able to match the required levels given their existing indebtedness.[44] There is no doubt, however, that the poorest, least creditworthy states will continue to face a binding constraint on their ability to earn or to obtain foreign exchange.

Two major themes, therefore, emerge for the IMF in the 1980s: the vulnerability of international dollar reserves to speculation and the need for finance for the LDCs.[45] On the first issue, the main discussion has centred around the proposed Substitution Account already mentioned. Since the report of the Committee of Twenty, the Interim Committee has continued discussion of, and in March 1979 expressed 'broad support' for, such an account in the Fund. The currently most acceptable scheme would be a voluntary one in which countries would deposit currency reserves into the account and receive SDR denominated claims in exchange. Still under consideration is the return on the SDR claims and whether or not it would be the same as on existing SDRs. There is support for the proposal on several fronts. It would tend to increase the relative importance of the SDR in international reserves, a cause to which the IMF is committed. Additionally, particularly if it reduced the attractiveness of holding reserves in international capital markets, there would be better control of international reserve creation. Finally, and especially attractive to the oil producing countries, it would furnish a means of diversifying foreign exchange holdings into an asset subject to international control. This would reduce the political risk of having assets frozen (as with Iranian funds held in the US market) and the oil producing countries having increasing influence in the IMF.[46]

The major difficulty with the scheme, however, is that the SDR and SDR denominated securities would have to be made more attractive if countries are to give up dollar (and other currency) assets in favour of the new issues.[47] As set out in note 47 the SDR is gradually being made a more attractive asset with net creditor positions now receiving an interest rate of weighted average short-term money market rates in the USA, UK, Germany, France and Japan. For the Substitution Account to be rendered attractive, however, yields will probably need to be higher still and the question then arises as to how such a yield is to be financed.[48] The predominantly dollar denominated 'backing' will only return money market rates and remaining IMF gold reserves would probably need to be put to use in the scheme. It is possible though that the OPEC countries, given the political fears mentioned above, may be willing to settle for a scheme which produced money market rates of return without the commitment, as at present, to one country's capital markets. A major movement of their funds would be a substantial aid to stabilising foreign exchange markets as fears of speculative flows subsided. Paradoxically, however, this solution may render more intractable the adjustment difficulties of the LDCs. A movement towards money market rates of return on SDR creditor positions implies that net users (from Table 3.2, clearly the LDCs) would be paying these rates. This would emphasise Chrystal's point[49] that the SDR becomes not a reserve asset, but an unused credit facility. If this is so, irrespective of whether an SDR-aid link is ever established, it does mean that future allocations of SDRs will have little effect in reducing the debt service burden faced by LDCs. Only if OECD and/or OPEC subsidy is available will this problem be overcome.

The oil price increases of recent years have thrown into relief the underlying structural difficulties faced by LDCs in adjusting their capacity to earn or to save foreign exchange. It has been argued that the IMF has not been sensitive to the time scale involved in correcting these fundamental difficulties.[50] Thus, the techniques of monetary and fiscal control stressed by IMF negotiators in arranging tranche and stand-by credits[51] so often useful in developed countries (where governments can deflect some of the opprobrium for the measures on to the IMF) are often inappropriate in the LDC context. Contractionary policy to cure payments deficits can often only succeed at the cost of large (non-marginal) reductions in national income, due to the inflexibility mentioned previously.

On the contrary, then, with present levels of LDC indebtedness, and the recession in the industrialised world, it would be appropriate if some radical initiatives on LDC financing were to render adjustment *during the course of growth* possible. Such an approach, while having obvious beneficial effects on the LDCs concerned, would also help to maintain, or to expand, LDC demand for the exports of the OECD nations. Indeed it has been estimated that, following the initial oil price increase in 1974, continued LDC spending financed by borrowing sustained OECD output nearly 1 per cent above what it would otherwise have been. This was roughly the equivalent of a strong expansion in the German economy.

Debt rescheduling for a number of countries has already pushed the

IMF into an assessment of medium- and long-term prospects for the economies concerned. *De facto* the Fund is becoming involved in *development* finance and, as it will have to be made available on the basis of an agreed development programme, increasingly close co-operation between the IMF and the World Bank would seem desirable.

Our narrative has followed the development of the IMF from an institution constrained by the politics of its birth into a much more powerful body, partly as a result of changing political circumstances. It has been at its best, however, when seizing the initiative in the face of opposition, and the role of the IMF in the structural adjustments following the oil crisis needs to be more innovative than its past performance would generally predict.

NOTES: CHAPTER 3

1 Reported by R. F. Harrod, 'Problems perceived in the International Financial System', in A. L. K. Acheson (ed.), *Bretton Woods Revisited* (London: Macmillan, 1972), p. 12.

2 See especially references to the sterling area and the financial role of London – paras. 28 and 31 of the first draft plan. All references are to the version as in *The International Monetary Fund 1945–65, Vol. 3 Documents* (Washington, DC: IMF, 1969), p. 3.

3 Particularly R. Triffin, *Gold and the Dollar Crisis* (New Haven, Conn.: Yale University Press, 1960) and as noted about American government proposals to the 'Committee of Twenty' by R. Solomon, *The International Monetary System 1945–76* (New York: Harper & Row, 1977), p. 242.

4 In the non-political sense of Chapter 2.

5 F. Hirsch, *Alternatives to Monetary Disorder* (New York: McGraw-Hill, 1977), pp. 27–9).

6 R. N. Gardner, *Sterling-Dollar Diplomacy*, 2nd edn (New York: McGraw-Hill, 1969), p. 134.

7 R. Solomon, op. cit., p. 12.

8 F. Hirsch, 'The development and functioning of the post-war international monetary system', *Finance and Development*, vol. 9, no. 2 (June 1972).

9 R. Triffin in Introduction to Gardner, op. cit.

10 *The International Monetary Fund, 1945–1965, Vol. 1 Chronicle* (Washington, DC: IMF, 1969), p. 324.

11 E. M. Bernstein, 'The Evolution of the International Monetary Fund' in A. L. K. Acheson, *et al.* op. cit., p. 62.

12 ibid., p. 63.

13 *The International Monetary Fund, 1945–1965 Vol. 1 Chronicle* (Washington DC: IMF, 1969), p. 370.

14 *Finance and Development*, No. 3 (1970), p. 17.

15 Hirsch, *Alternatives to Monetary Disorder*, op. cit., p. 33, and Solomon, op. cit., p. 24.

16 Solomon, op. cit., p. 31.

17 ibid., p. 43.

18 Quoted in B. Tew, *The Evolution of the International Monetary System 1945–1977* (London: Hutchinson, 1977), p. 113.

19 Solomon, op. cit., p. 37.
20 ibid., p. 42. It was also necessary, given the previously indicated inadequacy in the Fund's ability to lend to major borrowers.
22 See Bernstein, op. cit.
23 Harrod, op. cit., p. 18.
24 Solomon, op. cit., p. 49.
25 ibid., p. 72.
26 J. Williamson, *The Failure of World Monetary Reform, 1971–74* (London: Nelson, 1977), pp. 41–2.
27 Solomon, op. cit., p. 60.
28 Gardner, op. cit., Introduction, p. LV.
29 ibid., p. LV.
30 S. D. Cohen, *International Monetary Reform 1964–69: The Political Dimension* (New York: Praeger, 1970), p. 132.
31 ibid., pp. 132–3.
32 *The International Monetary Fund 1945–1965, Vol. 3 Documents* (Washington, DC: IMF 1969), p. 509.
33 *The International Monetary Fund 1945–1965, Vol. 2 Analysis* (Washington, DC: IMF, 1969), p. 528.
34 Reported in Solomon, op. cit., p. 187.
35 Williamson, op. cit., p. 61. The following section depends on this source.
36 Solomon, op. cit., p. 243.
37 See D. Williamson, 'Increasing the resources of the Fund: borrowing', *Finance and Development*, vol. 13, no. 3 (September 1976).
38 A. Kafka, *The International Monetary Fund: reform without reconstruction?*, Essays in International Finance (Princeton: International Finance Section, Princeton University, October 1976), p. 31.
39 ibid., p. 16.
40 ibid., p. 16.
41 F. Hirsch, *Alternatives to Monetary Disorder*, op. cit., p. 44.
42 '10 billion dollars for the IMF', *The Economist*, 13 August 1977.
43 See *The Economist*, 22 March 1980, International Banking Survey Supplement, p. 15.
44 ibid., p. 43.
45 It is being assumed that the OECD countries will continue to be able to raise 'recycling' funds through the Euro-markets.
46 Saudi Arabia, as the second largest creditor nation, now has a permanent seat in the Executive.
47 The SDR has already been improved in several aspects:
(1) On 1 July 1974 it was valued against a 'standard basket' of currencies and ceased to be linked with gold. It is calculated daily on the basis of sixteen major currencies with 'weights' determined by the trade of the relevant country. For example, in February 1980 the US$ had a 'weight' of 30.6 per cent.
(2) The SDR net creditor/debtor position interest rate is now 80 per cent of the weighted average of short-term market rates in the USA, UK, W. Germany, France and Japan.
(3) The reconstitution requirement mentioned in the text has been reduced from 30 per cent to 15 per cent.
(4) Participating central banks can now freely exchange SDRs for currency without IMF intervention. They can be lent or pledged as security for a loan by another central bank or government. Finally, they can be used in 'swap' arrangements or in forward operations.
     All these make the SDR a more satisfactory substitute for conventional reserves.
48 See, for example, *Midland Bank Review* (Winter 1979), pp. 22–3.

49 K. A. Chrystal, 'International money and international reserves in the world economy', paper presented to the International Economics Study Group, September 1977.
50 Vijay Joshi, 'Exchange rates, international liquidity and economic development', *World Economy* (May 1979), p. 258.
51 O. E. G. Johnson, 'The use of Fund reserves and stand-by arrangements', *Finance and Development*, vol. 14, no. 1 (March 1977), p. 20, for an account of normal policy 'advice'.

CHAPTER 4

The General Agreement on Tariffs and Trade (GATT)

The main objectives of the GATT are the reduction of tariffs, the prohibition of quantitative restrictions and other non-tariff barriers to trade and the elimination of trade discrimination. In addition Part IV of the agreement, added in 1965, extended these objectives in the interests of the less developed countries to include efforts to stabilise commodity prices and to give better access to the markets of the developed countries for exports from developing countries.

The purpose of this chapter is to evaluate the GATT's contribution towards attainment of these objectives and, more broadly, to consider the GATT's overall contribution to world economic welfare in the past and its potential contribution in the near future. The world economy has changed in many ways since the inception of the GATT. The key question is whether the GATT remains relevant or not.

THE GATT APPROACH

The GATT fulfils several functions. It provides:

(1) a set of agreed rules to govern trade between nations;
(2) rules and procedures to facilitate and discipline negotiations between nations on trade and commerce;
(3) a forum for international multilateral negotiations on trade as well as for the day-to-day bilateral negotiations and conciliation meetings which form a large part of the normal work of the GATT;
(4) a small but highly skilled and experienced secretariat which can assist in all these matters through research and documentation of the issue and by the exercise of leadership and diplomacy.

RULES

The General Agreement is a very complex, detailed and technical document which sets out the rules for the conduct of trade between the

members and the many exceptions to these rules which political necessity requires. However, three rules and their exceptions are of particular
importance. The first is the rule against discrimination in imports or
exports. This is the most favoured nation (MFN) clause of the agreement which we quoted in Chapter 1. The major exception to the principle is the provision permitting full customs unions or free trade areas.
Preferential arrangements which existed before GATT were allowed to
continue but subject to negotiation and to erosion as tariffs in general
came down.

THE MOST FAVOURED NATION (MFN) PRINCIPLE

The MFN principle has a long history of use in tariff negotiations.
Traditionally its main purpose has been to ensure that a party to a tariff
negotiation does not find that the concession of a reduced tariff on its
exports to the other party is eroded by a greater concession made to a
third country at a later date. The advantage is that adoption of the MFN
principle increases confidence in the long-term value of any concessions
obtained in tariff negotiations. From a world viewpoint there is the
additional advantage that tariff reductions will be spread by the operation of the MFN principle. For example, if A and B have a tariff treaty
and B and C enter tariff negotiations any concessions made by B to C
will have to be given equally to A wherever similar products are
involved. Within the GATT, where all members have agreed to the
MFN clause, the effect is to multilateralise all bilateral agreements, thus
speeding up the liberalising of trade.

The economic rationale for the principle of non-discrimination is
that this gives the best prospects for the supply of the imported good
being from the country which is the most efficient, that is, the lowest
cost producer of that good. This is the basic objective of free trade.
Current economic theory, however, takes the view that the situation is
in practice much more complex than that assumed in the classic
analyses of the gains from free trade. The real world is characterised by
many distortions apart from tariffs on final goods: subsidies, over-
valued or undervalued exchange rates, tariffs or subsidies on inputs,
monopoly and artificial pricing of the outputs of state industries, differences between nations in tax policies – all of these can influence the
degree of protection or assistance afforded to industries. Accordingly it
is not possible to say that non-discrimination will *necessarily* result in a
more efficient production pattern than would tariff reductions that discriminated between countries. In addition, considerations of income
distribution may argue for the giving of preferential reductions in
tariffs on goods exported by low income countries. This argument may
be reinforced by a variation on the infant industry argument. The

growth of manufacturing industries in the developing countries, for example, may be fostered by abolishing tariffs on goods exported by them while retaining tariffs on similar goods imported from industrialised nations.

Perhaps the most telling argument for the MFN principle is the practical one that without it many countries would be reluctant to negotiate reductions in tariffs for fear that their trading rivals may be given a better deal at a later date. If we also accept that progress towards freer trade is likely to promote higher standards of living in the world, then the MFN clause has a valuable role to play through spreading tariff reductions across all the GATT member nations who, between them, account for over 80 per cent of world trade. The MFN principle has probably made a major contribution to the immense reduction in tariffs which has occurred in GATT negotiations, from Geneva in 1947 to the end of the Tokyo Round in 1979.

The 'second best' arguments for distortions to balance distortions, beloved by economic theorists, have plausibility in certain limited situations, but when considering sweeping cuts in tariffs across many countries and for a wide range of goods it is implausible that this does not represent a greater progress towards an optimum allocation of the world's productive resources than would any attempt at nicely adjusted discriminatory tariff cuts. The MFN clause may also benefit poorer countries with low bargaining power, in that as members of the GATT they automatically benefit, through the MFN principle, from all the tariff cuts agreed through reciprocal bargaining among the more powerful and richer members. This may not mean much to countries near the bottom of the income scale because their exports are often raw materials and food products which have not figured much in tariff cuts, either because they are already free of duties or because they affect sensitive areas in the economies of the industrially developed nations. But developing countries which have a fair range of manufactured exports have certainly benefited and of course all gain indirectly from prosperity in their main markets. Finally, discrimination breeds discrimination. While any two countries or a group may gain more from a discriminatory reduction of tariffs retaliatory action by others is likely to ensure that the world as a whole is worse off.

EXCEPTIONS TO THE MFN CLAUSE

The pre-existing preference systems such as Commonwealth preferences were permitted as an exception to the MFN rule. While important at the time and the source of bitter dispute between the UK and USA they have faded into insignificance with the passage of time.

Other small exceptions to the MFN rule include permission to impose anti-dumping duties on the exports of a country which are sold at less than the normal value of the goods. This is fairly closely controlled and involves showing that the good is being sold below its normal value, for example, the domestic price in the home market of the exporting country, and that this is causing or threatening 'material injury to an established industry in the territory of a contracting party or materially retards the establishment of a domestic industry' (Article VI). Moreover the 'countervailing duties' may not be any more than the estimated subsidy on the offending goods.

The major exception to the MFN principle lies in the permission to form customs unions or free trade areas provided these do not increase tariffs or other obstacles to trade with contracting parties outside the union or agreement and provided that the union or agreement results in the elimination of duties on substantially all trade between the members (Article XXIV). This provision had in mind the political benefits that might be obtained from economic integration in Europe but was also influenced by the belief that any substantial dismantling of tariffs between a group of countries would represent a step towards freer international trade. Subsequent research has shown that this need not be the case. The effect of a customs union or a free trade area is both 'trade creating' and 'trade diverting'. This means that the location of production of any traded good may move either to a more efficient country or may be diverted from an efficient source outside the union to a less efficient source within it. An example may make this clear.

Suppose three countries A, B and C (which may stand for the rest of the world) have costs of production for bicycles as shown below:

A	B	C
£40	£30	£20

If A's tariff is 100 per cent A will be self-sufficient in bicycles. Should A now form a customs union with B, abolishing tariffs on trade between them, A would import all the bicycles its consumers want from B. World efficiency would have improved as more efficient production in B replaces the inefficient bicycle industry in A. This represents trade creation.

If A's pre-union tariff had been 60 per cent, trade diversion would have occurred as a result of the union. A 60 per cent tariff would have excluded B bicycles, but country C would have supplied A's entire market. The abolition of the tariff on B's exports to A, however, would make B's bicycles cheaper to customers in A than the tariff inclusive price of £32 for bicycles from C. The location of production of bicycles purchased in A would move from C, the most efficient producer, to B, a less efficient producer.

The formation of the European Economic Community has resulted in one clear example of trade diversion. Its system of protection for agriculture has reduced imports of foodstuffs from the low cost producers of North America, Australasia and the Caribbean in favour of the relatively high cost farmers in Europe.

Of course the pros and cons of a given customs union go far beyond the mere static welfare economics outlined here. The situation is much more complex when repercussions on consumption patterns, on scale of production, attitudes to competition, foreign investment and many other factors are brought into the analysis. But there can be no clear preconception that a customs union or free trade area will necessarily increase the welfare, even of the members, let alone the world as a whole.

In fact the contracting parties to GATT have been reluctant to pronounce on whether various customs unions and free trade areas are compatible with the GATT. Most have met with hostility from some members and operate either with the tacit (but not explicit) consent of GATT, or under specific waiver. Further consideration of customs unions and free trade areas can be found in Chapters 8 and 9.

QUANTITATIVE RESTRICTIONS

The second important rule is that concerning quantitative restrictions. Under Article XI most direct controls on trade are forbidden as a general method of protection. However, a long list of exceptions to this rule has robbed it of a good deal of its force. When written it could clearly be no more than an expression of piety. Hardly any country other than USA would have been prepared to abandon the use of controls on trade in that period of acute dollar shortage which followed the Second World War. Restrictions to safeguard the balance of payments were specifically authorised and were justified on this basis well into the 1950s. Since then, most countries have resorted to other weapons such as temporary surcharges on imports to meet temporary balance of payments crises rather than use quotas, despite the fact that quotas are acceptable under the GATT while surcharges are not.

The disapproval of quantitative restrictions on trade has backing in economic theory. A quota which produces the same reduction in imports as a given tariff will always involve a greater loss of economic welfare. The effects on domestic production and consumption are uncertain. It is liable to give monopoly profits to domestic producers. Economic rents, arising from the restriction on the supply of imports, may accrue to home or foreign firms and, depending on their relative bargaining strengths, the terms of trade may even move against the country imposing the quota.

Despite these objections to quotas, quantitative restrictions, especially in agricultural protection, form the most important barriers to trade at the present time. So-called 'voluntary quotas' have also severely affected the exports of Japan, and of a number of developing countries, particularly in the field of textiles, clothing and footwear.

REDUCTION AND BINDING OF TARIFFS

Rules governing tariff negotiations can be found in various parts of the agreement. The MFN clause is of course highly relevant, but Article XXVIII stresses the importance of 'negotiations on a reciprocal and mutually advantageous basis' to reduce tariffs and other imposts on trade. The agreement recognises that there are great disparities between tariff levels and states that, 'the binding against increase of low duties or of duty-free treatment shall, in principle, be recognised as a concession equivalent in value to the reduction of high duties'. It is also worthy of note that even in 1947 the special situation of developing countries was taken into account by acknowledging their need, 'for a more flexible use of tariff protection to assist their economic development and the special needs of these countries to maintain tariffs for revenue purposes' (Article XXVIII, Sec. 3(b)).

One point to stress is that negotiations were expected to involve *reciprocity*. At first sight this sits oddly with notions of the benefits of free trade and also with the MFN principle. The latter extends tariff reductions arrived at through negotiations between any of the contracting parties to all the other members of GATT whether or not they have reduced any of their tariffs. In practice reciprocity has been confined to the major trading nations who have done most of the bargaining and benefits have spilled over to the smaller and poorer nations. This is fortunate for they would have had little to offer by way of return.

The notion of reciprocity also seems at odds with theory for it appears to imply that the reduction of a duty on an import benefits only the exporting country. Each tariff cut is seen as a concession to be matched by a reciprocal concession from a trading partner, but the main gain from a cut in tariffs is the release of resources from inefficient use in producing goods directly, for use in increasing exports which can be exchanged to obtain imported goods more cheaply than they can be produced at home. A secondary gain stems from an increased stimulus to competition.

Despite these traditional arguments for unilateral tariff cuts one does not have to attribute an archaic mercantilism to the politicians to justify their preference for negotiations based on reciprocity. It is undoubtedly the case that multilateral tariff cuts bring greater benefits to a nation than simply cutting its own tariffs. For one thing the terms of trade are less likely to move against it. But slow adjustment problems, frictional unemployment, immobility of capital and other costs of reallocation of resources will also be less in a world in which demand for one's exports is rising commensurately with increased imports.

The once-over increase in world income resulting from the more efficient allocation of resources brought about by general tariff cuts will widen markets, bring additional economies of scale, enhance competition and generally improve managerial efficiency. These advantages would justify a nation, which firmly believed in the advantages of free trade, in holding on to its existing tariffs as bargaining counters to try, through exacting reciprocal tariff cuts, to see a much greater movement to freer trade than could be gained by unilaterally cutting its own duties, and lowering its exchange rate to maintain external balance-of-payments equilibrium.

Reciprocity, when interpreted narrowly, can have its own dangers in slowing negotiations and we shall return to this in considering the Kennedy Round and subsequent developments.

NEGOTIATIONS UNDER THE GATT

An important part of the work of the GATT is in dealing with disputes which arise between members. Procedures are laid down for aiding in the settlement of grievances. When one party feels that another member is failing to meet its obligations under the GATT it is advised to make direct representations to the offending member. Since 1958 such complaints have been circulated to all GATT members and any country which can claim an interest is entitled to participate in the discussions and any decisions are reported to all members. In this way the interests of all can be considered. Should no satisfactory conclusion be reached a panel of conciliation is appointed from independent experts selected from delegations not involved in the dispute. Normally the recommendations of such a panel are accepted, but on the few occasions when this has not happened the aggrieved party may receive permission to use retaliatory measures.

The more exciting activity within GATT, however, arises in the periodic grand multilateral negotiations which have occurred every few years since 1947. The first of these, the tariff negotiating conference in Geneva in 1947, was intended as a staging point en route to the creation of the International Trade Organisation (ITO). In the end the ITO never emerged but the conference itself was successful. Twenty-three countries took part in item-by-item negotiations. It resulted in 123 agreements relating to about half of world trade. The USA cut tariffs on 54 per cent of US dutiable imports. Tariffs on US dutiable imports as a whole were cut by 18.9 per cent, computed as a weighted average.

Reasons for the success in this first test of the GATT were the enthusiasm of the US government for liberalised trade, the bargaining power possessed by the USA as a result of its relative strength compared with the war-torn European economies and the willingness of the USA to trade tariff cuts on its own imports (which took effect immediately) against 'sham' tariff cuts in Europe and the other negotiating countries which would have no effect while they retained strict quantitative controls on their trade. The world as a whole benefited – Europe through its enhanced ability to earn scarce dollars from exports to the USA, and the USA through enhanced opportunities for employment in producing the goods which Europe could now afford to buy. American political objectives of a strengthened European economy, able to share the burdens of defence and less likely to turn to communism through economic frustrations, were also a more immediate payoff. In the longer run, of course, the USA also benefited from the reduced tariffs facing its exports when the European economies eventually relaxed their controls on imports.

The negotiating techniques typical of GATT, at least until the Kennedy Round, were on a product-by-product basis and started off by an exchange of lists between a pair of negotiators. Their lists contained offers to bind or reduce tariffs on goods in which the other country was the principal supplier and 'request lists' seeking reductions in tariffs facing the first country's main exports to the other country. This is just the same old procedure worked out in centuries of bilateral negotiations. The difference under GATT was that these lists were circulated to all participants who could then take them into account in their own negotiations and, where they had a major interest, join in the bargaining. As a result of the MFN clause all benefited by any concessions affecting goods which they exported even though they had taken no direct part in the bargaining. Consequently, at least some of the benefits of multilateralisation were achieved despite the basic item-by-item bargaining and the insistence on reciprocity.

The subsequent international tariff conferences up to the end of the fifth or 'Dillon Round' of GATT negotiations produced relatively small reductions in tariffs. The reasons for this were partly that they had different and more limited objectives such as dealing with the accession of new members or the effects of the creation of the European Economic Community. The unwillingness of Britain and Commonwealth countries to reduce Commonwealth preferences was also an obstacle in the earlier years. Other reasons, however, were the reduced negotiating authority of the US Administration, which was not extended significantly until Congress passed President Kennedy's Trade Expansion Act of 1962, and the belief that item-by-item bilateral negotiations had outlived their usefulness. The Kennedy Round represented a new and ambitious effort to put life into GATT negotiations.

THE KENNEDY ROUND 1964–67

The weakness of the traditional product-by-product approach to GATT negotiations was laid bare by the meagre successes of the conferences, from Annecy in 1949 to the end of the Dillon Round in 1962. There was general dissatisfaction with the method and wide support for linear tariff cuts across a wide range of products. One argument for this approach is that within a country the pressures from those who gain from the cuts may offset the cries for continued protection from industries which suffer. It may also encourage a more liberal approach to reciprocity. Other sources of dissatisfaction were the lack of progress in reducing restrictions in agricultural trade, the continuance of many non-tariff barriers and the apparent neglect of the special trading interests of the developing countries. The increased participation of the LDCs in GATT and in the UN, the creation of the EEC and EFTA all demanded new initiatives. These came from the Kennedy administration in the USA.

In his message to Congress commending the Trade Expansion Bill, President Kennedy listed 'five fundamentally new and sweeping developments (which) have made obsolete our traditional trade policy'. These were: (1) growth of the EEC, (2) pressure on the US balance of payments, (3) need to accelerate US growth, (4) the communist threat in aid and trade and (5) the need for new markets for Japan and the developing countries.[1] The Bill actually met little opposition in Congress and the Trade Expansion Act gave the President very great negotiating powers. He gained a general authority to reduce tariffs by 50 per cent over five years and to reduce to zero tariffs which were already 5 per cent or lower on an *ad valorem* basis. Provided agreement was obtained with the EEC he could (a) cut to zero tariffs on all goods where the USA and the EEC together supplied 80 per cent or more of world trade, (b) reduce to zero the tariff on any agricultural commodities if this would help US exports of the same commodities and (c) reduce to zero tariffs on tropical products not produced in the USA, if the EEC would do the same.

An escape clause was retained in the new act but with a radical innovation. If an import threatened serious injury to a US industry the President could: (1) adjust the rate of duty or use import restrictions, (2) conclude a 'market agreement' with the offending country to limit its export or (3) he could provide adjustment assistance to industries and their workers. This last provision was a surprisingly liberal and constructive approach to the problem. Another liberal move was to omit the traditional tightly defined 'peril points' for each commodity. Instead the Tariff Commission would advise the President as to the probable economic effect of tariff reductions. The 'dominant supplier' provision, which would have permitted reductions to zero on commodities where US and EEC supplies exceeded 80 per cent of world trade, while not contrary to GATT rules was discriminating in intention. It would have gone some way to establishing a free trade area between the USA and the members of an extended EEC since the removal of tariffs would be concentrated on goods of interest to them and not on goods where other countries were the major suppliers. In the event, France's veto of Britain's entry into the EEC in January 1963 ultimately destroyed the dominant supplier arrangement. The commodities eligible were reduced from twenty-five to two: vegetable oils and aircraft.

THE NEGOTIATIONS

In the preliminary discussions the idea of linear tariff cuts ran into immediate difficulties. The EEC countries, with some justification, drew attention to the problem of tariff disparities between the USA and the EEC countries. Eighty per cent of the EEC's external tariffs lay in the range 4–18 per cent while the American schedule showed a wider range of 2–38 per cent.[2] The EEC view was that very high tariffs had a lot of 'water' in them, that is, they would still exclude imports even if halved. An American spokesman had acknowledged the disparity in a statement to Congress in which he claimed that over one-sixth of the rates in the US tariff were above 30 per cent, whereas less than one-fifteenth of Europe's rates ran over 30 per cent.[3] The Six insisted on a levelling off of the high duties before acceptance of a single linear cut. They put forward a counter-proposal which aimed at a 50 per cent cut in the difference between the actual duty and an agreed target rate. The rates they suggested as ideal targets ranged from 0 to between 10 and 12 per cent, with the zero rates on raw materials and the rates rising with the state of processing. In practice the appearance of liberalism in these low rates is rather illusory since they would give fairly high *effective rates of protection* to manufacturing.

Further difficulties for the linear approach lay in the long lists of exceptions put forward by the participating countries. These had the unfortunate effect of pushing much of the work of the conference back onto a bilateral basis. Progress towards freer trade in agriculture was also slowed by the need for the EEC to settle its own policy. This delayed negotiations and turned out to be rather protectionist.

In the end, face-saving compromises were made and the slow process of negotiations went ahead from May 1964 to May 1967. The compromises did, however, erode the bold strategy of the simple linear tariff-cutting approach. Canada, Australia, New Zealand and South Africa did not participate in the linear bargaining, but negotiated *ad hoc*. The LDCs were also in the non-linear category since no reciprocity was expected from them. The whole agriculture issue was treated differently, the large exception lists involved a retreat to bilateral negotiations and the negotiations over the thorny problem of the American selling price system of protection in chemicals had to be split off from the main discussions.

THE ACHIEVEMENTS OF THE KENNEDY ROUND

Despite all the difficulties and the interminable haggling over reciprocity the achievements were considerable, far greater than in any other round of tariff negotiations. The main gains were in the reduction of non-agricultural tariff levels. Here, despite the difficulties of quantifying the gains from tariff reduction, it can be said that 'The average Kennedy Round reduction of 36–39 per cent by all major industrial countries was fully in keeping with the ambitious initial objectives. About two-thirds of tariff cuts were for 50 per cent or more, while a degree of tariff harmonisation greater than that inherent in linear cuts was achieved in the steel and chemical sectors as well as in scattered cases elsewhere.'[4] Smaller reductions were gained in textiles, iron and steel. This left textiles highly protected, but for iron and steel tariffs were already fairly low and unimportant as obstacles to trade.[5]

The agricultural negotiations showed relatively meagre progress, but even this was greater than had looked possible in the earlier negotiations. Substantial cuts were made in tariffs in both tropical and non-tropical products but little was achieved in the key areas of grains, meats and dairy products. The Common Agricultural Policy of the EEC proved a formidable obstacle. Arrangements for trade in grains, including price ranges for wheat and a joint food aid commitment, were agreed. The old International Wheat Agreement was replaced by the International Grains Arrangement to run for a three-year period starting on 1 July 1968. The purpose of the food aid commitment was to spread the load of supplying food aid to developing countries. Worthy though these two causes may be they have little to do with the traditional objectives of the GATT in fostering free international trade.

In the area of non-tariff barriers (NTBs) at least a start was made in the Kennedy Round. Some of the worst features of national anti-dumping regulations were eliminated in the new agreement on an international anti-dumping code. Ultimately the negotiations over the American selling price system brought the removal of several minor grievances, such as the uncertainty produced by arbitrary valuations by US customs in benzenoid chemicals, on one side, and the European road taxes which discriminated against large American cars, on the other.

ASSESSMENTS OF DEVELOPING COUNTRIES' GAINS

Although some twenty-seven developing countries took part in the negotiations the LDCs as a group were very dissatisfied with the results. Actually tariff cuts on non-agricultural exports of special interest to developing countries were substantial, averaging over 30 per cent if petroleum is excluded. However, this was less than for industrialised nations and the reason lay in the below average reductions in duties on textiles and processed agricultural products. They were justly incensed that even the modest tariff cuts on textiles were made conditional on the continuance of the GATT long-term quota arrangement which restricted severely their prospects for increasing exports of cotton textiles. It was in any case inevitable that the GATT negotiations brought most LDCs few immediate gains, given that over 80 per cent of their exports were raw materials which already faced low or zero tariffs. The negotiations were conducted on the basis that no reciprocal concessions would be asked of developing countries and the operation of the MFN clause ensured that all tariff reductions were passed on to them. For those LDCs that were actual or potential exporters of manufactures the benefits of the Kennedy Round were considerable. The rapid growth in manufactured exports from Brazil, Hong Kong, Taiwan, Singapore and South Korea over the late 1960s and early 1970s is in part due to the Kennedy Round.

GATT IN THE KENNEDY ROUND

The Kennedy Round represented one further step towards the GATT goal of multilateralisation. Even though the linear approach suffered many setbacks it did prove its worth in the end. A great many of the tariff cuts on industrial goods were a straight 50 per cent. The reciprocity principle, however, continued to be interpreted too narrowly by most of the negotiators. The professionals involved in the negotiations were perhaps apt to become involved in a bargaining game, losing sight of the overall objective of raising living standards in favour of the narrow view of gaining some margin for one's own exports in return for each 'concession' on imports, even though neither concession's effects could be measured with any confidence.

The failures of the Kennedy Round were not the result of either the institution of GATT or the principles involved in the new approach, but lay in the deep-rooted protectionist attitudes to agriculture embedded in European nations.

The GATT secretariat and Wyndham White (then GATT's Director General) played a crucial role in the negotiations. As a member of the US negotiating team put it, their 'technical support was objective, and the co-ordination of meetings was carried out so as to instill an impulse of progress but without becoming overbearing'. In the end the deadlock over chemicals was broken by the adoption, at the eleventh hour, of a package that was essentially identical with one proposed by Wyndham White two months earlier.[6]

GATT AND THE DEVELOPING COUNTRIES

The early history of GATT shows general indifference to or lack of awareness of the special problems of the less developed countries. True, Article XVIII released them from certain of the obligations of GATT membership but only under close scrutiny and annual examination of their situation. This proved too unattractive to most LDCs and in fact from 1947 to 1957 only Ceylon made use of Article XVIII. Their Minister of Commerce made clear in 1954 his dislike of that article. He declared[7] that its unattractiveness

> is evidenced by the fact that although there are so many under-developed countries who are members of the GATT, very few have cared to avail themselves of this article. Those of us who have had recourse to its provisions . . . find that the restrictions and limitations it places practically destroy the benefits that it professes to confer.

Most LDCs during this period simply made use of the balance-of-payments reason for applying quantitative restrictions. As most of the developed nations were doing the same thing they could hardly object. Participation by LDCs in GATT was minimal. Out of the twenty-three initial members in 1947 ten were LDCs. Ten years later this had grown only to thirteen. The lack of interest was hardly surprising. Real concern with the problems of the Third World is of relatively recent origin. In the aftermath of the Second World War most nations were preoccupied with reconstruction, development and reform at home. Development assistance was in any case the responsibility of the World Bank, not GATT.

By the mid-1950s, however, some signs of change were appearing. The GATT publication *International Trade* in 1954 showed a declining share of world trade for the LDCs. In 1957 increasing concern for the problems of LDCs led to the GATT appointing a group of experts to examine the issues. Their report, *Trends in International Trade, 1958* (the Haberler Report) drew attention to the role played by the trade policies of the rich countries in contributing to the difficulties of the LDCs. The authors were also critical of aspects of LDCs' trade policies which militated against exports and ran counter to their comparative advantage.

GATT reacted responsibly to the criticisms by setting up a new committee, Committee III, to deal with the special problems of LDCs. Its studies, followed up by its successor, the GATT Trade and Development Committee, and by the UNCTAD revealed the remarkable extent to which rich countries were hindering both the traditional exports of LDCs and their exports of manufactures. They found high tariffs, special internal taxes, quantitative restrictions and escalated tariffs which discriminated against LDCs' exports. Because they had few concessions to offer, developing countries had been unable to make much progress in bilateral negotiations to obtain reductions in these barriers to their trade. 'Of 4,400 tariff concessions made in the Dillon Round, only 160 were on items then considered to be of export interest to less developed countries.'[8]

The concept of 'effective protection' gained prominence both in academic literature and in international debate as a matter of particular concern to the LDCs. Nominal tariffs on elementary processed materials were often low, of the order of 10 per cent, but if the raw material entered duty free this could mean an effective rate of protection for the processing industry of as much as 80 per cent. The effective tariff rate is calculated on the value added in processing. This tends to be small for many actual and potential exports from LDCs and consequently the effective protection rate is high.

Despite plentiful documentation and discussion of the discrimination against LDCs' exports little was done to correct it. Finally, in 1963 twenty-one LDCs introduced a resolution calling for an Action Programme to stop new tariff or non-tariff barriers to LDC exports, and elimination by 1965 of all illegal quantitative restrictions, tariffs on primary products, reduction of tariffs on semiprocessed and processed products, and removal of internal taxes on tropical beverages and other mainly LDC exported products.

Some progress was made. Customs duties were eliminated from some tropical products, but divisions among the LDCs, between those whose exports benefited from EEC or Commonwealth preferences and those whose did not, inhibited a united effort to gain free entry of LDC exports to developed countries' markets.

A desire to meet the criticisms of GATT made by LDCs led to the adoption in 1965 of a new Part IV to the General Agreement. This dealt with trade and development and committed developed countries to assist the developing countries 'as a matter of conscious and purposeful effort'. While permeated with admirable sentiments Part IV contained few explicit commitments to meet the demands of the LDCs. It did, however, embody one principle of importance on reciprocity. This was the statement that

> The developed contracting parties do not expect reciprocity for commitments made by them in trade negotiations to reduce or remove tariffs and other barriers to the trade of the less developed contracting parties.

The idea was not new, it was already in the resolution setting forth the principles for the Kennedy Round and in any case had already been practised in trade negotiations, but inclusion in the agreement gave it greater force.

Developed countries also agreed to refrain from increasing barriers to LDC exports and to give high priority to the reduction of existing barriers including fiscal taxes. However, the phraseology used left plenty of scope for avoiding actually having to do anything. The GATT Committee on Trade and Development was set up at the same time to look after the concerns of the LDCs. In 1971 a 'Group of Three', the Chairman of the contracting parties, the Council, and the Committee on Trade and Development, got together to explore the possibilities of removing certain obstacles to imports by developed countries from LDCs and to advise on how Part IV was being, and could be, implemented.

As we noted above the LDCs had great expectations from the Kennedy Round in which one objective was to promote their interests. The outcome of course disappointed them, but they did benefit directly and indirectly in the ways noted in our discussion of the results of the Kennedy Round. The continual feeling among the governments of LDCs that they had not benefited from GATT as much as they ought built up pressure for an alternative organisation in which the issues of trade, aid and development could be handled together. This led directly to the United Nations Conference on Trade, Aid and Development in Geneva in 1964. We shall return to this later (Chapter 5).

Despite these expressions of disillusionment with GATT the LDC membership has increased greatly. Out of the hundred-odd countries which are members, or are applying GATT regulations pending decisions on whether to join or not, at least sixty-seven can be counted as LDCs. This may be partly due to a recognition that GATT does in the end bring results based on the acceptance of the hard realities of the bargaining process. UNCTAD speeches and resolutions are no substitute for that.

THE INTERNATIONAL TRADE CENTRE AND TECHNICAL ASSISTANCE

One further aspect of GATT and the LDCs is the valuable technical assistance which GATT has made available to their civil servants. Over the years many hundreds of officials from over seventy countries have attended five-month training courses on trade policy problems.

The International Trade Centre (ITC) was set up by GATT in 1964 to aid developing countries in promoting their exports. Since 1968 the centre has been jointly operated by GATT and UNCTAD. It makes its help freely available to all LDCs, providing assistance, on request, to plan and implement export programmes, helping with market research, marketing techniques and in training personnel for these activities. The ITC has a cadre of advisers who are available to provide short-term assistance of a specialised nature and it has established export promotion centres in many developing countries.

GATT TODAY

Developments of the 1960s raise sober doubts as to the permanence of GATT. . . . The Kennedy Round may emerge in the perspective of history as the twilight of the GATT.

These remarks by John W. Evans,[9] Assistant Special Representative for Trade in the Executive Office of the US President, typify the comments of many analysts of recent events. From 1947 to the end of the Kennedy Round GATT presided over a remarkable progress towards freer international trade. Protectionism, however, was never defeated and the aftermath of the Kennedy Round witnessed a powerful resurgence of protectionist lobbies, particularly in the USA. Led by the American chemical industry, but followed swiftly by others, an attack on the results of the Kennedy Round was mounted in Congress. Before the end of 1967 dozens of Bills had been introduced to provide for the imposition of quotas on imports. Support for protectionist measures came from the difficulties which the USA was experiencing with its balance of payments. Rampant protectionism in America seemed likely to undo the results of the Kennedy Round.

The Americans charged that they had been cheated. European nations had, in their view, substituted non-tariff barriers, adjustments in border taxes and reimbursement of taxes to exports which between them amounted to duties on imports and subsidies to exports. These charges had little or no basis in fact. The moves to harmonise taxes within the EEC did lead to changes in taxes on imports and in tax rebates to exports but these were not protectionist in intention, nor significantly so in practice. The widespread American belief that other developed countries had raised non-tariff barriers against them was based on misconceptions about the domestic tax changes in Europe and temporary surcharges placed on imports by Britain and France during their balance-of-payments crises.

If America, the world's largest trading power, turned protectionist and imposed widespread import restrictions the direct impact would affect half the world's trade immediately. The economic and political repercussions would set the course of free trade back for decades. Fortunately the American administrations up to now have fought off the protectionists.

AGRICULTURAL PROTECTIONISM IN EUROPE

Even before the Kennedy Round had got under way the EEC had chosen the protectionist route in agriculture. The variable levy system of the Common Agricultural Policy (CAP) adopted by the Community, while it may not have violated any specific GATT rule, was about as contrary to the spirit of GATT as could be. It effectively protected the least efficient producers of many commodities from foreign competition. The combination of the various agricultural policies in Europe gave rise to the absurdities of the 'butter-mountain' and of grain and sugar exports from Europe. The protection given to beet sugar was particularly damaging to the cane sugar producers of the Third World.

THE SPREAD OF DISCRIMINATION

During and after the Kennedy Round the spread of preferential trading blocs accelerated. New agreements included: the Arab Common Market, the Central African Economic and Customs Union, the New Zealand/Australia Free Trade Agreement, the association of several African states with EEC, the Caribbean Free Trade Agreement and the Trade Expansion and Economic Co-operation Agreement between India, the United Arab Republic and Yugoslavia. By 1969 seventeen regional arrangements covering over eighty member countries had been registered with GATT. Very few of them met the conditions laid down in the relevant sections of the agreement. The rapid extension of agreements between EEC and the Mediterranean nations in 1970 added yet another large bloc of trade discrimination. However, the real shock to countries outside of Europe and Africa came with the renewed prospect of a union of the EEC with the EFTA countries.

Three years after the Kennedy Round the structure of international trade was very different from the prospects that faced negotiators in 1962. The share of world trade to which MFN duties applied had already diminished noticeably, and the impending enlargement of the Community promised a further drastic contraction.[10]

The subsequent entry of Britain, Ireland and Denmark has, of course, fulfilled that promise. The inclusion in the EEC of Greece, Spain, Portugal and possibly Turkey would reinforce the point.

PREFERENCES FOR LESS DEVELOPED COUNTRIES

The second major breach in the GATT principle of non-discrimination came in the eventual adoption by most of the developed nations of some system of generalised preferences for manufactured exports from LDCs. The idea was put forward at the 1964 UNCTAD meeting and after years of delay somewhat bowdlerised versions of the principle have emerged. Most sensitive areas such as textiles and leathergoods have been excluded by most of the industrial nations, but in other industries they have allowed duty free entry to LDCs' exports.

VOLUNTARY QUOTAS AND OTHER RESTRICTIONS ON IMPORTS

Another fundamental principle of GATT is the outlawing of quantitative restrictions as a protective device. Recently, however, they have proliferated in a new guise. Japan and many LDCs have been coerced into the adoption of 'voluntary' limitations of exports to America and the EEC by threats of more severe unilateral restrictions if they do not comply. The USA has introduced quotas on colour television sets from Japan and on shoes from Taiwan and South Korea, and Japan has shown few inhibitions in maintaining non-tariff barriers by one device or another.

European car manufacturers complain bitterly of bureaucratic administration of new car acceptability regulations in Japan as well as tightly controlled dealerships which exclude them. Italy responded with a tight quota against imports of Japanese cars. Britain concluded a voluntary export restraint agreement with Japanese car manufacturers and there have been demands from the motor industry in the rest of Europe for similar measures.[11] With the reduction of tariffs to their present low levels non-tariff barriers have certainly increased in relative importance. They may have increased absolutely as well.

THE MARCH OF EVENTS

The environment of world commerce has changed in many ways since the inception of GATT. The growth in importance of the developing countries is one significant change that we have already noted. Another, with profound implications, is the growth of the multinational corporations and the increase in the mobility of capital and technology between nations.

Increased mobility of factors serves the overall GATT objective of more efficient use of world resources, but the multinationals bring with them many complications for the economy and polity of nations. It is an anomaly that GATT has no provisions for dealing with the problems which they raise in the commerce of nations: concentration of economic power, risks of cartelisation or other restriction on trade, intra-firm trade and transfer pricing, government controls on foreign investment, to name but a few.

ECONOMIC CRISES

The late 1960s and early 1970s have been fraught with perils to the GATT ideals. A series of monetary crises culminating in the oil crisis of 1973 spelt the end of the era of Bretton Woods. The dollar exchange standard with pegged exchange rates which were changed reluctantly and only in conditions of fundamental disequilibrium has given way to an international monetary system of floating exchange rates subject to varying degrees of official intervention. These crises and their monetary implications were considered in Chapter 3 on the IMF. Here we are concerned with their implications for world trade and how they may influence the role of GATT.

Faced with the problems generated by the huge flows of finance involved in their oil deficits, exacerbated by the post-Iranian Revolution price increases, some countries may be tempted to use competitive devaluations, restrictions on trade or domestic deflation in efforts to control inflation and current balance-of-payments deficits. Such actions could have a multiplier effect, through the reactions of their trading partners, leading to a worldwide depression. If countries seek to find their own salvation through bilateral agreements with oil producers, and attempts to earn balance-of-payments surpluses from other net oil importers to pay for oil imports, they are likely not only to destroy international co-operation and the existing intergovernmental institutions, but also themselves in the process.

Further tariff-cutting in a world in which the annual rates of inflation greatly exceed the average height of tariffs might seem of little importance but the argument for the gains from international specialisation does remain. When low tariffs are cut to zero there are significant gains to trade simply from ending their nuisance value. Low nominal tariffs also sometimes give high effective protection, but it is true that non-tariff barriers are the chief obstacles to trade today. A return to protectionism would do nothing to solve the immediate crises while destroying much of the gains painstakingly achieved through years of negotiations within the GATT. The solution most likely to save the world from the worst economic crisis since the 1930s lies in further development of the international co-operation which has served so well in the past. Protectionism would lead to a shrinking of world trade and this would deal a further crippling blow to the exports of the majority of the developing countries. Policies which expanded, or at least helped to prevent the contraction of, world trade would benefit all, including the oil exporters. GATT remains the obvious intergovernmental organisation to handle these issues. It has become all the more important for nations to support the GATT principles, because these may be all that stand between order and chaos in trade relations.

THE CHANGE IN STATUS OF THE UNITED STATES

Up to the mid-1960s the power and prestige of the United States supported a liberal trade regime, but over the decades since the first Geneva Round of tariff negotiations there have been profound changes in international relationships. The overwhelming dominance of the United States in politics and economics declined. The rise of the EEC and Japan established new centres of economic and political power. The problems of the developing countries were pushed to the centre of the stage. The Organisation of Petroleum Exporting Countries (OPEC) suddenly changed from a 'paper tiger' to the real thing in 1973. Trade with the Eastern bloc Centrally Planned Economies (CPEs) became significant. All of these developments raised new problems in trading relationships or exacerbated old ones. The progressive weakening of the dollar and increasing US balance-of-payments difficulties throughout the 1960s and early 1970s, together with the Vietnam debacle, weakened American self-confidence and enhanced attitudes of particular self-interest as compared to the magnanimity with which US leaders had in earlier years borne discrimination against their exports by Europe, Japan and the LDCs. These changes in attitudes influenced the negotiations and outcomes of the Tokyo Round.

THE TOKYO ROUND OR MULTILATERAL TRADE NEGOTIATIONS (MTN) 1973–79

Despite the skeptics who wrote off the GATT after the Kennedy Round yet another grand negotiation in the GATT was mounted and brought, eventually, to completion. It sought to deal with many of the issues which arose from these new developments in trade relationships outlined above. For example, the 'Tokyo Declaration' adopted in September 1973 by the ministers of about one hundred countries laid great stress on securing 'additional benefits for the international trade of developing countries'. Reference to the need to pay special attention to the needs of developing countries runs like a refrain through almost every section of the text. Particular aims of the negotiations were to include reduction or elimination of non-tariff measures, an examination of emergency safeguards procedures – especially the operation of Article XIX of the GATT, to take account of the special characteristics and problems of trade in agriculture, treating trade in tropical products as a priority sector. Finally, it was emphasised that 'the policy of liberalising world trade cannot be carried out successfully in the absence of parallel efforts to set up a monetary system which shields the world economy from the shocks and imbalances which have previously occurred'.

THE DELAYS IN THE TOKYO ROUND

It was originally intended that negotiations should be completed by 1975, but the European Economic Community was not able to agree on its negotiating stance among its members until early 1975 and the enabling legislation in the USA was not completed until President Ford signed the Trade Reform Act in January 1975. By then the US government was moving into a pre-election period and, in effect, most important economic and political decisions were postponed until President Carter and the new administration took office in January 1977. Despite this political hiatus technical discussions made some progress. Seven groups were set up to consider the following specific topics: (1) tariffs and the appropriate negotiating schemes; (2) non-tariff measures, covering in sub-groups, quantitative restrictions (including voluntary restraints), technical barriers, customs issues, subsidies and countervailing duties; (3) agriculture (grains, meat and dairy products); (4) safeguards; (5) the 'sector' approach, that is, to look at the possibilities for co-ordinated reduction or elimination of all barriers to trade in selected sectors; (6) tropical products; (7) 'special and differential treatment for developing countries'.

THE RESULTS OF THE MTN[12]

A general assessment of the results of the MTN is that they did make some progress towards the achievement of some of the original objectives, but that they failed to contain the spread of protectionism, and despite all the 1973 rhetoric about the importance of securing special gains for developing countries, the upshot was that the negotiations were very largely among the rich nations. The developing countries took relatively little part in the main debates and most of their gains from the MTN were incidental. These points can be established by examining the results in each of the main areas of negotiation.

TARIFFS

The main controversy here centred on the formula to be used as the basis for the linear or across-the-board tariff cuts on manufactures. The main protagonists as in the Kennedy Round were the USA and the EEC. The Community's tariff level, because of the averaging process used to arrive at the EEC's common external tariffs, tends to be fairly uniform at about 8–9 per cent, while the US tariff rates show a much greater dispersion about their average level of about 7.9 per cent. Each proposed a formula that would produce the larger cut in the protection level of the other party. The Americans conceded a little to harmonisation – a cut of 60 per cent on tariffs above 6.66 per cent and of slightly smaller amounts (down to 50 per cent) on lower duties. Whereas the EEC proposed that a given tariff be cut by its own percentage four times so that high tariffs would be reduced a great deal and low tariffs by very little. A compromise was eventually achieved on a formula proposed by the Swiss, whereby the final tariff would equal $AX/A + X$ where X is the original tariff rate and A is a parameter that could be set by each country. This produces a considerable degree of harmonisation with a parameter of 14 to 16. The Swiss actually proposed 14 but the EEC eventually adopted 16. The effect of the latter is to reduce a 5 per cent tariff to 3.8 per cent while a 50 per cent tariff falls to 12.1 per cent. On the original US formula the 5 per cent tariff would drop to 2.5 per cent while the 50 per cent tariff would fall to 20 per cent. Ultimately most tariff offers in the negotiation roughly approximated the Swiss formula, and eight years was settled as the time over which the tariff reductions would be phased in to effect.

Attempts to quantify the effects of the tariff negotiations are fraught with difficulty, but all estimates agree that the effects on trade, employment and resource allocation are small. This was inevitable given the low initial level of most tariffs in manufactures and the resistance of the EEC to deep cuts in the common external tariff which is one *raison d'être* for the community's existence. The GATT secretariat estimate is that when fully introduced, tariff levels on all industrial goods traded among the ten developed import markets would fall by about a third on a weighted average basis and the 'total value of trade affected by MFN tariff reductions and bindings at prevailing rates amounts to more than \$125 billion'.[13] Also differences in the national tariff levels were considerably reduced by the effects of harmonisation. But the average tariffs on all industrial products pre-MTN were only 7.2 per cent on a weighted basis and post-MTN they become 4.9 per cent – a rate of reduction of 33 per cent.[14] Such changes are fairly insignificant. The welfare impact of these tariff reductions – which has been estimated to range from an increase of 0.53 per cent in gross domestic product for Ireland to a mere 0.02 per cent for Germany, with an overall increase of 0.08 per cent for eighteen industrialised countries – is not great.[15] However, they do serve to promote a more open, nondiscriminating international trading system. The tariff cuts are deeper on finished products than on intermediate goods and raw materials, so effective tariffs are cut rather more. This should prove of some benefit to developing countries that wish to move into processing their own raw materials for export as semi- or finished manufactures. But tariff cuts on products which at present figure prominently in developing countries' exports were generally less deep than average.

One sectoral agreement was achieved, which has abolished all obstacles to trade in products that fall under the civil aircraft agreement between the major industrial countries. This was proposed by the USA and was facilitated by the amount of co-operation and joint production which takes place between the USA and European aero-engine and airframe industries.

As with the Kennedy Round, reductions in protection in temperate zone agricultural products have fallen far short of the aspirations of exporting countries. Average tariffs have declined minutely from 7.9 per cent to 6.9 per cent and non-tariff barriers continue to restrict trade severely.

Many developing countries were anxious that tariff cuts should not erode their benefits under the Generalised System of Preferences. The overall effect appears to be that 'for agricultural products, supplies from developing countries would benefit from increased m.f.n. duty-free admission and increased GSP coverage. For industrial products, the GSP coverage would be marginally reduced while duties on supplies not benefiting from the GSP would in general be reduced significantly'.[16]

NON-TARIFF MEASURES

More progress was made in the field of non-tariff distortions to trade. This was a specific US objective, to control the spread of subsidies and other non-tariff practices that were impeding US trade. Agreements were reached on eight specific types of non-tariff measures. The best known of these is the Code of Subsidies and Countervailing Duties, perhaps the most contentious issue in the whole negotiations. This code clarifies and extends the interpretation of the pre-existing GATT Articles VI, XVI and XXIII. These permit the imposition of countervailing duties on imports where there is evidence that they have benefited from a subsidy, provided that the subsidy is causing or threatening *material injury* to an established domestic industry or to retard materially the establishment of a domestic industry. The amount of any countervailing duty is limited to an amount equal to the estimated value of the subsidy. The chief interest of the EEC in this code lay in the risk that US domestic legislation might be invoked to restrict nearly $500 million of Community exports to the USA because of regional subsidies, remission of VAT and other measures. Existing US law required only proof of subsidy, not material injury, to justify countervailing. US law has now been brought into line with the new code and requires objective evidence of material injury before retaliation. The new code contains detailed guidance on interpretation of the key questions and provision for settlement of disputes.

The USA gained from the code a more precise definition of what constitutes a subsidy, and the inclusion of some agricultural products in curbs on subsidies. For some time, the USA has objected to domestic subsidies given by the EEC, particularly in its Common Agricultural Policy, which reduced the market for US agricultural exports. But the code still respects the right of nations to give subsidies in depressed areas and for other domestic social and economic reasons.

GOVERNMENT PROCUREMENT

Another significant agreement was that on government procurement. Previously GATT provisions permitted governments to discriminate in their purchases in favour of domestic supplies. The aim of the new agreement is to promote greater international competition in supplying goods to governments and public agencies, but excluding certain key areas such as defence. When the new code comes into force in January 1981 it should lead to equality of treatment for foreign and national supplies. Contracts have to be widely publicised in English, French or Spanish. But there remain difficulties over interpretation, and technical standards can remain as a barrier. Japan has maintained that the code does not apply to semi-private companies. This provoked loud protests from the USA because Japan's main buyer of telecommunications equipment falls into this category. The code is in breach of the GATT MFN requirement as it applies only to those who have signed this particular code. Limited as it is, it nevertheless represents a remarkable achievement given the tradition in most countries of using government contracts as a method of achieving domestic, social and economic objectives.

OTHER AGREEMENTS

Agreements were reached on: methods of customs valuation, to increase their clarity and uniformity between nations, in the *Customs Valuation Code*; *Technical Barriers to Trade* (the *Standards Code*) to harmonise technical specifications between countries so as to facilitate trade; *Import Licensing Procedures* which aimed at preventing the use of delaying mechanisms and the exercise of bureaucratic methods as covert means to restrict imports.

AGRICULTURE

In addition there were agreements on topics in agriculture: an *International Dairy Arrangement, Bovine Meat* and a *Multilateral Agricultural Framework*.

Progress in the field of agriculture trade has always been difficult because of a combination of economic and political factors. The USA and Australasia are major exporters of food products and have a keen interest in opening up markets in Europe and Japan. But the agricultural industries of Japan and the European Community are politically powerful. Even in the UK, where agriculture employs less than 3 per cent of the labour force its spokesmen claim that it is the largest single industry. But in Japan 20 per cent of employment is in agriculture, in Ireland 27 per cent, in France 14 per cent and in Italy 19 per cent. Moreover, since in these countries it tends to be a labour intensive industry tariff cuts in that sector would produce much greater job losses than equivalent tariff cuts on manufactured products.

Both in Japan and in the EEC agriculture is politically sensitive. Agricultural groups form a substantial part of Japan's Liberal Democratic Party's constituency. The Common Agricultural Policy is now the most important common feature of the EEC, buttressed by powerful agricultural lobbies, defence arguments and national sentiment. Attempts to change or even mildly reform the CAP are resisted as a betrayal of the ideals of the Community, especially by France. Barriers to agricultural imports in Japan and the EEC are very high. The tariff equivalents of the quotas and levies used are in some cases as high as 300 per cent in the EEC and over 100 per cent in Japan. Moreover the EEC uses revenues from import levies to subsidise exports of agricultural surpluses which arise from excessive support prices paid to Community farmers. These damage the interests of the major agricultural exporting nations and some developing countries.

This clash of interests has bedevilled attempts to liberalise trade in agriculture which has remained stringently controlled and protected while trade in manufactures has progressed to a stage of near free trade. The prospective memberships of the EEC for Greece, Spain and Portugal has compounded the difficulties since they, too, are heavily dependent on agriculture and produce several goods which compete with US exports.

87

In the final analysis slightly more progress was made in tariff cuts and bindings than in the Kennedy Round, but the gains to the US and other agricultural exporting nations were still very small – perhaps an increase in US exports equivalent to about 2 per cent of total US agricultural exports.

Attempts to conclude an extension of the International Grains Agreement failed. Minor agreements were achieved in dairy products and meats, but these are largely consultative arrangements likely to have little effect and having nothing whatever to do with trade liberalisation.

The code on subsidies is much weaker on agricultural exports than on manufactures. It requires negotiators to agree not to displace the 'exports of another signatory bearing in mind the developments in world markets'. They are also not to give subsidies 'in a manner which results in prices materially below those of other supplies'. This may give aggrieved parties the legal basis for bringing complaints against EEC policies, but it is rather vague and action could be stymied by EEC votes required to permit action under this code.

THE MULTILATERAL SAFEGUARD SYSTEM

In accepting a movement towards free trade countries have to weigh the benefits of lower prices to consumers and increased productivity against the costs of adjustment to industry and employment. To reduce the risks of dismantling trade barriers it helps to have available some means by which a country can temporarily replace barriers against an unexpectedly rapid rise in particular imports which threaten serious injury to a domestic industry. GATT provides such a means in Article XIX, 'Emergency Action on Imports of Particular Products'. But the 'serious injury' must be 'a result of unforeseen developments'. The nation wishing to invoke Article XIX must give advance notice to the contracting parties of the GATT, must consult with all exporters of the product and if they are not satisfied they have a right to retaliation by withdrawing substantially equivalent concessions or other obligations if the first nation goes ahead with the action of withdrawing concessions or imposing controls on imports.

Because of these limitations upon their freedom of action many nations have increasingly stepped outside the GATT rules and negotiated voluntary export restraints (VERs) or orderly marketing arrangements (OMAs) with those countries whose exports threatened their domestic industries. These arrangements violate the fundamental non-discrimination principle of the GATT as they are selective between exporters of the same good. They have been used to restrict the exports of Japan and of many of the newly industrialising countries (NICs) such as Hong Kong, Taiwan, South Korea and Brazil. In recent years they have become a major instrument of protectionism instead of an instrument to give a temporary respite to enable structural adjustment. As Sidney Golt has put it, 'The lack of internal constraints on their use by the government of the importing country, the absence of consultation with other domestic interests, and especially consumers, and the wholly extra-legal character of their operation are among the characteristics which make them both habit-forming and infectious'.[17]

Developing countries saw reform in this area as crucial to their aims of maintaining and insuring access for their exports to markets in developed countries. They sought the outlawing of VERs and OMAs; and the barring of selectivity in the application of safeguard action (except for small suppliers and new entrants who should be exempted), differential and more favourable treatment for developing countries, acceptable criteria for determining 'injury', the degressive application of restrictions and an obligation to link import restraint to efforts to make structural adjustment in the developed country imposing the restraint, the possibility of compensation to exporters and multilateral surveillance. But their remonstrations had little effect.

Most of the debate was between the USA and the EEC. The American proposals seemed to conform to the spirit of the GATT and contained many of the provisions which the developing countries had adopted in their proposal. They wanted: specified procedures to determine injury, public hearings, time limits and degressive application of restrictions, but the elimination of rights to retaliate or demand compensation as long as the rules had been followed, and concessions to small suppliers and developing countries until they matured. Selective application of restrictions would only be permitted with the consent of the exporting country. This was the main bone of contention with the EEC who were strongly in favour of selectivity and basically seemed unwilling to reduce their independence to take action against 'disruptive imports'.

Negotiations eventually broke down over how much surveillance of selective safeguards was appropriate. The Europeans maintained the right to act unilaterally while the Japanese and the developing countries as the obvious targets insisted on the need for international approval. Negotiations continued after the initialling of the Tokyo Round Agreement in April 1979 but failed to resolve the differences. The final decision in November 1979 was to continue with the existing Article XIX but to strive in the future for an improved safeguards system through elaborating and supplementing Article XIX, and a committee was set up to continue the discussions and report in June 1980.

THE TOKYO ROUND AND THE DEVELOPING COUNTRIES

A major commitment of the Tokyo Declaration, as we noted, was to secure in the negotiations additional benefits for the trade of the developing countries, substantial improvement in conditions of access for their exports and measures to attain stable, equitable and remunerative prices for primary products. There was also recognition of 'the importance of the application of differential measures to developing countries in ways which will provide special and more favourable treatment for them'. Most of this turned out to be empty rhetoric.

As we have seen, developing countries achieved little or nothing on the multilateral safeguards issue which was probably the most important one as far as combating the rising tide of protectionism against their manufactured exports was concerned. On most of the other issues developing countries should gain; for example, reductions in tariffs and non-tariff barriers in general will incidentally increase their present and future access to markets in the developed countries. But in relatively few of the areas settled by the MTN were their 'additional benefits' for developing countries. In most areas there were fewer gains for them than for the industrial nations. On tariffs their net gains were fewer because few of the goods in which LDCs are major exporters were much affected and some of their gains from MFN tariff cuts would be offset by the erosion of their differential advantages under the Generalised System of Preferences. Their attempts to secure 'special and favourable treatment' were largely in vain. Although it is true that the MTN provided a firmer legal basis for differential treatment, developed countries and particularly the USA insisted on the acceptance of the principle of graduation. The more advanced among the developing countries had to accept more obligations and disciplines upon their policies, for example, with regard to subsidies and reciprocity. The Code on Government Procurement makes certain concessions to developing countries and to the least developed among them, but they are unlikely to win many contracts as the threshold value (SDR 150,000) below which countries need not go out to international tender may be too high for most of them and much of the work may be too technical. On tariff escalation and on trade in tropical products their gains were exceedingly modest and far short of their hopes.

LEAST DEVELOPED COUNTRIES

These were to receive specially favourable treatment in the Tokyo Round, but little attention was given to their problems in the negotiations. A draft protocol which some of them put forward late in 1978 suggested their exports should be exempted from tariff and non-tariff barriers, strict non-reciprocity, and the application of MFN treatment to them in all developed countries, including parity of treatment with the partners in common markets. But the least developed countries are given very few mentions in the Report of the Results of the Tokyo Round. Apart from the government procurement code, where special consideration is given to them but from which they are unlikely to benefit, they gained only what was made available to any developing country save for vague promises to take account of their special situation and problems.

CONCLUSIONS ON GATT

The results of the MTN were a disappointment to most nations, but far from undermining the GATT there is widespread recognition that it is essential to preserve the rule of law in the field of international 'economic' relations. Without agreement on a set of rules to govern trade governments are tempted to use expedients such as quotas or VERs on imports which may benefit them in the short run but which damage other nations' interests and in the long run will damage their own interests. The GATT supplies a minimum set of rules and some form of international surveillance. The Tokyo Round's achievement was to make a little progress towards freer and more disciplined trade at a time when there were great pressures in the direction of a breakdown of the system of free trade and a retreat into protectionism. It did not succeed totally in containing the threat of growing protectionism: the pressures remain. The clamour for more protection for more industries continues. The 1980s will be fraught with at least as great difficulties for the maintenance of a relatively free international trading system as the 1970s but further development and reform of the GATT is probably the only hope for the preservation of that free trading system which has scored pretty well through most of the post-Second World War era. We shall return to these issues in Chapter 12.

NOTES: CHAPTER 4

1   E. H. Preeg, *Traders and Diplomats. An Analysis of the Kennedy Round of Negotiations under the General Agreement on Tariffs and Trade* (Washington, DC: The Brookings Institution, 1970) gives a detailed account of the campaign to win support for the Trade Expansion Bill.
2   Karin Kock, *International Trade Policy and the GATT 1947–1967* (Stockholm: Almquist and Wicksell, 1969), p. 102.
3   Preeg, op. cit., p. 55, footnote.
4   Preeg, op. cit., p. 257.

5 Details of the effects of Kennedy Round tariff cuts on non-agricultural imports can be found in GATT Press Release No. 992, 30 June 1967 or in Preeg, op. cit., p. 238, Table 14.1.
6 Preeg, op. cit., p. 180.
7 Kock, op. cit., p. 228.
8 K. W. Dam, *The GATT, Law and International Economic Organization* (Chicago and London: University of Chicago Press, 1970), p. 230.
9 J. W. Evans, *The Kennedy Round in American Trade Policy. The Twilight of the GATT?* (Cambridge, Mass.: Harvard University Press, 1971), p. 318.
10 Evans, op. cit., p. 320. See also his analysis on pp. 319–20.
11 *The Times* (London), 29 October 1974. Of course Japanese manufacturers face rather similar non-tariff barriers in Europe but seem to show greater willingness to overcome them.
12 The following section is based on the report by the Director-General of the GATT, 'The Tokyo Round of Multilateral Trade Negotiations' (Geneva: GATT, April 1979).
13 op. cit., p. 118.
14 op. cit., p. 120, table headed *Tariff Average*.
15 Alan V. Dearndorff and Robert M. Stern, *An Economic Analysis of the Effects of the Tokyo Round of Multilateral Trade Negotiations on the United States and the Other Major Industrialized Countries* (Washington, DC: US Government Printing Office, June 1979), p. v.
16 Report of the Director-General of GATT, op. cit., p. 127.
17 Sidney Golt, *Developing Countries in the GATT System*, Thames Essay No. 18 (London: Trade Policy Research Centre, 1978), pp. 11–12.

CHAPTER 5

The United Nations Conference on Trade Aid and Development (UNCTAD)

The first United Nations Conference on Trade Aid and Development was held in Geneva in 1964. It met as a result of sustained pressure by an alliance of developing countries, the Soviet Union and Eastern European centrally planned economies acting within the General Assembly of the United Nations. Their general aim was to create one organisation that would deal with all the trade and aid issues involved in promoting economic development in the Third World. As such it was a revival of some of the original ideas of the International Trade Organisation mooted at the Havana Conference in 1948.

In the Bretton Woods system most matters concerning trade were dealt with in GATT, but international commodity agreements were the concern of committees of the UN Economic and Social Council (ECOSOC) along with the UN Food and Agricultural Organisation (FAO). Aid questions were handled by the World Bank for most multilateral aid and by the Development Aid Committee of OECD for most bilateral aid. Problems of international monetary co-operation were normally discussed within the IMF. Clearly all of these topics were relevant to economic development of the developing countries and there is a reasonable case for making sure that all aspects of the problem in their interrelated complexity should be properly considered within one central organisation. However, there were real and imagined conflicts of interest between rich and poor nations in the proposals put forward for achieving this through UNCTAD or some new body set up by UNCTAD.

VOTING AND DECISIONS

The UN General Assembly accords an equal vote to all countries whatever their size, wealth or political power. The specialised agencies such as the World Bank and the IMF operate rather differently. Decisions in these bodies reflect the economic and political power of the members through weighting systems on the votes and through their dependence on the rich nations for co-operation and funds. In GATT what matters most is 'horse trading'. Countries bargain bilaterally or in groups for concession against concession on matters of trade. It is true that within GATT there is recognition that poor developing countries should not be expected to make reciprocal concessions, but the fact that they have in any case few attractive concessions to offer means that they cannot take the initiative in actions to obtain trade concessions for themselves. These political facts of life naturally produced a desire on the part of developing countries (and of Soviet bloc countries, which were in any case not members of the IBRD, IMF or, in general, GATT) to create a body for discussing all matters of trade, aid and international finance within a UN body where their overwhelming voting power could prevail. For the same reason the USA, Japan, Western Europe and Australasian countries were opposed to such a new body and argued that all such topics could be perfectly well handled within the existing agencies.

By 1962 the Western powers finally accepted the inevitable and a unanimous resolution of ECOSOC resolved to convene a United Nations Conference on Trade and Development. This was endorsed later that year by the UN General Assembly.

UNDERLYING PHILOSOPHY

The economic philosophy underpinning the existing institutions such as GATT and the IMF stressed the desirability of free international trade and the effectiveness of market forces in allocating economic resources so as to maximise world output. Bilateral aid flows, while perhaps influenced to some extent by economic efficiency criteria, were largely determined by political criteria. Multilateral aid flows, while perhaps not altogether uninfluenced by politics, were mainly influenced by criteria related to economic efficiency more than equity.

The proponents of UNCTAD were in general much more interventionist in matters of trade. Most of the developing countries were very dissatisfied with the existing trading arrangements. They believed that their export prices were subject to severe short-term instability and doomed to decline *vis-à-vis* the prices of the manufactured products which they required to import. Trading relations between rich and poor countries seemed to them exploitative in view of differences in relative bargaining power between buyers and sellers. Their exports to rich countries also faced barriers in the form of tariffs, quotas, internal taxes and subsidies on competing products produced in developed countries. Since most of their own manufacturing industries were young, small and inexperienced they felt that they required protection

94

against competition from developed countries' industries within their own countries and assistance by way of preferential tariff treatment when exported to rich countries. All of these factors led them to demand intervention to improve their acquisitions of foreign exchange through more generous aid, through international commodity arrangements designed to reduce the ill-effects of instability and to increase revenues, and through tariff preferences in rich countries for developing countries' manufactured exports.

The theoretical underpinning for most of these attitudes comes from the 'theory of the peripheral economy' associated mainly with the writings of Raul Prebisch and which found expression in the report 'Towards a New Trade Policy for Development' written by Prebisch in his capacity as the first Secretary General of UNCTAD. Before his appointment to that office Prebisch had been Secretary General of the UN Economic Commission for Latin America. In that role he published a number of academic journal articles and ECLA documents giving expression to his ideas on the problems of economic development in Latin America.[1] These ideas were subsequently generalised to embrace the difficulties facing developing countries as a whole.

THE PREBISCH THESIS

The main tenets of this thesis are: (1) that the prices of primary commodities, which form the main exports of developing countries, have declined relatively to the prices of manufactured exports and that this is an inevitable and continuing process; (2) as a result of this tendency most of the gains from international trade accrue to the richer nations while developing countries gain little from their participation in existing international trade relations.

The empirical evidence advanced in support of the view that the commodity terms of trade have shifted against primaries or against developing countries cannot in fact sustain that judgement. The problem is that any trend up or down can be produced by a judicious selection of the base period and final years. If the early 1950s are chosen as a starting point a clear downward trend can be shown throughout the 1950s and 1960s in developing countries' terms of trade, simply because of the vastly inflated prices for raw materials and food products caused by the Korean War. On the other hand, if we take the decade 1961–71 we find that developing countries' terms of trade remained nearly constant. If we include 1973 and 1974 they have risen sharply.

This problem of analysis cannot be overcome by simply taking a sufficiently long series of years, for then the validity of the indices becomes extremely suspect. What is being compared is a weighted average of prices for a representative bundle of goods exported by developing countries with a similar weighted average of prices for a representative bundle of their imports of largely manufactured goods from developed countries. But over time two serious difficulties arise. First, the composition of the exports will certainly alter as tastes change and new goods become available. Secondly, the quality of the manufactured goods is likely to alter significantly over time. Modern earthmoving equipment used in road building and dam construction is enormously more productive today than twenty years ago. Rubber tires have a much longer useful life nowadays. Modern high-fidelity sound reproducing equipment is immensely superior to old gramophones. Small cheap electronic calculators today are more powerful and versatile than large expensive computers of ten years ago, and so on. The introduction of new goods and the improvement in quality of existing goods both tend to introduce an upward bias into an index of prices for manufactures. Typically, new manufactured goods when originally introduced are very expensive. Imitation, competition and mass production follow causing costs and prices to fall over time until a long-run equilibrium price is achieved. Ballpoint pens, transistor radios and electronic watches and calculators are familiar examples of this production cost pattern. Omission of such new goods from the index will consequently introduce an upward bias in the estimate of price movements of manufactures. Improvements in the quality of goods included in the index has the same effect. If earthmoving equipment sold today costs twice as much as ten years ago, but can shift four times as much earth in a given time, its real cost has halved rather than doubled since one bulldozer can now do the work of four old ones.

These methodological difficulties make it hazardous to generalise about long-term trends in commodity terms of trade. Any confident assertions in this area should be treated with extreme scepticism. There are a number of studies of these trends,[2] which vary considerably in their conclusions and do more to strengthen agnosticism than to support faith in a secular decline in the commodity terms of trade of the developing countries. Moreover, whatever the strength or weakness of the historical evidence it could not prove anything about future trends in relative prices.

The theoretical arguments advanced in support of an inevitable tendency for a worsening in developing countries' terms of trade are equally unconvincing. In fact it is not so very long since economists were arguing the opposite hypothesis, that diminishing returns in agriculture and mineral extraction would inevitably result in rising relative prices for their products. More recently proponents of the limits to growth school of thought have been predicting the dire fate that awaits the world as a result of the pressure of demand upon food and non-renewable natural resources such as oil and other minerals.[3] If their predictions proved correct the prices of food products and raw materials would start rising fairly sharply, well before the end of this century. In practice most of the basic assumptions about existing reserves of minerals in *The Limits to Growth* were too conservative and insufficient allowance was made for the tendency of known reserves to increase rather than decrease or for the degree of substitutability possible between materials.[4] But if the neo-Malthusians are to be taken with a pinch of salt the same must be said of the Prebisch school arguments for an inevitable tendency for primary commodity prices to fall relative to manufactures.

In a study on institutions there is insufficient space to dwell on disputes in theory so only a brief summary of the arguments can be given here. There is an extensive and readily accessible literature covering the issues which readers can turn to for a fuller explanation.[5] The main systematic explanation put forward by Prebisch, for a secular trend against developing countries' relative export prices, is that trade unions in developed countries can secure for themselves the benefits of increased productivity so that wages rise when productivity rises and product prices for manufactures do not fall. For countries on the periphery, lack of organisation among workers and a high degree of competition among producers leads to productivity increases being passed on to consumers through falling prices. As a result the fruits of progress pass to the nations at the centre through increased prices for their exports and decreased prices for their imports. This tendency is reinforced by asymmetric responses to cyclical swings in the world economy. Trade unions prevent wage cuts and so prices of manufactures fall only slightly in a slump while commodity prices plunge. In the boom, although prices of primaries soar, manufactured prices will also rise sharply.

Other reasons advanced are based on differences in the demand characteristics of primaries and manufactures. It is claimed that primaries are faced by low income elasticity of demand and that technological change in the industrial nations leads to economy in their use of raw materials and to substitution of synthetic for natural products. Together these add up to a growth in demand for primaries which is much slower than for manufactures.

It is also claimed that the price elasticity of demand for primaries is low so that lowering their prices through either productivity increase or through devaluation of exchange rates leads to relatively little increase in quantities sold.

The difficulty with the claims of low income and price elasticities is that as a generalisation it fits some commodities but not others. Oil, the major primary export from developing countries, is income elastic but has a low short- to medium-term price elasticity. Income elasticities for rubber, copper and aluminium are likely to be high. Then again, the price elasticity facing the total exports of a specific commodity may be low, but that facing any single exporting country is likely to be very high. Hence any single developing country can increase its export earnings by lowering prices and increasing the volume of its sales. Of course, it would do this partly at the expense of other exporters, some of whom may be developing countries. Nevertheless, all developing countries as a group can benefit from a reallocation of exporting along the lines of their comparative advantage; for example, the expansion of African coffee and cocoa while Latin American countries switch resources out of these products into other lines of activity.

Prebisch's argument based on productivity and trade union pressure does not stand up well under analysis. Suppose two countries A and B export, respectively, manufactures and food products. Assume that they start off with equilibrium in their balance of payments. Now assume that productivity increases occur in both, but in A incomes rise and output prices remain constant while in B incomes stay constant but prices fall. The terms of trade would shift in favour of A initially as Prebisch predicts but that this should persist is highly unlikely, for citizens of A and B will now tend to buy more of the food products and less of the manufactures. This will push B into balance-of-payments surplus and A into deficit and to correct this A would have to devalue sufficiently to reduce manufactures' prices relative to primary prices to restore equilibrium. Only with rather special assumptions about price and income elasticities would the terms of trade move permanently in favour of A. At least it should be clear that the Prebisch theory is not the self-evident proposition it might appear to be.

Even if it were true that the commodity terms of trade tended to move against developing countries' exports this would not in itself demonstrate that there were no significant gains to be had from trade. Both rising real purchasing power over imports and increased real returns to factor inputs can be consistent with falling export prices if these are associated with proportionately larger volumes of exports and increased productivity per unit of factor inputs.[6]

In fact none of this argument about trends in the terms of trade is necessary to the main policy objectives of developing countries within UNCTAD. Other more acceptable arguments can be advanced to justify increased aid and measures to increase the export earnings of developing countries. Unfortunately it continues to colour the rhetoric of spokesmen for the developing countries and to flourish in development literature. Many pronouncements by the UNCTAD secretariat appear to take it for granted.

TOWARDS A NEW TRADE POLICY FOR DEVELOPMENT

The Prebisch Report which heavily influenced discussion at the first UNCTAD and has continued to dominate UNCTAD thinking to this day contains a general analysis of the major problems facing developing countries. If they were to achieve a minimum 5 per cent growth of GNP throughout the 1960s they would require heavy investment, much more than they could raise by domestic savings, and require imports of raw materials and capital goods greatly in excess of their ability to earn foreign exchange. This trade gap between required imports and export proceeds was estimated, without much explanation, at about $20 billion by 1970.

Unstable and declining primary export prices and restrictive commercial policies of the rich nations make the closing of this gap impossible without a great deal of help in the form of capital aid, commodity agreements, compensatory financing schemes, removal of barriers in developed countries to developing countries' exports and preferential access for manufactured exports. In addition the Prebisch Report advocated regional integration among developing countries, increases in trade between developing countries and the socialist countries and the establishment of a new international trade organisation within the UN framework.

In all this, there were two points of some novelty. The first was that Prebisch acknowledged that much import substitution in developing countries, behind high levels of protection, had been grossly inefficient. Moreover, import substitution or 'inward looking industrialisation' was becoming increasingly more costly and difficult. Consequently, he advocated a new form of the infant industry argument whereby new exporting industries would be assisted by tariff preferences in the rich nations. The second point of interest was the advocacy of international commodity agreements and compensatory finance schemes, not simply as devices to moderate fluctuations in commodity markets, but explicitly as a means of transferring income to the exporters. Both of these ideas will be considered later.

THE FIRST UNCTAD, GENEVA 1964

The Prebisch Report's proposals were faithfully reflected in the conference committees. These were entitled: (1) International Commodity Problems; (2) Trade in Manufactures and Semi-Manufactures; (3) Invisible Trade and Financing for Expansion of International Trade; (4) Institutional Arrangements; (5) Expansion of

International Trade; (6) Implications of Regional Economic Groupings. The work of these committees was not very effective since they tended to produce confrontation between emotionally voiced demands from delegates representing the developing countries aligned in the 'Group of 77' and the refusal of the major trading nations to make concessions to them. When it became clear that deadlock was being reached on most issues, discussion was moved into smaller, less formal conciliation committees in which some progress was made. However, in the end the 1964 Conference fell far short of achieving the aims of the developing countries. To gain acceptance most of the resolutions were much diluted from their original forms but even so they were only accepted because of the 'voting machine' of the 'Group of 77' in which the developing countries had formed themselves for the duration of the conference. The rich nations opposed or abstained from many of the sixty major resolutions in the final act of the conference.

Nevertheless, the 1964 UNCTAD did result in some achievements. For one thing, it achieved the status of a permanent organ of the UN, meeting at prescribed intervals. Membership is open to all members of the UN and UN specialised agencies. Between the major conferences the Standing Committee of the Conference, the Trade and Development Board, acts as the permanent executive organ. It reviews the progress on implementation of conference recommendations, initiates research studies and carries out the preparatory work for conferences. Under its aegis are four specialised committees dealing with: commodities, manufactures, shipping and invisibles. The permanent secretariat was headed by Prebisch until March 1969. He was succeeded then by Perez Guerrero of Venezuela who was in turn succeeded by Gamani Corea of Ceylon in 1974.

Apart from this, little of direct concrete significance was achieved. Probably the main impact of the conference was to dramatise the wants of the developing countries, thrusting their grievances and demands into the public consciousness of the rich nations. It also showed that the developing countries could, on occasion, submerge their differences in order to speak with one voice on some major issues. The first UNCTAD stimulated thinking on development issues and did put forward some schemes for alleviating what were perceived as major problems. Probably the most important of these was the generalised system of preferences (GSP) for exports of manufactures and semi-manufactures from developing countries. While it gained no support at the time from the major industrialised nations (the USA and UK voted against it) the idea was kept alive and now most rich countries have adopted some version of a GSP.

Another scheme to emerge was the British/Swedish proposal for supplementary finance to provide compensation for unexpected shortfalls in developing countries' export proceeds. This has continued to figure in various forms in discussions over the years. The IMF has created a special borrowing facility, the Compensatory Financing Facility (CFF), for developing countries faced with such export problems, which goes some way towards the compensatory financing idea.

THE NEW DELHI CONFERENCE 1968

Little if any progress was made towards UNCTAD goals during the intervening years. Despite the UNCTAD resolution to increase aid to 1 per cent of national income the proportion of the rich nations' national incomes allotted to financial flows to developing countries declined. The Kennedy Round of tariff cuts did not appear to do much for the exports of the developing nations. Growth targets were not achieved and the gap between rich and poor nations increased.

Before the New Delhi Conference the 'Group of 77', by then in fact eighty-nine developing countries, met in Algiers to agree common policies. This resulted in the Algiers Charter which listed their proposals. The OECD nations had no comparable list of objectives but did at least approve in principle the adoption of a general scheme of preferences for manufactured exports from developing countries. This was a major shift in attitude for the USA and the UK.

The actual conference was a vast unwieldy affair; 1,600 delegates from 133 member nations and 44 international organisations. The preference issue caused rifts to appear among both the developing and the developed countries. Countries which already had access to preferred markets, through the Commonwealth preference area or the Yaoundé Convention between many African countries and the EEC, felt that they would lose from a move to a GSP. The Americans and the French could not agree over the reverse preferences which French exports enjoyed in the Francophone countries. The French did not wish to relinquish these quickly while the USA insisted that they could only accede to a GSP if a timetable for the abolition of reverse preferences was agreed in advance.

The approach of the British and the French to commodity problems was almost diametrically opposed, with the French urging the interventionist line of organised markets with fixed prices while the British pursued the line of compensating countries for adverse export fluctuations.

The general view of commentators was that the second UNCTAD was a failure. The one achievement was to set up an intergovernmental group to develop a workable scheme for generalised preferences. Other resolutions of note included one on shipping agreements, raising of the aid target from 1 per cent of national income to 1 per cent of GNP (a larger but conceptually less defensible measu.e of ability to afford aid) and recommendations on international action for over a dozen commodities.

LATER UNCTADS

A third, equally ineffective, UNCTAD was held in Santiago in 1972, a fourth in Nairobi in 1976 and in 1979, UNCTAD V met in Manila. The last two took place in a rather different atmosphere. The use of the oil weapon and OPEC's success in raising oil prices put new heart into advocates of commodity cartels and aroused interest in international commodity agreements (ICAs) among both producers and consumers. Even the British became advocates of ICAs at the Commonwealth Conference in Jamaica in 1975. The rise in oil prices also had the other effect of making the needs of many large and very poor countries more urgent. Major new proposals from the UNCTAD Secretariat for an Integrated Commodity Programme with a Common Fund dominated the Nairobi meeting and subsequent discussions between LDCs and the OECD nations. In the end an emasculated Common Fund was eventually agreed in 1979 but little progress has been achieved in setting up effective ICAs. These issues and a later proposal from the Manila Conference for a Complementary Financing Facility for stabilisation of commodity export earnings will be considered more fully in Chapter 6.

A CRITIQUE OF UNCTAD

Have the activities of UNCTAD either achieved or improved the prospects of realising a more efficient and/or more equitable use of the world's resources? This is the criterion by which we have chosen to judge international institutions, and by that standard UNCTAD has not been a great success. Most UNCTAD proposals show an almost total disregard for efficiency in the sense of concern for maximising the value of output produced from currently available inputs. Instead such measures as ICAs, compensatory financing and discriminatory preferences sacrifice efficiency in order to redistribute resources from rich nations to poor ones. This might be justified if these measures could be expected to promote a substantially improved distribution of income without incurring very high costs in terms of sacrificed output or growth of world production, but their effects could be inequitable as well as damaging productive and distributive efficiency.

ICAs designed to transfer income to exporting nations have to operate by restricting the volume of exports. This is normally done by fixing export quotas which may bear little or no relationship to the relative efficiency of the producers and tends to freeze the pattern of production and exports, frustrating the development of efficient producers and retaining the inefficient. Moreover, the number of commodities which are suitable for control is rather limited by reason of the existence of good natural or synthetic substitutes produced in developed countries. ICAs are exceedingly difficult to instigate and to administer effectively once instigated. They create powerful incentives to smuggling and corruption, and if the managers of the agreement make incorrect predictions of trends in demand or supply they can seriously destabilise markets or force destruction or dumping of food or raw material products. They raise revenues by imposing a regressive tax on consumers and may transfer these revenues to wealthy producers or exporters or to governments whose policies with regard to either growth or equity leave a great deal to be desired.

Compensatory financing (CF) schemes, if designed to enhance export incomes, are equally subject to the criticism put forward in the preceding sentence, but at least have the merit of not directly influencing the quantity or pattern of production. They may do so indirectly by influencing incentives but this is unlikely to be as important or as damaging as quantitative controls on exports or production.

If either ICAs or CF schemes are recognised as a form of aid to developing countries there is a serious risk that other forms of aid would be reduced. The net aid effect of ICAs might then be negligible or even negative.

The objective of assisting economic development by transferring resources to Third World nations is likely to be achieved more efficiently by putting the same resources through multilateral aid channels such as the World Bank or regional development banks. They are now likely to be influenced in their aid policies by considerations of both stimulating economic growth and concern for distribution of the benefits of growth to the most needy in the least developed nations.[7] Under ICAs or CF schemes revenue allocations are determined by considerations which need have no relation to either poverty or capacity to make good use of aid.

The example and the urging of OPEC has raised the spectre of producer cartels in a number of other primary exports. OPEC has forced joint consideration of oil prices with commodity arrangements for other raw material exports of Third World countries. The prospects for long-lived cartels in almost all other primaries are poor,[8] but attempts to organise and implement cartels can disrupt supplies and push up prices temporarily. Partly to avoid this the OECD nations are showing some interest in the revival of proposals for ICAs with producer and consumer participation. They may indeed be willing to trade higher prices for more assured long-term supplies. But on the whole the revival of interest is a reflection of shifts in the balance of power rather than any change in views about the economic effects of ICAs.

THE GENERALISED SYSTEM OF PREFERENCES (GSP)

Perhaps the most constructive and hopeful proposal put forward at UNCTAD was for generalised non-reciprocal preferences for manufactured exports from LDCs in developed countries' markets. Admittedly it had a hostile reception from the USA and UK in 1964 but they were won round to acceptance of the idea by 1968. Of all the main UNCTAD proposals the GSP is the only one which has achieved a fair measure of implementation. Most developed nations have now made some arrangements for preferential entry. Indeed, some schemes have been in existence for many years (Australia's was begun in 1966) and have undergone revisions to make them more liberal. [9]

Unfortunately it is not yet possible to make a thorough analysis of the real effects of the GSP. Schemes of major countries, such as the USA and Canada, are relatively recent and even for other countries the necessary data for a proper evaluation of the welfare effects is lacking. However, some judgements are possible from *a priori* reasoning – data on the volumes of trade likely to be affected, and some early attempts at quantitative analyses. [10]

Several students of the issue have concluded that the benefits flowing from the GSP would be small, based on: (1) the low volumes of manufactures presently exported by developing countries; (2) their concentration in a few countries such as Hong Kong, Singapore, Taiwan and Mexico; (3) the exclusion of textiles, leather goods and processed agricultural commodities common in most countries' adopted GSP; (4) the market disruption clauses and quota limitations imposed by most developed countries on goods admitted under preferential arrangements; (5) the low level of tariffs on manufactures after the Tokyo Round of multilateral tariff negotiations in GATT. However, this is too static a view. Exports of manufactures from developing countries have been growing very fast even before any effects of the GSP could have registered. Over the period 1965–72 exports of manufactures from LDCs increased in value at an annual average rate of 19.5 per cent and in 1972 formed over a quarter of their total exports. There is a growing trend for American and Japanese firms, in particular, to establish labour intensive parts of their production processes in LDCs. [11]

The existence of the GSP is bound to have increased the incentives for such foreign direct investment, joint ventures and technological transfer agreements. While profits from these activities will have to be shared with the foreigners there will nevertheless be a significant amount of local value added for LDCs. Where the preferential rate is a zero tariff the gains are greater than appear at first sight because of the reduction in administrative time spent on customs matters. One would expect the incentive effect of reduced tariff barriers to form a strong stimulus to the creation of new export industries in developing countries.[12] This is reinforced by the tendency for the effective as opposed to the nominal tariffs to be specially high on exports from LDCs (see Table 5.1).

Table 5.1 *Averages of Nominal and Effective Tariffs on Industrial Countries' Imports of Manufactures*

	Nominal	Effective
Total imports	6·5	11·1
Imports from developing countries	11·8	22·6

Source: I. Little, Scitovsky and Scott, *Industry and Trade in Some Developing Countries* (London: Oxford University Press, 1970), p. 273.

It is true that most of the systems so far established have been hedged by quota restrictions *ab initio* or arrangements for the introduction of controls whenever any risk of 'market disruption' arises. However, progress has been made in liberalising these restrictions and GATT keeps a wary eye on unjustified use of 'market disruption' clauses in trade agreements. It is almost certainly the case that the quantity of LDC exports affected has been much greater than the derisory amounts suggested by Patterson or Murray.[13]

THE WELFARE EFFECTS OF THE GSP [14]

The basic argument put forward at UNCTAD for preferences was a variant of the infant industry arguments for government assistance. The main difference was that the subsidy should be paid by foreigners rather than the citizens of the LDCs. However, if the industries were genuine infants which would successfully mature, all would benefit from the reduced real cost to the world of obtaining these goods. If the goods were standard, non-differentiated products like copper wire the preference receiving countries would act as price takers. They would sell at the tariff ridden price in the developed country's market and would receive a windfall gain equal to the tariff revenue on exports previously collected by the government of the preferences giving country. The extra profits made by the developing countries' exporters would encourage increased production of the good for export which would displace exports from the rest of the world to the preferential market. If internal and external economies of scale resulted from expansion of LDC's production of copper wire the real cost to the world economy of obtaining these products would fall. Since processing at source of a mineral, such as copper, normally reduces the transport cost element in the final cost there is likely to be another source of gain to the world economy from a shift of production from a country that imports crude copper to one that has its own copper mines. Another, potential welfare gain may arise from shifting industries, such as mineral refining and processing, away from the crowded and polluted industrial centres of Europe and North America to areas of the world where external diseconomies of industrial concentration are much less significant (not of course to the congested and polluted cities of the Third World such as Sao Paulo or Calcutta).

If social costs (private costs plus externalities) do not fall but rise as a result of diverting production of the goods to developing countries, there would be a loss of efficiency to the world economy. This would occur when costs of production in the developing countries are higher than in the rest of the world and/or rise as output increases in response to the increased revenue deriving from the preference. However, even were this the case it would be possible for the transfer of income from richer people to poorer people resulting from the preference to more than compensate for the loss of efficiency.

All of the foregoing relies on the assumption that the rest of the world's supply of copper wire is perfectly elastic. This enables one to assume that the effects on the rest of the world are very small, amounting to little more than the short-term costs of shifting resources from wire production to other activities in which they would earn the same incomes. The assumption of a highly elastic world supply of the kinds of goods which LDCs are likely to export is not unrealistic, but it must be remembered that the displacement effects may, on occasion, be concentrated on labour-intensive industries located in narrow geographical areas within developed countries. This is the major reason why most countries reserve the right to limit preferential access to their markets and are unwilling to extend preferences to textiles. Even liberal regimes have to recognise that resources may not be very mobile from such industries in such areas. High regionally concentrated unemployment is a sensitive issue for most governments.

If the good we are concerned with is a differentiated product such as a bicycle the giving of a tariff preference can be expected to result in a lowered price and expanded sales for these exports from LDCs. Some of the increased sales will be at the expense of home country producers, some from developed countries which export bicycles. The first involves trade creation (a shift from a higher to a lower cost source of supply), the second, trade diversion (a shift from lower cost exporters to higher cost LDC exporters). However, if expansion brings economies of scale in production, development and marketing to the LDC exporters these static effects may be negligible in comparison to the dynamic ones.

It is not possible to state definitely what the overall effects on world economic efficiency are. However, attempts to measure the static efficiency effects of much bigger moves towards discriminatory free trade, for example, in large customs unions such as the EEC, have shown very small quantities are involved. It seems likely that the net trade creation and trade diversion effects of the GSP would also be rather small. The consumption effects through reduced prices to consumers would be beneficial. Even though economies of scale both internal and external are hard to quantify they are almost certain to occur as a result of preferences. Moreover, the stimulus to foreign firms to locate production in LDCs is likely to mean an optimum combination of capital and technology from developed countries with unskilled labour in developing countries. Since creation of jobs for the burgeoning youthful populations of developing countries is of the utmost importance this is a key result in evaluating the overall impact of a GSP. The dynamic effects of the GSP may take time to develop but they are likely to be distinctly beneficial and quantitatively much more important than the once-over reallocation effects which economic theory analyses with more confidence.

Recent empirical research on a comparison between rates of growth of developing countries which have adopted outward looking, export-oriented policies rather than inward looking, import-substituting policies bear out the value of the GSP approach. Both sets of countries used government policy to direct resources. The contrast is not between successful *laissez-faire* policies and unsuccessful intervention, but between interventions which stimulated exports rather than import substitution. The research shows the former countries to have come out ahead.[15]

Finally, the general trend in tariffs in the world is downward. There were fears after the Kennedy Round that little more progress would be made, and these fears have been exacerbated by recent world recession. Nevertheless, the multilateral negotiations for tariff reductions did go ahead in the Tokyo Round and despite protests such moves towards free trade will gradually erode the preferences, forcing industries in LDCs to become competitive.

On balance, the GSP has probably brought more benefits than most commentators have allowed. Moreover, its potential remains high. If it merely encourages developing countries to remain outward looking in their development policies and to diversify their exports it will have achieved substantial benefits.[16] It is also true, however, that the benefits are likely to accrue mainly to the more fortunate developing countries, those whose per capita incomes, rates of growth and share of manufacturing in national income are already relatively high. But these countries' increased prosperity will increase their demands for food, raw materials and other goods, substantial amounts of which come from other developing countries. The gaps in standards of living may increase, but all are likely to be absolutely better off.

UNCTAD'S ACHIEVEMENTS

The concrete achievements of UNCTAD have been small. They amount to: (1) A Cocoa Agreement, which has had no economic impact having never bought or sold any cocoa or in any way influenced cocoa sales or prices. (2) The Generalised System of Preferences, which has brought some gains to a number of developing countries, but because of the limitations and safeguards imposed by developed countries the gains have been much circumscribed. It can be, and has been, maintained that LDCs would in any case have gained much more from straightforward, non-discriminating tariff cuts under the GATT negotiations.[17] (3) The Integrated Programme for Commodities, which has yet to see any effective commodity agreements in being and whose main drive for the establishment of a Common Fund for financing ICAs has brought forth a mouse of a fund. These and the later proposal (UNCTAD V) for a Complementary Financing Facility are considered below in Chapter 6. (4) Attempts to control the activities of transnational corporations and promote transfers of technology to LDCs, which amount so far to little more than pious hopes for an unenforceable code of conduct on the transfer of technology.

Despite the lack of concrete progress in trade and aid matters perhaps a claim can be made for some success on a political level. Christopher Brown puts this view forward in a recent book.[18] Despite all its failures UNCTAD continues to draw support from its members for expansion of its staff and activities. Brown feels that this must be because members derive benefits from 'an intangible symbolic function of a higher order than actual paper output and meaningful agreements concluded. UNCTAD embodies a basic ideology that everyone can accept: that is, countries and people should be in communication with one another and they should make the world a better place . . . Perhaps what little it produces in a conventional sense is less important than the fact that it confronts important issues, such as inequities in trade between rich and poor countries'.[19] It provides a forum for political debate, a safety valve for the expression of the pent-up resentment of poor nations against the rich, perhaps also as a means of diverting attention from the results of errors in domestic policies towards the alleged barriers to progress caused by trade relations with the industrially developed nations.[20]

NOTES: CHAPTER 5

1   See, for example, UN, ECLA; *The Economic Development of Latin America and Some of its Problems* (New York: UN, 1949) and R. Prebisch, 'The role of commercial policies in underdeveloped countries', *American Economic Review, Papers and Proceedings* (May 1959). See also Hans Singer, 'The distribution of gains between borrowing and investing countries', *American Economic Review, Papers and Proceedings*, May 1950.

2   UN, *Relative Prices of Exports and Imports of Underdeveloped Countries* (New York: UN, 1949); A. H. Imlah, 'The terms of trade of the United Kingdom', *Journal of Economic History* (November 1950); C. P. Kindleberger, *The Terms of Trade: A European Case Study* (New York: Wiley, 1956); P. Lamartine Yates, *Forty Years of Foreign Trade* (London: Allen & Unwin, 1957); T. Morgan, 'Trends in terms of trade and their repercussions on primary producers', in Roy Harrod and D. C. Hague (eds), *International Trade Theory in a Developing World* (London: Allen & Unwin, 1963). Unpublished report of a Committee of Experts on the Terms of Trade set up by UNCTAD. It reported that there was no convincing evidence that the terms of trade had moved against LDCs (*New York Times*, 26 May 1975 and *Guardian* (London), 2 June 1975). P. Bairoch, *The Economic Development of the Third World Since 1900* (London: Methuen, 1975). G. F. Ray, 'The "real" price of primary products', *National Institute for Economic and Social Research Review* (August 1977).

3   Danella Meadows, Dennis Meadows, Jorgen Randers, and William Behrens III, *The Limits to Growth* (London: Potomac Associates, Earth Island Ltd., 1972).

4   The Meadows study has been subjected to much criticism. A recent paper by Nicholas G. Carter of the IBRD, 'Population, environment and natural resources: a critical review of recent models', paper presented to the Stockholm Seminar on Population in September 1973, attacks the mechanics of the model. Other critics have attacked the ignoring of price and substitution, still others the basic assumptions about existing resources, for example, H. Cole, Christopher Freeman, Marie Jahoda and K. Pavitt (eds), *Thinking About the Future: A Critique of the Limits to Growth* (London: Chatto and Windus, 1973) (for the Science Policy Research Unit of Sussex University).

5   J. Viner, *International Trade and Development* (London: Oxford University Press, 1953) Ch. VI; G. Harbeler, 'Terms of trade and economic development', in H. S. Ellis, (ed.), *Economic Development for Latin America* (London: Macmillan, 1961. Gerald Meier, *The International Economics of Development* (New York: Harper, 1968). See M. J. Flanders, 'Prebisch on protectionism: an evaluation', *The Economic Journal* (June 1964), for an extensive critique of the underlying Prebisch model.

6   See Viner, op. cit., or Meier, op. cit.

7   See Chapter 11 on the World Bank.
8   Benison Varon and Kenji Takeuchi, 'Developing countries and non-fuel minerals, *Foreign Affairs* (April 1974); Hugh Corbet, *Raw Materials, Beyond the Rhetoric of Commodity Power* (London: Trade Policy Research Centre, 1975); Carl Van Dryne, 'Commodity cartels and the theory of derived demand', *Kyklos*, Vol. 28, fasc. 3 (1975); D. K. Osborne, 'Cartel Problems', *American Economic Review* (December 1976); S. Harris, Salmon and Smith, *The Analysis of Commodity Markets for Policy Purposes*, Thames Paper (London: Trade Policy Research Centre, 1979) pp. 52–7. Jere R. Behrman, *International Commodity Agreements* (Washington DC. Overseas Development Council, October 1977).
9   See UNCTAD/TD/B/C.5/22 'Second general report on the implementation of the generalised system of preferences' (Geneva: UNCTAD, April 1974).
10 See Gardner Patterson, 'Would tariff preferences help economic development?', *Lloyds Bank Review* (April 1965); T. Murray, 'How helpful is the generalised system of preferences to developing countries?', *Economic Journal* (June 1973); R. E. Baldwin and T. Murray, 'MFN tariff reductions and LDC benefits under the GSP', *Economic Journal* (March 1977) and Jaleel Ahmad, 'Tokyo Rounds of trade negotiations and the generalised system of preferences', *Economic Journal* (June 1978).
11 See G. K. Helleiner, 'Manufactured exports from less developed countries and multinational firms', *Economic Journal* (March 1973).
12 Uncertainty (due to the escape clauses typical of most versions of the GSP), however, does weaken this incentive. Complexity of regulations and lack of information have also reduced LDC gains from the GSP.
13 ibid.
14 See H. G. Johnson, *Economic Policies Toward Less Developed Countries* (London: Allen & Unwin, 1967), Ch. VI for a more thorough analysis of the static welfare effects of a GSP.
15 Anne Kreuger, *Liberalization Attempts and Consequences* (Cambridge, Mass.: National Bureau of Economic Research, Ballinger, 1978).
16 It is unfortunately impossible to explore all of the arguments for and against the GSP in a work on institutions. There is an enormous amount of documentation from UNCTAD and GATT on the subject.
17 Baldwin and Murray, op. cit.
18 C. P. Brown, *The Political and Social Economy of Commodity Control* (London: Macmillan, 1980).
19 ibid., p. 215.
20 ibid, pp. 215–16.

CHAPTER 6

International Commodity Agreements

International Commodity Agreements (ICAs) represent attempts to modify the operation of commodity markets so as to achieve various objectives such as price stabilisation or price enhancement. Support for such intervention stems from apparent weaknesses in the operation of market forces in achieving an efficient allocation of resources, appropriate levels of privately held stocks in some commodities and an equitable distribution of income from their export as between exporters and importing countries.

ICAs are to be distinguished from producers' or exporters' cartels by the feature of consumer agreement to the scheme and representation on the governing body. Apart from an international wheat agreement in 1933 and sugar in 1937 none of the agreements set up before the Second World War had consumer representation. Basically, the interwar agreements were simply cartels which tried to both stabilise and raise prices of various commodities including coffee, tea, rubber, copper and tin. Despite temporary successes, they all failed and probably caused more disruption to markets than would have occurred in their absence.[1] Experience of these failures influenced the UN Havana Conference in 1947–8 to lay down principles and procedures for setting up and operating ICAs. These included adequate representation of producing and consuming interests, a guarantee of a sufficient supply and of increasing use of the most efficient producers under agreements that involved controlling supplies.

ICAs SINCE THE SECOND WORLD WAR

Considering the number of primary commodities which enter international trade and which are of interest to developing countries the actual number of ICAs since the Havana Conference has been remarkably few. They have usually taken endless negotiations (over ten years for cocoa) to set up. Only wheat, sugar, tin and coffee have lasted a number of years, and few appear to have achieved much before their demise. This is eloquent testimony to the difficulty of obtaining agreement between producing and consuming nations and of running ICAs to the satisfaction of all members. Despite these failures in the past there remains a strong and persistent lobby for ICAs. Recent events in the oil market, the commodity boom of 1973–74 and the subsequent world recession and slump in commodity prices have added stimulus to the search for solutions to commodity price fluctuations. The surge in world rates of inflation has aroused interest in 'ratchet' effects of unstable commodity import prices on the rate of increase in domestic price levels in industrial countries. It has also led to pleas from LDCs for indexation; the gearing of commodity prices to indices of the price level of the manufactured imports of developing countries; and for a comprehensive approach to commodity problems. This has included, recently, the UNCTAD proposal for an integrated programme of buffer stocks for at least ten core commodities (with possible extension to eighteen): copper, tin, coffee, cocoa, sugar, tea, cotton, jute and jute manufactures, rubber and hard fibres, together with such measures as multilateral contracts, compensatory financing schemes and at UNCTAD V the proposal for a complementary facility for commodity related shortfalls in export earnings.[2]

OBJECTIVES OF ICAs

Most schemes have as their main objectives to stabilise and/or increase the world price of the commodity, producers' incomes, foreign exchange earnings of exporting countries and government revenues from taxes on the commodity. More stable prices are desired because wildly fluctuating prices may cause hardship and are likely to increase the costs of both producers and consumers through increasing uncertainty and producing exaggerated responses in production and consumption. Where these responses are lagged one or more seasons behind the price change they can be particularly damaging in producing 'cobweb' cycles. High current prices for coffee, for example, may stimulate planting of new coffee trees that will only bear fruit five or more years hence when prices may become, as a result, very depressed. More stable earnings for producers becomes a particularly important objective when the producers are small farmers with low incomes and little or no reserves, though most countries have national measures such as marketing boards which try to stabilise producers' earnings. Greater stability in export revenues should reduce uncertainty in economic planning and where taxes are geared to export revenues, as is the case for many primary exports, this objective is reinforced.

The aim of raising prices, incomes or export earnings above the levels that would prevail without intervention has to be seen as a form of disguised economic aid or as compensation for declining terms of trade. The charters of several ICAs also include the aim of expanding the markets for their primary products by developing new uses, reducing trade barriers and increasing sales promotion.

As is often the case in economics many of these objectives are mutually incompatible. A world price stabilised within narrow limits could cause greater instability in export earnings for some commodities, whereas a raised price may involve lower incomes and will certainly militate against expanded markets. Obviously these possibilities depend on assumptions about elasticities of demand and supply for specific commodities, but are in fact more than likely. For example, where demand shifts are the main cause of fluctuations, but demand is price elastic, an export quota agreement will destabilise export earnings. Similarly, where supply variations are the basic cause, holding price stable through a buffer stock can destabilise income[3] if the price elasticity of demand is greater than 0.5. A stable price can also involve lower total export earnings.[4] But recent research shows these results are less likely than was previously considered to be the case, particularly if the band within which a buffer stock seeks to confine price movements is fairly wide. In practice the conflict between price stabilisation and stabilisation of export earnings for most countries' export earnings is unlikely.[5]

METHODS ADOPTED BY POSTWAR ICAs

The major target of all recent ICAs has been stabilisation and support of price. Each ICA has made use of one of three methods: multilateral contracts, export quotas and buffer stocks, or a combination of these.

MULTILATERAL CONTRACTS: THE INTERNATIONAL WHEAT AGREEMENT

Successive international wheat agreements illustrate the multilateral contract approach. Most of the exporters have been rich nations reflecting the dominance of North America and Australia in the production of foodgrains while most of the advocacy for ICAs has come from less developed countries envisaging ICAs as a form of assistance to them.

As with all ICAs the wheat agreements took some time to get started. The Fifth International Wheat Conference in March 1947 introduced the plan, but two-and-a-half years elapsed before it was implemented. There was a continuous series of three-year agreements in wheat from 1949 to 1965. The 1965 Agreement was extended for two years pending the negotiation of a new convention after the discussion on trade in grains in the Kennedy Round within GATT. An International Grains Arrangement was negotiated in 1967 which continued until June 1971.

113

This was followed by a new International Wheat Convention (1971) and a Food Aid Convention, but this new arrangement contained no contractual arrangements to govern prices or quantities bought and sold. Effectively the multilateral contract system was in force from 1949 to 1971 with a one-year gap in 1967/68. Negotiations for a new wheat agreement are presently (1980) underway in GATT and the International Wheat Council.

Objectives

The agreements aimed at assuring supplies of wheat to importing countries and markets for wheat to exporting countries at equitable and stable prices. Subsidiary aims of expanding trade in wheat and increasing international co-operation in dealing with world wheat problems were included in the Articles.

The Methods

The original agreement of 1949 set a price range in terms of one specific grade of wheat, Canadian Manitoba No. 1, and permitted other types of wheat to be bought and sold at a variable discount or premium (subsequently this proved to be a difficulty). About two-thirds of the world trade was covered by the contracts to sell at the maximum agreed price of $1.80 a bushel in times of scarcity and to buy at the minimum agreed price of $1.50 in times of surplus. This left a residual unregulated market in which prices could fluctuate in response to supply and demand.

The agreement neither imposed quotas nor held stocks. Exporting countries and importing countries merely entered into contracts to sell or buy agreed quantities at the stipulated maximum or minimum prices, whenever the free market price reached these limits.

When the third agreement was negotiated in 1959 the principle of fixed quantity contracts was abandoned in favour of undertakings by the importing members to buy a minimum *percentage* of their commercial needs from the exporting members, so long as prices were within the agreed range. The exporters were still obliged to sell at the stipulated maximum price an amount equal to the annual average of importers' purchase over the previous four years. The general effect of this change was to allow importing nations to adjust their purchases in accordance with their domestic wheat production – a factor of some importance to the EEC and its Common Agricultural Policy. The Wheat Trade Convention (1971) contained no price or quantity provisions and was basically just a mechanism for international consultations. Despite fairly continuous efforts to negotiate a new International Wheat Agreement none has been signed to date.

The Working of the Agreements

The initial membership of the 1949 Agreement was forty-one countries, but the number has waxed and waned over the years depending on market conditions and individual countries' assessments of the benefits and costs of membership. In January 1971, forty-four countries plus the EEC were the total membership. Voting power in the Wheat Council was divided equally between the exporting and the importing groups. Within each group votes were based on their relative importance in the grain trade.

The original agreement in 1949 provided for guaranteed amounts equal to about two-thirds of the world wheat trade. During its period of operation world prices, in fact, ran continuously above the agreed maximum price. Importers consequently exercised their rights to buy the agreed quantities at the fixed agreement price. As a result the 1949 Agreement operated almost entirely in the interests of the importing nations.

The 1953 Agreement tried to change this by raising the maximum and minimum prices. This was achieved but only at the cost of withdrawal from the scheme of the major importer, Britain. The British took the view that the general trend in prices would be downward as a result of growing wheat supplies. This turned out to be correct and other importers withdrew. The proportion of world trade involved in transactions within the agreement dropped to less than 30 per cent of world trade.

Several other problems emerged in the course of the operations of the wheat agreements. Up to 1967 the prices were only fixed for one grade of wheat, thus apparently avoiding the knotty question of quality differentials. However, this soon led to discontent as exporters of other types could increase their sales, when there were surpluses, by lowering prices through exaggerating quality differentials. Canada, whose Manitoba wheat was the reference standard, had much less flexibility to do this and pressed for a fundamental renegotiation of this aspect in 1967.

A major weakness throughout most of the life of the wheat agreements was the absence of large nations such as Britain, Russia and China. The presence outside the scheme of the Soviet Union was a particular embarrassment as it was an importer in some years and an exporter in others. When the Russian harvest was good the Soviet Union could undercut the agreement's minimum price to the disadvantage of the members.

The Wheat Agreement had no success in reducing excess production and by the mid-1950s both the USA and Canada were holding very large stocks of wheat which represented a severe threat to the agreement's ability to maintain prices. Only their willingness to hold these stocks prevented the collapse of the Wheat Agreement. Crop failures in 1963 and 1965, together with large imports by the USSR and India, mopped up these excess supplies and wheat prices rose sharply in 1965 and 1966.

The Grains Agreement of 1967 raised both the maximum and minimum prices by about 10 per cent and in response to the Canadian complaints attempted to fix the price range for fourteen different grades of wheat. The higher price range encouraged further production and the price of the principal grade (No. 2 Hard Red Winter Ordinary f.o.b. at Gulf Ports) fell from around $1.73 at the end of 1968 to a low of $1.42 in October 1969. The International Grains Agreement came under increasing pressure from rising world production in both exporting and importing countries. Competition from non-member countries became severe and the floor prices became inoperative. New negotiations in 1971 failed to achieve any agreement on the price range and the agreement has continued purely for consultative purposes.

After 1972 grain prices once more soared. A disastrous harvest in Russia, failures of the monsoon in Asia, drought in Africa and a swing in tastes towards grain-fed beef in affluent countries like Japan combined to push the wholesale price index for wheat from 107 in 1971 to 300 in 1974. These shocks to both rich and poor nations led to renewed interest in an international grains agreement but negotiations proved difficult and protracted mainly because of the apparent irreconcilability of the EEC and the US positions on trade in agricultural products.

INTERNATIONAL QUOTA AGREEMENTS

The International Coffee Agreement, ratified in October 1973, also intended to use a quota system but its economic clauses were never operative.

Both the Coffee and Sugar Agreements combined the objectives of stabilisation (in the sense of moderating fluctuations in prices about their longer-run trend) with support for prices.

THE INTERNATIONAL COFFEE AGREEMENT (1963–73)

Basic quotas were set for each exporting member at the beginning of the agreement and in each subsequent year. The Coffee Council then divided these into quarterly allocations so as to maintain the desired balance between supply and demand throughout the year. Penalties could be imposed on countries for exceeding their quotas. There were no fixed price targets apart from the aim of keeping prices above the low levels of 1962. The council was left to determine quotas in the light of market considerations and producing and consuming nations shared the votes equally. Importing countries had to take all their coffee from exporting members save for small historically determined amounts from non-members.

Coffee is one of the few commodities where production and exports are almost entirely in the developing countries. It is also a very valuable commodity accounting for a substantial share of the total foreign exchange earnings of a number of poor countries in Latin America and Africa. This makes it an attractive commodity for both stabilisation and price support. It has also technical advantages in being storable at reasonable cost[6] and having a low price elasticity of demand in the main consuming countries. Despite these advantages the Coffee Agreement ran into many problems and effectively came to an end in 1972.

Goals

The Coffee Agreement had three main goals: (1) reduction of short-term fluctuations in coffee prices; (2) at first tacitly and in the 1968 Agreement explicitly, support of coffee prices above the trend which would have occurred in the absence of intervention; (3) diversification.

Problems

The main problems could be classified in terms of resolving conflicts: (1) between producers and consumers over prices, (2) between producing countries over market shares and (3) the problem of enforcement.[7]

The International Coffee Agreement probably only got off the ground because of a need felt by the Kennedy administration to make some grand gesture to Latin America. Without American involvement and support no quota agreement could survive, simply because the USA is the dominant consumer. Support from the main consuming nations was essential for enforcement – to prevent non-member producers from taking advantage of the agreement to undercut its prices and expand their sales. Equally the co-operation of consumers was required to police the so-called 'tourist coffee', that is, sales by members outside of their quota to non-member countries from which it was trans-shipped to consuming countries which were members.

This need for the co-operation of consumer nations and for American leadership in this, required compromise on prices. Up to a point, consuming nations might be willing to see coffee prices rise above free market levels in expectation of political gains but, in general, they would oppose high prices. This is a general problem for ICAs.

The issue of market shares was particularly thorny in the case of coffee. The dominant suppliers were Brazil and Colombia, but most growth in demand and production was in the robustas (used in soluble coffee) produced in East Africa and Ivory Coast. This led to frequent disputes over the size of the quotas and demands for separate treatment for robusta coffee. Some flexibility was introduced into the methods of adjustment of quotas but the problem was never fully resolved and it

117

remains true that the agreement tended to freeze the pattern of market shares and thwart the African suppliers. This caused continual friction between the African and Latin American members of the Coffee Council. There was also a tendency for countries to increase production in order to provide an argument for a larger export quota. These continued pressures and frictions always threatened the stability of the agreement.

One factor which assisted in the creation and continuation of the agreement was the dominance of Brazil as both the largest producer and the possessor of enormous stocks. The constant threat that Brazil could flood the market with coffee at any time it wished helped to keep other producers in line. Brazil's stocks amounted to over 95 per cent of one year's basic quotas for most of the life of the Coffee Agreement. Its position had some obvious similarities to Saudi Arabia within OPEC.

Achievements

The mere survival of the Coffee Agreement for some ten years in the face of these problems was in itself an achievement. The provision that exports above quota could be made to markets with low coffee consumption – 'new markets' – without restriction, helped as a safety valve. However, it carried with it the danger of re-exports to traditional markets making the success of the scheme even more dependent on the goodwill of the consuming nations in abiding by the rules for enforcement of the agreement.

It is difficult, if not impossible, to judge the effect of the agreement on prices either in terms of reduction in fluctuations or in terms of raising prices above free market levels. It has been suggested that it may have effected a small resource transfer from consuming to producing nations. Price and earnings fluctuations continued to be rather wide for many members within the agreement.

Some diversification took place and there was an increase in processing of raw coffee in Brazil. Both of these are desirable objectives but it is difficult to say how much they were assisted by the agreement. Most of the diversification took place in Brazil and Colombia, both of whom would have pressed on with such policies, even in the absence of an agreement or its diversification fund. Similarly the existence of huge stocks of surplus coffee in Brazil meant that it could always have adopted a discriminating pricing policy on raw coffee, selling it to local processors more cheaply than to foreign countries. In fact, the existence of the Coffee Agreement and Brazil's desire for its continuance gave American coffee processors some leverage in discussions on Brazil's success in capturing 14 per cent of the US soluble coffee market. The whole International Coffee Agreement very nearly came to grief over the issue during the negotiations for its renewal in 1968.

The agreement broke down in 1972 over the issue of price. Brazil demanded an upward adjustment of coffee prices to compensate for the devaluation of the US dollar. This demand was rejected by the USA. In fact prices subsequently rose sharply because of frost damage to the crop.

THE INTERNATIONAL SUGAR AGREEMENT

Sugar is a commodity produced widely by both rich and poor nations. In the tropical developing countries the raw material comes from cane sugar, largely a plantation crop, but also grown by small peasant producers in many countries. In the developed countries sugar is produced from sugar beet. Normally tropical cane sugar is significantly cheaper and developing countries have a substantial comparative advantage in sugar production. Unfortunately strategic considerations during two world wars led to the establishment of large areas of beet crops in the USA and Europe. These have continued to exist behind high protection. In fact the degree of self-sufficiency in sugar production in developed countries has gone on rising since the Second World War.

The structural imbalances in the sugar market due to protection in the industrial countries are made still more complex by the various politically-motivated preferential arrangements between importers and exporters. In 1954 over 60 per cent of world trade in sugar was covered by such arrangements. Throughout the last twenty years three principal preferential trade sectors have existed. The United States quota arrangements covered about one-quarter of world trade and reserved US import requirements to offshore areas of the USA such as Hawaii and Puerto Rico, and countries with special trade relations with the USA such as the Philippines. Prices have usually been very favourable.

The Commonwealth Sugar Agreement (CSA) guaranteed imports of agreed quantities of sugar by the UK at negotiated prices to Commonwealth producers. There was a supplementary allowance for developing countries. Prices, though less attractive than the US scheme, have since 1965 been guaranteed for three years and were usually substantially higher than free market prices. The CSA covered about 10 per cent of world trade in sugar.

After the USA suspended Cuba's quota in 1960 a special arrangement between the USSR and Cuba has given price and quantity guarantees to Cuba on very favourable terms. Other bilateral arrangements between some EEC members and developing countries came to an end in 1968 with some compensatory direct grants to aid rationalisation.

The existence of preferential arrangements covering over 60 per cent of trade in sugar together with a degree of self-sufficiency in the major importing areas, amounting to over 60 per cent of their total requirements in an average year, produced severe problems for the residual free market in sugar. The problems are instability and access. Comparatively small variations in beet sugar production in these conditions can produce large changes in import requirements in the face of a very low elasticity of supply of cane sugar exports. This has produced wild swings in free market sugar prices. In fact beet sugar production is subject to quite large fluctuations and has thus been a major cause of instability. The main tasks of an international sugar agreement are to bring some stability into the situation and to improve access for tropical sugar into industrial countries and protected markets.

The Agreements

The first post-Havana International Sugar Agreement (ISA) ran from 1954 to 1958, and covered about 30 per cent of world exports. Voting power was divided equally between exporting and importing countries. The main aim was stability in prices at levels that would be reasonable to producers but would not encourage any expansion of sugar production in developed countries. Subsidiary objectives included expansion of trade in sugar and enhanced earnings for developing countries. All trade under preferential arrangements continued outside the agreements.

Basic quotas for sugar exports to the 'free market' were allocated to exporting countries on a historical basis and arrangements were made to provide for quota adjustments to restrict exports when prices fell below target and to expand them when prices rose too high. Importing countries were restricted in the amounts of sugar which they were permitted to buy from non-participating countries and cut price imports were also banned with certain limited exceptions.

From 1959 onwards, with a second agreement, all the major exporters and importers were members, but this still amounted to only 35 per cent of world trade because of the exclusion of the preferential sectors. A third ISA was negotiated in 1968 and lapsed in 1973. Between 1973 and 1977 there was no ISA but it was successfully renegotiated in 1977, but excluding the European Community.

The agreements also contained provisions about stocks. Exporters were supposed to carry stocks of at least 10 per cent of their basic quota, but not exceeding 12.5 per cent of their previous year's output.

The Effects

Sugar prices continued to fluctuate wildly and it is difficult to argue that the ISA had much effect in reducing short-term instability. Alton Law points out that, even ignoring the exceptional year 1961–62, the average annual price fluctuation was more than 75 per cent greater in the twelve years of ISA control than in the eleven years before and between the agreements.[8] It was equally unsuccessful in reducing tendencies to surplus or in supporting prices. Jung and MacAvoy contend that the USA and other industrial countries' production and import policies had much greater effects on developing countries' export prices for sugar than either the 1953 or 1958 ISAs.[9] For most of the period stocks in the exporting countries frequently exceeded the stipulated maxima. The sugar market was, of course, thrown in chaos by America's abolition of Cuba's preferential quota and her substitution of preferential arrangements with other suppliers. A huge world crop in 1960–61 forced prices down to about 2 US cents a pound as compared with the agreement preferred range of 3.25–3.75 cents per pound. A meeting in 1961 to readjust basic quotas failed to reach any accord, partly because Cuba's demands were unacceptable to most of the other members. As a result the market intervention provisions of the ISA were suspended. Control mechanisms were reintroduced in 1969 under the third ISA but were suspended once more at the end of 1973. The ISA continued purely on an administrative and consultative basis with no economic provisions until 1977 when it was reconstituted on a basis similar to the third ISA.

The ISA really did very little to deal with the main problems of the sugar market. It did not even attempt to restrict the growth of inefficient production behind tariff walls in the industrial nations. The basic quotas showed little concern for efficiency. Peru, which may have been one of the lowest cost producers in the world, was given a relatively tiny quota in the 1953 Agreement. It withdrew protesting that 'Neither the United Nations nor the present Conference could press an efficient producer to become an inefficient one.'[10]

Various estimates have shown that free international trade in sugar would have brought greatly increased earnings to developing country exporters, amounting to over $500 million per annum in the late 1960s according to Johnson.[11]

Prices would also, in all probability, be much more stable in a free market. Sugar production is very widely dispersed so that large fluctuations on the supply side due to weather or disease are unlikely. The income elasticity of demand in the main consuming nations is very low so that cyclical fluctuations are also an unlikely cause of instability. Only stock variations due to wars or similar dramatic events are likely to cause surges in demand.

This is one market where free competition would in all likelihood bring the best results in terms of stability, efficiency and equity. The ISAs were palliatives diverting attention from the much greater priority of persuading the rich nations to reduce their protection of beet sugar.

INTERNATIONAL COCOA AGREEMENT 1973

No economic provisions of the Cocoa Agreement ever came into force. It was however similar to the Coffee and Sugar Agreements in relying mainly on quotas as the method of market intervention, with buffer stocks as a secondary device. It took over ten years of negotiations to set up a Cocoa Agreement which had no effect on cocoa prices and faced termination in April 1980 by the producer countries who apparently saw this as their last chance to dispose freely of funds accumulated in their buffer stock rather than see them absorbed in the Common Fund.[12]

THE INTERNATIONAL TIN AGREEMENT
(BUFFER STOCK AND QUOTA)

After the Second World War an International Tin Study Group was set up to consider proposals for a tin agreement. Tin has a prewar history of instability and of producers' agreements to control output and support tin prices. These early arrangements may have moderated fluctuations in tin prices and supported them above free market levels but they also had the effects of retaining inefficient high cost mines and of stimulating a successful search for methods of economising on the use of tin.

Plans put forward by the Study Group in 1948 and 1950 were rejected and it was not until 1953–54, when the USA stopped its strategic purchasing policy for raw materials, that a sufficient stimulus to find a solution resulted in the creation of the first International Tin Agreement (ITA) in 1953. Delays over ratification, however, prevented its coming into operation until 1956. There have been five successive Tin Agreements, but they have all retained essentially the same provisions. It is the only agreement where it is the intention to rely on a buffer stock for market intervention with quotas as the residual means to support flow prices.

Aims
As usual the main aim has been stabilisation of the price. Maintenance of employment and increasing export earnings for the producing countries are also declared objectives. The need to develop new sources of supply, to improve efficiency in mining, smelting and concentrating tin ores is also supposed to be borne in mind.

Methods
In conformity with the Havana principles the ITA allows for voting power to be shared equally between the exporting and the importing nations. Among each group votes are distributed according to average tonnages traded in the latest three years.

Although purchases and sales from the buffer stock of tin form the main method of market intervention the agreement also allows for the imposition of export quotas. The International Tin Council, representing most of the exporting nations and with some notable exceptions most exporting countries, sets the policy for the scheme. The producers contribute to the buffer stock on a basis related to their share in production. A lower and an upper price range are agreed and the manager of the buffer stock is given directives on purchasing and selling tin from the stock in accordance with these. In the 1956−61 scheme, for example, the management had discretion to buy when the price lay between £640 and £720 per ton and to sell when it was between £800 and £880. Between £720 and £800 the management was not permitted to buy or sell. Outside the limits of £640 and £880 the management was obliged to respectively buy tin or sell it. These limits were adjusted many times in the course of the several tin agreements, with the range constantly moving upwards. The management were also given greater discretion in the fourth agreement to buy or sell as they saw fit within the defined ranges. One major purpose of this was to reduce the risk of one-way speculation by professional speculators and it also generally increased the flexibility of the scheme. The financial resources required to operate the stock were until the late 1970s almost entirely supplied by the exporters and there is no obligation on importing members to buy exclusively from exporting members. Their sole responsibility is to assist with the administrative costs. Few importing countries (and that only recently) have made some contribution to the financing of the tin buffer stock. Lately several tin producing countries have been able to draw on the IMF for funds to cover part of their subscriptions to the stock under an IMF scheme for this purpose.

If the stock exceeds a certain quantity the Tin Council can impose export quotas proportional to historical exports.

Operation

The ITA covers members with over 75 per cent of world tin production which ought to give it greater prospects of success than, for example, the Sugar Agreement. However, neither the USA, a large importer, nor the USSR, sometimes a major exporter, joined the earlier ITA. In addition the United States had enormous stocks of tin throughout all of the ITA's life. In 1962 the ITA buffer stock stood at a mere 3,200 tons while the USA had 350,000 tons which was equal to two years' world production of tin. In the same year the rest of the world held 50,000 tons of tin in stocks.

On the whole the ITA has succeeded in holding the tin price above the agreement floor in most years, but to do this has required that the operations of the buffer stock be buttressed by the imposition of export quotas with their attendant dangers of inefficiency. The ITA resources have never been sufficient to enable it to hold large enough stocks to even out swings in the tin market.

A recent careful study of the Tin Agreement has concluded that it made only a marginal contribution to the reduction of instability in tin prices and producer incomes. The US strategic stockpile transactions were much more important. To be effective the ITA would have required a maximum stock at least five times larger than it possessed. The authors of the study argue that: 'the longevity of the International Tin Agreement may owe a good deal to its ineffectiveness'.[13] Nevertheless, the ITA can claim some successes over its thirty years or so of existence. It has shown some capacity to influence independent national stockpiles, to attract consumer contributions, to extend consumer membership and to provide some objective criteria for a price adjustment mechanism. Moreover, it has emerged as a useful forum for producers and consumers to gather and exchange information which in itself may exert some price stabilising influence.[14]

THE UN'S INTEGRATED PROGRAMME FOR COMMODITIES[15]

Most of the political pressure for ICAs comes from spokesmen for the developing countries. This is reflected in countless resolutions in UNCTAD and in the grandiloquent mid-1970s demands for 'A New International Economic Order', basically a collection of old ideas in a fashionable package. Stabilisation and support for primary commodity prices remains the main objective and ICAs the main mechanism for achieving it. The only novel features in the UNCTAD proposals for an integrated programme were the suggestion for a Common Fund for financing international stocks and the simultaneous negotiation of a broad group of ICAs. The UNCTAD report stressed, 'That years of studies, discussions and consultations in various forums have succeeded in establishing international arrangements for only a few commodities, hardly any of which have proved to be effective or durable.'[16] Instead of drawing the conclusions that such a dismal record might indicate basic flaws in these forms of market intervention UNCTAD demanded urgent negotiations for creating a package of up to eighteen ICAs with buffer stocks and a Common Fund without wasting further time in research or consultation.

But of those eighteen commodities three already had existing price control agreements (tin, coffee and cocoa); two had existing and successful producer price raising schemes (bauxite and phosphates); four were unsuitable for buffer stocks schemes either because of the absence of organised markets or perishability (iron ore, bauxite, meats, bananas). Price enhancement for copper, cotton, iron ore, vegetable oils and oil seeds, sugar and meats was unlikely and inequitable because developed countries produced a large proportion of them, and for rubber, jute, hard fibres and cotton because of the ready availability of synthetic substitutes.[17] A rather similar appraisal can be found in Rangarajan's book where he says, 'of the 18 commodities in the list, the stock mechanism is suitable for four, of which two already have operating mechanisms and one does not need to be stocked in the near future ... It is difficult to avoid the conclusion that the stock mechanism was first chosen as a saleable proposition and the Integrated Programme then fitted round it.'[18]

If it is accepted that ICAs are a good thing then there is a case for a simultaneous approach and for the creation of a common fund for stocks. The attraction of dealing with a large group of commodities simultaneously is that it can have something in it for everyone. Countries which have interests in some commodities as consumers but in others as producers can offset gains from one agreement against losses on another. Against this can be set the sheer complexity of the task and the tremendous demands that would be created for the simultaneous presence at various negotiating tables of the same groups of ministers, civil servants and commodity experts. There are also a number of countries which do not export any of the affected commodities. Viewing the possibility of a simultaneous price increase (since that is the most likely effect of the start of the large number of stockpiles recommended) in a wide range of important imports is unlikely to raise much enthusiasm on their part for such proposals. It may be possible to give a little disguised aid in the form of an agreement on sugar or coffee without the electorate noticing what is afoot, but if similar transfers through raised prices are intended for ten or more commodities strong opposition from consumers is very likely.

A common fund for buffer stocks offers several advantages. First, if the market behaviour for some commodities is out of phase with movements in prices of others some buffer stocks could be selling at the same time as others are buying. These offsetting movements could reduce the overall size of the required fund as compared with the aggregate of individual commodity funds required to achieve the same policy objectives. If, however, the main cause of instability was cyclical – fluctuations in demand which caused all commodity prices to rise and fall together – this economy in funds would be zero or negligible.

A large single fund might obtain finance on better terms than would several smaller ones. Lending risks would be pooled and reduced, and dealing in large sums of money would yield some economies of scale. UNCTAD envisages the buffer stocks as representing investments which could attract funds on a near commercial basis from OPEC members, but this is a very doubtful proposition. It depends on either rather wide swings between purchase and sale prices or very accurate prediction of trend on the part of the stock managers. The combination of administrative, brokerage, storage and deterioration costs in stocks tends to absorb a very large part of the gross margin between purchase and sale prices making it unlikely that the fund could support high interest charges.[19]

Negotiations for a Common Fund were eventually concluded in 1979. It was set up with 'two windows'. The first is intended to help finance international buffer stocks and internationally co-ordinated national stocks. Its second window will finance such measures as research and development, marketing and diversification. The financial structure of the CF is envisaged as government contributions of $470 million of which $400 million is for the first, and $70 million for the second window. Of the $400 million, $150 million is to be contributed in cash, $150 million on call and $100 as on call for backing the Fund's borrowing.[20] UNCTAD's earlier estimate of $6 billion for stocking the ten 'core' commodities (thought by many to be an underestimate) may not be directly comparable to this because of differences in the financial arrangements, but the obvious disparity in size is so huge as to suggest that the CF is unlikely to have any significant impact upon commodity trade instability.

In any case it has often been remarked that the main obstacle to ICAs has seldom been lack of finance. Negotiations have almost always broken down over the issues of the target price and the allocation of quotas. Even if they could be set up it is not known whether ICAs could succeed in moderating fluctuations in the export prices and revenues of developing countries. Past experience does not justify optimism. Nor does the evidence of theoretical and empirical research, including simulation studies, suggest that the task of keeping actual prices within, say, plus or minus 15 per cent of a target price which keeps in touch with long-term trends in supply and demand, is anything but extremely difficult in technical terms, let alone in the real world of clashing interests between producers and consumers and among producing nations.[21]

COMPENSATORY FINANCING

Two other schemes for alleviating the effects of commodity trade instability have been operating for a number of years. These are the IMF's Compensatory Financing Facility (CFF) started in 1963 and the EEC's STABEX scheme which was established by the Lomé Convention between the Community and forty-six African, Caribbean and Pacific countries in 1975. Both operate on the basis of partially compensating countries for shortfalls in export earnings which result from fluctuations in commodity markets. No attempt is made to intervene in the markets to influence quantities or prices. Countries are simply permitted to borrow on easy terms when they have an export shortfall and the loans normally have to be repaid within a few years.

The IMF's CFF defines a shortfall as the gap between the current year's merchandise export proceeds and the average for five years including the two previous years, the current year and forecasts for the two subsequent years. Initially drawings were limited to 25 per cent of the member's quota in the IMF, were not additional to ordinary drawings and required the member to co-operate with the Fund in finding a solution to its balance-of-payments difficulties. Partly because of these limitations and partly because the 1960s were a period of relative stability the CFF was little used. Over the years the scheme was liberalised. Major changes were made in 1975 in the wake of the oil crisis. the limit on drawings was raised to 75 per cent of quota and could be additional to ordinary drawings. The permitted net amount of outstanding drawings in any twelve-month period was raised from 25 to 50 per cent of quota. Because the calculation of the shortfall is necessarily delayed until after the end of the current year countries were permitted to draw on their ordinary quota in anticipation of a shortfall and then convert this to a CFF drawing at any time up to eighteen months later. Shortfalls have to be for reasons outside the country's control and the member still has to co-operate with the IMF in finding a solution. A rule which prevented a country from borrowing if its current exports were 5 per cent or more than the average of the two previous years was eliminated. This proved crucial in the inflationary years of the 1970s.

After the 1975 reforms drawings shot up. In the subsequent sixteen months drawings by forty-nine member countries reached SDR 2.4 billion or twice the amount in the previous thirteen years.[22] By April 1980 the drawings by the non-oil LDCs had amounted to 4.6 billion SDRs and their net outstanding credits were 2.5 billion SDRs.[23]

Nevertheless, it has been criticised for providing far too little assistance to the NOLDCs. UNCTAD Secretariat calculations show that drawings against the CFF by the NOLDCs have on average not exceeded 12.5 per cent of shortfalls. Even in 1976 – the year of maximum drawings – it was only 12.7 per cent.[24]

It may well be time for the CFF to meet a much larger proportion of export shortfalls, and most suggested reforms point that way, but several factors should be borne in mind. First, the IMF assumes that most countries will use their own reserves, borrowing from other official sources and commercial sources as well as drawing upon the CFF. Secondly, the 1976 drawings were in relation to the shortfalls of 1975 which was a quite exceptional year. Primary commodities hit their peak in 1974 and their trough in 1975, recovering substantially in 1976 and 1977. Many LDCs should have accumulated reserves from the preceding commodity boom in 1973/74 and the IMF had created several emergency funds to assist in this world crisis, for example, the Oil Facility and the Trust Fund. The NOLDCs did draw on these.

The CFF scheme is in principle a much easier system to operate than ICAs. It is much more comprehensive in that it covers all merchandise exports (and could easily include invisibles as well) and it is much less demanding of political necessity to obtain agreements, or technical skill in forecasting future prices of individual commodities and designing optimal stocking policies than is the case for ICAs. CFF-type schemes emerge in a favourable light from simulation exercises and in practice the IMF scheme seems to have worked in the right directions even if the amounts of compensation have seemed small in relation to the recent problems of the NOLDCs.[25]

Increases in LDCs' Fund quotas, the inclusion of invisibles, and calculation of shortfalls in real terms (allowing for changes in the price of imports) are all possible reforms which could increase the value of the CFF to NOLDCs.

STABEX

The STABEX scheme was designed to stabilise earnings from exports of the African, Caribbean and Pacific (ACP) countries to the Community. It covered seventeen agricultural commodities and iron ore. The original forty-six ACP countries later rose to fifty-two so that it involves a substantial number of developing countries, many of them rather small, poor and vulnerable. But the commodities whose earnings are intended to be stabilised amount to only 20 per cent of the export earnings of the ACP countries. in 1976, its first year of operation, seventeen ACP countries drew SDR 72 million. In the same year ACP countries drew SDR 124 million from the IMF scheme and NOLDCs' total drawings for 1976 were SDR 1,575 million.[26]

The total sum allocated to STABEX for the whole period 1976–80 was only about $420 million and conditions for eligibility were quite stringent. The exports had to be in crude or very elementary processed form. Individually they had to account for at least 7.5 per cent of the country's total merchandise exports to all destinations. The shortfall, calculated in nominal terms, had to be at least 7.5 per cent below the average earnings from that product to the EEC over the previous four years. For the least developed, land-locked or island economies these two conditions are dropped to 2.5 per cent.

The terms of repayment are liberal. Compensation payments to the least developed countries are in the form of grants and for the others the loans are interest free and repayable as and when export earnings recover.

The STABEX can be criticised for discriminating between ACP and other LDCs and for being too limited in coverage and funds. This has the effect of making it liable to political influence when decisions have to be made on rationing funds between intending borrowers. The idea of making compensation payments grants to the least developed countries is widely commended as an appropriate change for adoption by the IMF, CFF. But is it sensible to confuse transfers intended to promote development with assistance intended to deal with temporary financial embarrassment? The criteria for allocating funds for each of these purposes should be quite different. Of course situations may arise where what was intended as a short-term loan has to be rephased. Instead of exports rising in the next three years they may drop still further or there may be a drought forcing up food imports. Such unforeseen events need special *ad hoc* arrangements and that basically is the attitude of the IMF.

A COMPLEMENTARY FACILITY FOR COMMODITY-RELATED SHORTFALLS IN EXPORT EARNINGS

This is the most recent proposal of the Group of 77 at UNCTAD V in June 1979. There they requested that the UNCTAD Secretariat in consultation with the IMF staff carry out a detailed study for a complementary facility 'to compensate for shortfalls in each commodity, taking account of its financial requirements, possible sources of financing, its financial feasibility, institutional arrangements and the modalities and considerations that would provide adequate compensation in real terms to developing countries . . . '.[27] It is intended that this should be additional to improvements in the CFF of the IMF and other IFC arrangements. Most of the OECD nations voted against this resolution or abstained.

CONCLUSION

International commodity agreements are technically difficult to design and operate and politically difficult to negotiate and manage. They take many years of negotiation to set up and are prone to break down or be emasculated within a few years. These are the lessons of history. But theoretical reasoning, the diversity and complexity of commodities and their substitutes, and the experience of the market operators all suggest that even given the political will, it would be very difficult to run schemes which would successfully smooth out fluctuations in commodity prices and make a significant contribution to smoothing out fluctuations in LDCs' export earnings. It may be worthwhile experimenting with a few ICAs but it would ensure a waste of resources to try to set up many before we have hard evidence that some can be made to work.

If the major worry of the LDCs is fluctuations in their export earnings (and this is what has usually been maintained) the CFF approach offers much greater prospects of success. There is scope for reforming and expanding it, but not in the direction of turning it into a mechanism for long-term transfers of resources to LDCs. The criteria for long-term assistance ought to differ significantly from the relatively automatic provision of short-term finance to meet balance-of-payments problems induced by export instability.[28]

NOTES: CHAPTER 6

1 See J. S. Davis, *International Commodity Agreements: Hope, Illusion or Menace* (New York: Committee on International Economic Policy, 1947); Peter Bauer, *The Rubber Industry* (Cambridge, Mass.: Harvard University Press, 1948); J. W. F. Rowe, *Primary Commodities in International Trade* (Cambridge: Cambridge University Press, 1965), part IV; P. Lamartine Yates, *Commodity Control: A Study of Primary Products* (London: Jonathan Cape, 1943).

2 UNCTAD, 'An integrated programme for commodities: Report of the Secretary General of UNCTAD', TD/B/C.1/766 (Geneva. UNCTAD 9 December 1974), and 'Report of the UN conference on trade and development on its fifth session', TD/268 (Geneva; UNCTAD, 13 July 1979), p.15.

3 See A. I. MacBean, *Export Instability and Economic Development* (London: Allen & Unwin, 1966), p. 266; M. Radetzki, *International Commodity Arrangements* (London: Hurst, 1969), pp. 6–9; C. P. Brown, *Primary Commodity Control* (Kuala Lumpur: Oxford University Press, 1975), pp. 55 and 135–7.

4 Brown, op. cit., pp. 140–4.

5 See D. T. Nguyen, 'The effects of partial price stabilisation on export earnings instability and level, in A. Sengupta (ed.), *Commodities Finance and Trade* (London: Frances Pinter, 1980).

6 Actually storage for large quantities of coffee proved to be much more difficult than expected.

7 Bart S. Fisher, *The International Coffee Agreement: A Study in Coffee Diplomacy* (New York: Praeger, 1972) gives a detailed account of the politics of the Coffee Agreement.

8 Alton D. Law, *International Commodity Agreements: Setting, Performance and Prospects* (Lexington, Mass.: Heath, 1974), p. 51.

9 Helen Jung and Paul MacAvoy, 'A baleful look at prospects for commodity agreements', in F. G. Adams and S. A. Klein (eds), *Stabilising World Commodity Markets: Analysis, Practice and Policy* (Washington Food Foundation Conference, 1978) (Lexington, Mass.: Lexington Books, 1978), pp. 271–86.

10 See V. Timoshenko and B. Swerling, *The World's Sugar* (Stanford, Calif.: University of California Press, 1959), p. 338.

11 R. H. Snape, 'Some effects of protection on the world sugar industry', *Economica* (February 1960) and H. G. Johnson, *Economic Policies Towards Less Developed Countries* (London: Allen & Unwin, 1967), Appendix D, use similar approaches and derive essentially similar conclusions.

12 *Neue Zurcher Zeitung* 5/6 April 1980, quoted in Helen Wasserman, 'Breakdown of the international cocoa agreement', *Journal of World Trade Law* (July/August 1980), p. 361.

13 Gordon Smith and George Schink, 'The international Tin Agreement: a reassessment', *The Economic Journal* (December 1976), p. 721.

14 C. P. Brown, *The Political and Social Economy of Commodity Control* (London: Macmillan, 1980), p. 20.
15 UNCTAD, op. cit., TD/B/C.1/166 and Supplementary Papers TD/3/C.1/166 Supps 1–5.
16 ibid., p. 3.
17 Brown, *The Political and Social Economy of Commodity Control*, p. 92.
18 L. N. Rangarajan, *Commodity Conflict* (London: Croom Helm, 1978), p. 305.
19 See UNCTAD, TD/B/C.1/166, Suppl. 2 (December 1974) and TD/B/C.1/184 (24 June 1975) for Secretariat views on the advantages of a common fund.
20 I. S. Chadha, Adviser to the Commodities Division UNCTAD, 'The integrated programme for commodities: an assessment', *Bulletin*, vol. 1 (1980), p. 24 (Institute of Development Studies, Sussex).
21 Smith and Schink, op. cit.; Brown, *Primary Commodity Control*, and *The Political and Social Economy of Commodity Control*, Ch. 5.
22 Louis Goreux, 'The use of compensatory financing', *The Journal of Finance and Development* (IBRD/IMF) (September 1977), p. 21.
23 IMF, *International Financial Statistics* (June 1980).
24 Iqbal S. Gulati, 'Compensatory financing: inadequacy of present arrangements and new proposals', in A. Sengupta (ed.), *Commodities Finance and Trade* (London: Frances Pinter, 1980), pp. 181–2.
25 See, for example, T. Morrison and L. Perrez, 'Analysis of compensatory financing schemes for export earnings fluctuations in developing countries', *Journal of World Development*, vol. 4, no. 8, (1976); Louis Goreux, op. cit., and also in IMF, *Staff Papers* (1977), pp. 613–41.
26 For comparative analysis of the two schemes see Guy Erb, 'North–South dialogue and compensatory financing' (Washington, DC: Overseas Development Council, June 1977) and L. N. Rangarajan, *Commodity Conflict* (London: Croom Helm, 1978), pp. 241–4.
27 UNCTAD TD/268, 'Report of UNCTAD V' (Geneva: UNCTAD, July 1979), pp. 15–16.
28 See the forcefully presented arguments of the Canadian delegate to UNCTAD V. TD/268/Add 1 (20 July 1979), pp. 22–3.

CHAPTER 7

The Organisation for Economic Co-operation and Development (OECD)

Unlike its predecessor, the Organisation for European Economic Co-operation (OEEC), and unlike the other institutions discussed in this volume, the OECD is not closely identified with any one, overriding, central theme. Whereas international trade issues are clearly the domain of the GATT, and international financial collaboration is, in principle, the preserve of the IMF, the OECD is essentially a general forum for consultation between the advanced industrial countries.

Since the signing of the OECD Convention in 1960, the diffuse nature of its concerns has led to major initiatives being taken in the specialised bodies mentioned. More particularly the OECD's original economic co-ordination role in Europe has been superseded by the EEC. Thus in reviewing the activities of the OECD it has to be recognised that tangible achievements are few, and that there is strength in the criticism that the institution is something of a 'talking-shop'.

None the less, developments in the world economy with a reduction in the industrial pre-eminence of the USA, the emergence of OPEC and the increased unity that LDCs have developed in international negotiations all suggest that a 'first world' forum may, increasingly, be necessary. That there has been some revival of interest in the OECD as such a body[1] is the justification for the following review.

ORIGINS AND COMPOSITION

Although in some ways there was a rather distinct break in continuity between the two, the OECD is generally regarded as the successor to the OEEC and there is much in common in organisation and intent. With regard to the latter General Marshall's Harvard speech in June 1947 indicated that Europe's recovery, given the common problems of all of the countries, should be embarked upon as a co-operative venture. As the major constraint was a shortage of dollars with which to import (mainly) US food and essential equipment, Europe would be well advised to regard itself as a unit and to seek a joint programme that

132

would maximise the benefit from the aid funds. There were two aspects to this when the Convention on European Economic Co-operation (which designated the tasks of the OEEC) was signed in Paris in April 1948. First, the USA wished to avoid dictating a programme to the Europeans, and one function of the OEEC was therefore to advise the Americans on aid allocation. Secondly, it was recognised that, even with the aid funds, dollars would be in short supply, resulting in a need to maximise the efficiency of use of local European resources so as to permit a satisfactory level of economic activity without 'extraordinary outside assistance'.[2] Thus the Convention, under Articles 4, 5 and 6, envisaged progress on the liberation of intra-European trade. Article 4 also envisaged a multilateral system of payments for Europe as an urgent requirement for such trade liberation. The OEEC was established primarily to bring these plans to fruition.

The multilateral payments system was indeed crucial in the liberalisation programme and, following an American intitiative, the European Payments Union (EPU) was established by agreement of OEEC members in September 1950. This was essentially an arrangement for the Bank for International Settlements in Basle to cancel out the claims and debts of each country against its various European partners, month by month, leaving for each nation a residual claim or debt towards the EPU. 'In the following seven years these multilateral compensations . . . sufficed to cancel almost half of the gross surpluses and deficits incurred without recourse to either gold or credit.'[3]

The second feature of the EPU was to assist the settlement of payments remaining after this process. About 60 per cent of these were to be financed by mutual EPU credits and the remainder by gold and dollars (or currencies acceptable to the creditor countries). As a means to encouraging corrective policies by net debtor countries the gold portion of the settlement was to increase gradually towards 100 per cent as that country's 'quota' deficit was exceeded.[4]

The mechanism described removed the need for bilateral settlements on a continual basis and the door was thereby opened for a major expansion of intra-European trade. The OEEC Code of Liberalisation was the instrument used to reduce the impediments to the increased trade made possible by the improved financial arrangements. Under the code the members committed themselves to abolishing restrictions on specified percentages of their imports from all other countries—first, by a fixed percentage of total private imports, and secondly, in specified proportions in the case of three major categories: food, raw materials and manufactured products.

In terms of our present interest there are perhaps two distinctive features in what emerged from the developments within the OEEC just described. First, a comprehensive view was taken of the problems of member countries. Thus the Trade Committee and the Steering Board of Trade which presided over the Code of Liberalisation co-operated closely with the Managing Board of the EPU when countries ran into major payments disequilibria. Monetary and trade matters were highly co-ordinated, as for instance in the crises following the Korean War. Emphasising the comprehensive approach, the OEEC Council in March 1952 initiated an annual review of the economic condition of the member countries.

Economic policy of member countries was examined from the stand-point of the others who would be affected by way of trade flows. This general approach reflected a tendency to stress faster economic growth and to discourage deflationary measures, to seek out policies to relieve bottlenecks in the growth process (e.g. manpower, productivity) rather than to reduce growth itself.[5]

The second point to note about the OEEC experience is that the quick progress towards liberalisation and the willingness to submit to (and be influenced by) a critical review of each country's economic policies required a very high degree of concurrence on what it was that was to be achieved. For the European powers of the time the joint goal was reconstruction growth, and the liberalisation of exchange between themselves. Although the OECD in 1960 inherited the approach to economic policy of the OEEC, as discussed, it was less clear that the same degree of common interest between the enlarged membership remained.

Indeed, 1958 and the emergence of the EEC marked a serious rift between Britain and the 'Six' over the future of free trade in Europe. The issue was the degree of supra-national authority in the free trade area as British proposals to minimise such authority emerged from the OEEC (the Maudling Committee). French and other European hostil-ity to the institution followed. The OEEC had lost authority and it had lost a large part of its initial *raison d'être*. By 1958 non-resident convert-ibility of the major European currencies had been achieved and quanti-tative restrictions on intra-European imports had been drastically reduced through the Code of Liberalisation.

With reconstruction largely completed the most obvious task remain-ing was a return to non-discrimination in trade, and it was therefore desirable that the organisation evolve into one with direct US represent-ation. Although closely involved, the latter had not been a member of the OEEC.[6] In addition to concern over the growing inadequacy of the OEEC as an organisation for discussion of the economic relations of the countries of the Atlantic arena, the USA was increasingly sensitive to the demands for economic aid from the developing world. As the USA had begun to experience payments problems herself towards the turn of the decade, she was anxious that the revived European powers contribute in this area. The result of this latter concern was the establishment of the Development Assistance Group in 1960, later transferred into the OECD as the Development Assistance Committee (DAC).

The search for a new Atlantic forum culminated in the signing of the OECD Convention in Paris in December 1960, and the nature of this body reflected political preferences on both sides. The suspicions of the Europeans, notably the French, required that the OECD be not too powerful or involve international commitments that might conflict either with EEC policy or with national sovereignty. The Americans, in turn, mindful of the suspicions aroused in Congress by the emergence of the GATT, would not permit an institution which could formulate binding commitments not approved by national legislatures. Thus Articles 5 and 6 of the OECD Convention were so worded that such commitments were out of the question.

With this background the OECD could not be the same as the OEEC as the latter aimed at formal international agreements and binding decisions. The objectives of the OECD had to be both 'broader and vaguer' than those of the OEEC.[7] The stated aims under Article 1 of the Convention were as follows:

(1)   To promote the stability and growth of its members.
(2)   To promote the economic development of non-members.
(3)   To expand world trade on a non-discriminating basis.

Despite the vagueness of these aims and that (notwithstanding (3) above) the Code of Liberalisation could not be carried over due to American sensibilities, the OECD shared much with the OEEC. Thus, on the structural level, the supreme body is the Council, as in the OEEC. However, whereas formerly this was composed of representatives of the member countries, the new Council meets either at ministerial or permanent delegate level. The rule of unanimity with provisions for abstention was continued, with a proposed course of action not applying to the abstaining member. The Executive Committee meets more frequently, being a smaller body which prepares business to be placed before the Council. It sometimes acts as a co-ordinating group for OECD work, especially when different committees and their 'working parties' are involved. Of these specialised committees the Economic Policy Committee (EPC) is concerned with the 'dead centre of economic policy, the true focus of the OECD'.[8] It is also the committee where two of the features of the OEEC, commonly regarded as of vital importance, have been carried over into the working of the OECD. First, the committee's working parties 2, 3 and 4 on long-term problems of economic growth, policies for better international payments equilibrium and on cost, production and prices, respectively, stress the co-ordination of different aspects of economic policy already noted as a distinguishing feature of the OEEC. The importance of this committee ensures that highly placed national officials participate regularly alongside permanent delegates.

Secondly, associated with the EPC is the Economic and Development Review Committee, the forum in which the annual confrontation sessions concerning the totality of economic policies of member countries are held as initiated by the OEEC.

PAST AND PRESENT WORK OF THE OECD

With the constitution and composition outlined above the OECD has conducted 'useful but for the most part rather low key activity'[9] in a broad spread of international and economic issues. Following the accession of Japan to the Convention in 1964 the OECD incorporated all of the main non-Communist industrialised countries.[10] Indeed, the negotiations over Japan's entry helped to rehabilitate that economy into the world system. European countries began to grant her MFN status, and Japan's trade policies were brought under scrutiny in the manner already described for other members. The process permitted the development of Japanese/European official contact in the general field of economic relations on a continuing basis.

Two natural issues for such a forum emerge: first, trade and trade related issues between the major industrial countries; secondly, aid policy towards LDCs. Immediately, on trade related issues, the OECD enters the field which is the responsibility of negotiations under the GATT. This does not necessarily imply conflict, however, and early work, originally started in the OEEC, continued under the OECD. The Code of Liberalisation of Invisible Transactions was an instance where substantial progress had been made in the OEEC period and further developments in liberalising transactions in certain kinds of insurance and reinsurance, among others, continued into the OECD era. Additionally, in 1957, just prior to the realisation of non-resident convertibility for the major currencies, the Committee for Invisible Transactions proposed to the OEEC Council firm commitments to liberalise capital movements. These included obligations to liberalise movements of capital between member countries for long-term direct investment and for the transfer of proceeds of such investment if liquidated. In 1959 a Code of Liberalisation of Capital Movements followed and in 1964 it was enlarged to cover new international capital issues.

Transactions such as those mentioned above are clearly an ideal area for negotiation in a body such as the OECD where the most affected parties are indeed the advanced industrial countries and where formal agreement is not the aim. In this kind of area it may be reasonable to regard the OECD, at least potentially, as an 'antechamber' of the GATT. Thus tentative accord may be reached between the developed nations primarily affected by certain practices, and, subsequently, generalisation may be possible through the GATT. The obvious case here is the priority given to non-tariff barriers in the recently completed MTN negotiations under the GATT. Such barriers had long been considered at the level of specific cases in the OECD Trade Committee and its general working party.

Currently, further steps are being taken following an initial Council recommendation in 1967 concerning restrictive business practices which affect international trade. Based on that recommendation, a 1979 version goes further in the direction of notification and consultation between countries when one of them proposes legal or legislative action against a practice which may affect the interests of another. Additionally, subject to safeguards, it is suggested that the authorities and firms of one member country be allowed to submit information to the authorities of the country taking action.

This clearly is relevant to the domain of international business where one member country may find that its interests are seriously affected by a restrictive business practice of a firm located in another member country. In this case the affected country may enter into negotiation with the other country to get the practice stopped. In cases where two countries cannot agree on a mutually satisfactory solution, the OECD Committee of Experts on Restrictive Business Practices is recommended as a conciliation forum.[11]

A further example concerns the OECD Code covering aspects of international investment and multinational enterprises. The original instruments adopted in June 1976 covered guidelines for multinational enterprises, the principle of 'national treatment' and the effects of international investment incentives and disincentives. This remains the only operative, though of course, voluntary, code for multinational firms. A mid-1979 review by the OECD Council at ministerial level concluded that the guidelines would stand a better chance of being accepted if left unchanged, but one new principle concerning the transfer of workers from a foreign affiliate 'for the purpose of unfairly influencing negotiations with employees' was added.[12] This provision followed trade union alarm voiced through the Trade Union Advisory Committee to the OECD over the 'Hertz Case' in Denmark.

Additionally, and although voluntary, the guidelines have taken on a 'moral suasion' element in 'inviting' multinationals to notify their concurrence with the guidelines in their annual report to shareholders.

They are also invited to include, in subsequent reports, brief accounts of their experience with the guidelines, for example, steps taken to ensure their observance and difficulties encountered. It would perhaps be wrong to trivialise such developments as it is presumably through an *evolutionary* procedure that satisfactory international social regulation of large international firms will be achieved. Governments have agreed, at least, that while carrying out national policies in this area, they will report regularly to the OECD International Investment and Multi-national Investment Committee on progress made. *The Economist* has commented that this could be the end of 'a pretty hefty wedge' as far as multinationals are concerned.[13]

While it is difficult to assess the merits of such potential developments it is likely that a more uniform legislative climate would be a desirable one in so far as governments can achieve broad agreement on their aims. For example, legislation on (say) environmental questions affecting multinationals (as well as national enterprises) would be somewhat dangerous if imposed by one government alone, in that future multinational investment may merely move to another state if significant costs are involved in compliance.

More directly of concern recently, however, have been the two other aspects of the 1976 accord. The American authorities have been pressing for more progress in member governments' willingness to treat multinational firms or branches operating in their territories in the same way as nationally owned enterprises. While the 1979 ministerial review felt that there had been a significant improvement in the 'transparency' of exceptions to national treatment since the 1976 measures, and that some countries had broadened national treatment,[14] the Americans remain unimpressed. There is the continued belief that firms do not complain of discriminating treatment for fear of further such treatment. It is likely that the OECD will be the forum from which progress in this area will have to come.

Similarly with international investment incentives, the third item of the 1976 measures, the American authorities are applying as much emphasis in this area as they did with industrial subsidies in the recent GATT negotiations. Their belief is that mutual government self-control in offering inducements to multinational investment is preferable to the application of import controls against the products of a plant, which is later regarded as being subsidised, and therefore justifying protective action to be taken against it. They have also voiced concern in the OECD at the proliferating use of performance requirements negotiated by governments with firms in exchange for generous government financial assistance. One example would be a minimum export ratio of final output, or the use of a certain value of locally made components.

Again this is a highly complex, contentious area in which the OECD is likely to be used to marshal facts (as the USA wants in this instance) and to come to a general level of agreement between the developed nations. They are the most heavily affected, being generally both the home base for some firms and hosts for others. It is then intended to move towards formal GATT negotiations when some such basis has been worked out.[15]

In concluding this review of OECD activities to date the role of the Development Assistance Committee and aid policy must be noted. Of course, the OECD is not *exclusively* an advanced country organisation, given the membership of Greece and Turkey, and financial consortia have been arranged for these countries by *ad hoc* working parties. The most recent pledged $900 million to Turkey in early 1979 to assist that country in overcoming major economic difficulties. In addition the World Bank agreed to a $150 million programme loan and a consortium of commercial banks was to provide $400 million in new funds with the OECD acting as a co-ordinator. In addition to the normal short-term examinations of Turkish economic policy, a medium-term review would be conducted by the Secretary General of the OECD as part of the package.

More generally, however, it has been the DAC which has been the focal point of OECD aid activity. Here, again, at the frequent meetings of the committee aid policies of members have been subject to critical scrutiny. Early goals, which have remained, were to increase the quantity of aid given but to improve also the terms of that aid. An associated body, the Development Centre, was established by the Council in 1962, devoted to research, documentation and training for LDCs. Notably, the Centre has often given assistance in drafting, implementing and evaluating programmes. Aubrey, in his review of the early years of the OECD, suggests that the conscience element, as a result of the DAC 'confrontation' sessions, did benefit the level of aid given and the development of financial consortia. Thus testimony before the US Congress revealed that increased contributions by other countries to the UN Special Fund could be traced directly to DAC meetings. Furthermore, the UK announced the easing of aid in advance and specifically linked this to a DAC resolution. Finally a general softening of terms between 1962 and 1965 seems to have been at least partly due to OECD influence.[16]

Unfortunately the progress noted by Aubrey has not been maintained (at least on the general level – Sweden, Norway, Denmark and the Netherlands are exceptions). We may compare the series given in Table 7.1 with the DAC target for net official development assistance to LDCs and multinational agencies.

The disappointing overall performance is much affected by the

Table 7.1   *Net ODA from DAC countries to LDCs and multilateral agencies as percentage of donor GNP*

	1966–68 mean (%)	1970 (%)	1975 (%)	1977 (%)	1978 (%)	1979 (%)	1980[a] (%)
DAC Average	0· 4	0·34	0·36	0·33	0·35	0·34	0·34
USA	0·41	0·32	0·27	0·25	0·27	0·19	0·18
Sweden	0·26	0·38	0·82	0·99	0·90	0·94	0·95
Germany	0·39	0·32	0·40	0·33	0·37	0·44	0·44
Japan	0·28	0·23	0·23	0·21	0·23	0·26	0·27

[a] Estimates.

Source: Column 1 taken from *DAC 1978 Review.* Remainder from: *World Development Report, 1980* (Washington, DC: IBRD/Oxford University Press, 1980) Tables A5 and 16, respectively.

adverse trend of the (absolutely) largest donor, the USA. This observation, however, should not obscure the depressing performance of Germany and Japan, the two DAC countries which, from economic size and balance-of-payments viewpoints, should have been in a strong position to improve their performance. The case of Sweden is included to illustrate the possibilities when the political will is present in an advanced industrial society.

Whether or not the performance would have been worse but for the DAC is, of course, a moot point but the willingness of the DAC to single out named countries for criticism in its publications[17] and to engage in country policy 'confrontation' is likely to be of some benefit. It is arguable, however, that more success has been recorded in terms and conditions of aid. A high level (ministerial) meeting of the DAC in October 1972 put forward a recommendation in this area and in February 1978 a new one superseded it. The funds covered were Official Development Assistance (ODA) going both the LDCs and multilateral agencies with the intention of promoting economic development and welfare. The funds had to have a 'grant element' of at least 25 per cent, the latter being defined as the difference between the face value of a loan and the discounted present value of the debt service and amortisation flows (using a 10 per cent opportunity cost discount rate) expressed as a percentage of the face value.

The specific recommendation in regard to these funds was that members should endeavour 'to maintain or achieve as soon as possible an average grant element in their ODA commitments of at least 86 per cent.'[18] The extra provision was that countries with ODA commitments as a percentage of GNP substantially below the average for DAC members would not be regarded as having met the terms target. However, these are not, in fact, onerous recommendations; all but two of the DAC countries met the 86 per cent requirement in 1977 and the second target is relative not to the DAC target of 0.7 per cent but to the existing average of 0.4 per cent. An additional grant element target of 90 per cent was noted for ODA to the least developed countries, but again only two countries actually fell short of this target in 1977. None the less publicity and concentration upon terms and conditions, especially for the least developed countries, is an important contribution, given mounting problems of meeting debt service payments on previously received foreign financial flows. Unfortunately, however, whatever progress is made in this area for ODA terms can only have a small influence if the *shortage* of such funds forces the developing world (and especially the least developed) to borrow increasingly at commercial rates on world capital markets. The DAC recognises that this is exactly what is happening,[19] but continues to exert influence where it can. Current policy, for instance, is to increase stress in ODA targets on the least developed countries. Using a ratio of ODA to donor's GNP it is suggested that the figure for recipients in this category be 0.35 to 0.4 per cent to complement the overall ODA/GNP target of 0.7 per cent.

Considering the paucity of achievement in this area, the extent to which the DAC has improved on what would otherwise have occurred is highly debateable.

CONCLUSIONS AND THE FUTURE OF THE OECD

That there is need for co-ordination of policies between the advanced industrial nations in the economic sphere, well beyond that which the OECD has so far managed to achieve, is fairly clear. New issues which call for a common reponse are emerging and we end by reviewing attempts by the OECD to co-ordinate policy in two areas of vital interest for the 1980s. The first concerns the reaction of the OECD membership to the OPEC related oil crisis. Secondly, there is the emerging response towards the manufactured imports from the Third World. The response of the membership to the oil crisis was the establishment in 1974 of the International Energy Agency and a proposed Financial Support Fund, the American view prevailing that the OECD would be a suitable umbrella organisation for these new arrangements. The Financial Support Fund[20] was never in fact put into operation. The IEA did, however, come into being with a key provision for the sharing of available supplies in the event of a repeat of the 1973 oil embargo or when supplies were cut by more than 7 per cent.

Current work of the IEA, however, involves close monitoring of the emerging demand/supply situation, with one instance of action being in March 1979 when the decision was taken to reduce consumption of oil by 5 per cent. It had appeared to become necessary at the end of 1978 when the monthly collection of data on oil shipments from member governments indicated a shortfall of supply with respect to emerging demand for 1979 as a whole.[21]

It is not possible to be clear on the effectiveness of these measures; IEA oil imports for 1979 were similar to those for 1978. It may be noted, however, that part of the restriction was supposed to be effected through the 'implementation of flexible stock policies', that is, a controlled run-down of inventories. In the event 1979 was characterised by 'more . . . competition than we should have liked'[22] and IEA member stocks were at record levels by year end following major and destabilising activity on the Rotterdam spot market.

Nevertheless, following the Tokyo Summit Meeting the IEA did agree on country-by-country ceilings for oil imports, setting targets for both 1980 and 1985. Additionally, some principles have been agreed on 'equitable burden sharing' if downward revision of targets looks necessary in view of changes in supply. Clearly, some such mechanism is an essential development if chaos is not to follow future supply disturbances, although on the practical level a cynical view of the targets so far envisaged must be noted. Thus, the target demand for IEA countries, when added to demand by the rest of the world, appears to exceed best estimates of 1980 supplies, and in envisaging a standstill on 1979 levels, the base year was influenced by considerable stock building to which reference has been made. It remains, of course, to be seen how well the downward target revision mechanism will work if it should be needed.

A further, embryonic, beginning of advanced country co-operation in what is an increasingly important area is represented by discussion within the OECD of positive adjustment policies. Thus member countries need to move in the direction of policies that will facilitate the movement of factors of production (labour and capital) out of industries experiencing secularly falling demand for their output and which are facing, or are likely to face, increasingly severe overseas competition such as that from newly industrialising countries.

It is recognised that the whole range of government economic policies are relevant here, possibly justifying the OECD as a focus. First, it is seen as a necessary policy to counter increasing demands for trade protection from declining industries. In maintaining free trade and in promoting the efficiency with which factors of production are used across economies the use of expansionary fiscal/monetary policies is less likely to collapse into inflation rather than genuine expansion. At a less aggregated level, regional policies, it is argued, must be such as to facilitate change rather than to support existing activity. Labour market policies are required, as are dynamic approaches to innovation and research and development.

Certainly, these are policies that any national government should be striving toward, but a mutual renunciation of protectionism and an increase in the transparency of state assistance to different sectors may provide the necessary extra support for more enlightened policies. It is easier, for example, for one industry to ask for protection when a similarly placed industry in another country is receiving it than if the trend is away from such practices. Indeed this may be another example of where initial advanced country co-ordination of industrial, man-power and regional assistance policies could eventually be codified under the GATT.

In a world economy no longer dominated by one country (the USA) progress must involve consultation prior to formal commitments based upon shared interests. Given the magnitude and complexity of some of the issues considered above it is perhaps to be hoped that the OECD will emerge from its present relative obscurity.

NOTES: CHAPTER 7

1   M. Camps, *'First World' Relationships: The Role of the OECD*, Atlantic Papers, Vol. 2 (Atlantic Institute for International Affairs, 1975).
2   Ninth Report of the OEEC, *A Decade of Cooperation Achievements and Perspectives* (Paris: OEEC, 1958), p. 26.
3   ibid., p. 79.
4   ibid., p. 80.
5   H. G. Aubrey, *Atlantic Economic Cooperation: The Case of the OECD* (New York: Praeger, 1967), p. 18.
6   Membership of the OEEC comprised: Austria, Belgium, Denmark, France, Germany, Greece, Iceland, Italy, Luxembourg, The Netherlands, Norway, Portugal, Sweden, Switzerland, Turkey and the UK. OECD membership in 1960 added Spain, the USA, and Canada, with special status for Yugoslavia and Finland.
7   H. G. Aubrey, op. cit., p. 102.
8   ibid., p. 150.
9   Camps, op. cit., p. 9.
10 Australia and New Zealand joined rather later.
11 *OECD Observer* (November 1979).
12 *OECD Observer* (July 1979).
13 *The Economist*, vol. 270, 31 March 1979, p. 60.
14 *OECD Observer* (July 1979), p. 41.
15 *The Economist*, vol. 270, 31 March 1979, p. 60.
16 Aubrey, op. cit., pp. 105–6.
17 e.g. *Development Co-operation: Efforts and Policies of the Members of the Development Assistance Committee* (Paris: OECD, November 1978), p. 20.
18 ibid., p. 172.

19 ibid., pp. 121–2.
20 *The Economist*, vol. 255, 12 April 1975, p. 99.
21 *OECD Observer* (March 1979).
22 Ulf Lantzke, Executive Director of the IEA quoted in *OECD Observer* (January 1980).

CHAPTER 8

The European Economic Community (EEC)

INTRODUCTION

The primary aim of this chapter is to examine the impact of the European Economic Community (EEC) on international trade. There are two immediate difficulties, however, in an assessment of this institution. First, as an *Economic Community* it embraces more than a straightforward free trade area between a number of countries or a customs union. A free trade area involves the abolition of tariffs, etc., on intra-partner trade and the customs union supplements this with a common external tariff (CET) on all goods imported from outside the union. An economic community however seeks to develop towards *economic union* between the members. In addition to the CET, eventual removal of all impediments to the free movement of goods and of factors of production (labour and capital) between members is contemplated. Such impediments might be differing national tax treatments and company laws, differing social security legislation and non-tariff barriers to trade. 'National' purchasing in government and public sector procurement would be an example of the latter.

For the present study, therefore, the outline above suggests that we need to consider more than the direct impact on trade of internal tariff removal and the establishment of a CET. Some assessment is also needed of the indirect impact on trade of additional measures aimed at economic union.

Having defined the focus of assessment a second complication lies in the way of economic analysis of the EEC. Arguably, unlike the other institutions considered in this volume, the driving force behind the establishment of the EEC was not predominantly economic. The celebrated remark of W. Hallstein, former President of the EEC Commission, that 'We are not in business at all; we are in politics' serves to emphasise the point.

Indeed the political process in the EEC has a distinct impact on the economic sphere and this must be considered in what follows if the nature of progress in the Community, and the relevant constraints, are to be understood.

POLITICS AND POLICY MAKING IN THE COMMUNITY

The first political point to note is that the creation of the EEC was the result of extraordinary political circumstances generated by the galvanising impact of the aftermath of the Second World War. For Europe it was the experience of two devastating conflicts involving France and Germany within a single lifespan that prompted Jean Monnet in 1943 to say[1]:

> There will be no peace in Europe if States re-establish themselves on the basis of national sovereignty, with all that this implies by way of prestige policies and economic protectionism. If the countries of Europe once more protect themselves against each other, it will once more be necessary to build up vast armies.

The blurring of economic and military concepts of 'protection' is perhaps indicative of feelings at the time. In the same interview he argues that expensive military alliances would beggar Europe when the might of the USA and USSR necessitated the creation of a single European market as a prerequisite for economies of scale and attendant prosperity.

Alongside these 'European' pressures for change, the USA, during negotiations on the Marshall Plan following 1947, made it clear that it was in favour of some form of European economic integration. The Committee on European Economic Co-operation was established to put forward proposals on the use of the Marshall Funds and the USA made it clear that these should be linked to advances toward integration. The US desire was to foster a militarily and economically strong Western Europe and the Organisation for European Economic Co-operation (the aid agency of the committee) was established with this in view. Thus those in favour of European integration benefited at that time from considerable US support.

Given these auspicious background conditions it was possible, despite British and Scandinavian opposition to any notions of supranationality, for the 'European idea' gradually to gain ground. Thus, in 1954 the three 'Benelux' countries (their customs union was formed in 1948) called for a general common market for Europe *on the grounds that political unity would prove difficult to achieve*. That is, economic integration would be the forerunner of political integration.

This process of economic integration, however, involved political compromise from the outset. Thus, two treaties were signed in Rome on 25 March 1957, one concerning the EEC, and the other Euratom. As Monnet notes[2] the Germans had strongly favoured the creation of a

Common Market while the French viewed unfettered competition from German industry with some reservations. However, the French interest was served by the development of Euratom as a means of increasing security of energy supplies following the Suez crisis. The two treaties were therefore necessary to provide sufficient inducement to each party to proceed on the integration path. This linkage of issues has continued to characterise Community developments as will be indicated in what follows.

In addition to establishing free trade between the signatories Benelux, France, W. Germany and Italy, the 1957 Rome Treaty abolished obstacles to factor movements between members. In the same Article 3 a common policy on agriculture was stipulated. Common policies in transport, competition and economic co-ordination were also mentioned.

The 'European idea' gained constitutional support by the provision for qualified majority voting in the supreme decision-taking body of the Community – the Council (Article 148).

The Treaty established, under Article 4, that there would be four governing institutions: an Assembly, a Commission, a Council and a Court of Justice. Of most relevance to an economic assessment of the Community, developments in the Commission and the Council might be noted.

The Commission, effectively the civil service of the Community, was originally (Article 157) to have nine members (no more than two from each state) chosen on grounds of competence for the tasks at hand. It has three functions – initiation, mediation and administration – with the first being generally regarded as the paramount role. The mediative role was provided for in the Treaty by allowing the Commission to deliver opinions on Treaty provisions and to participate in the shaping of measures taken by the Council. The administrative role allows the Commission to ensure implementation by member states of agreed Treaty provisions, with recourse to the Court of Justice if required in cases of recalcitrance.

As noted above, however, it is the initiative role of the Commission, to 'formulate recommendations or deliver opinions on matters dealt with in this Treaty, if it expressly so provides or if the Commission considers it necessary' that is critical (Article 155).

This would permit the Commission to forward to the Council as the supreme decision-taking body of the Community (consisting of government ministers of the member states) policy proposals for the Community which, in principle, the Council could accept (on a qualified majority) or reject. If the proposal were to be rejected, however, an amendment to the proposal would require unanimity of the Council (Article 149).[3]

The intention therefore was that the Commission should 'draft detailed proposals which would form the basic structure of common policies'. However, 'this formal procedure has acquired a symbolic status as part of the mythology of the Communities but in practice the Community process has evolved very differently'.[4]

The basis of this argument concerns the loss of political initiative by the Commission due to increasing bureaucratisation (partly attributable to enlargement of the Community in 1973). With a total of thirteen commissioners friction occurs in the allocation of portfolios to different nationalities. These portfolios organised under different Directorates General are often split artificially. Thus the DG for Industrial and Technological Affairs is under a different commissioner than that for Competition Policy.

This lost initiative has been gained by the Council, composed of national government ministers. The ministers involved depend on the topic under discussion but those of Agriculture and Foreign Affairs tend to be the senior partners and are called in when other colleagues are in deadlock.[5]

In addition to this shift in influence the Commission is influenced by the Committee of Permanent Representatives (COREPER) made up of the heads and deputies of permanent national delegations to the EEC. Although this ostensibly meets to prepare Council sessions, defining areas of disagreement, it has a more pervasive effect. Thus,[6]

> The Commission, as the executive of the Community, has the right to make policy proposals. In preparing them though it is drawn into a process of inter-governmental bargaining, because it is required to consult with the Permanent Representatives in Brussels of the member countries.

Add to this the non-realisation of qualified majority voting on the Council and the constraints on truly 'European' initiative in policymaking are evident. These institutional developments are highly relevant, moreover, for the development of EEC policy towards nonmembers. Thus political scientists note that progress in the Community has been a process of converting *high politics* (matters of acute national concern) into *low politics* through a process of major concessions.[7] The EEC/Euratom joint agreement has been explained in these terms already but it should be noted that the key inducement to France to tolerate free industrial competition was the Treaty commitment to a Common Agricultural Policy (CAP).

This bargaining process however has tended to mean that the interests of non-members are ignored and there is a reluctance to reopen issues, once settled internally, for the benefit of negotiations with non-members.[8] The prime example of this, of course, is that of the CAP. During the Kennedy Round of tariff negotiations (May 1964– May 1967) one of the main difficulties was the understandable desire of the US Congress to include agricultural goods in the tariff-cutting negotiations; understandable because agricultural products constituted $1,600 million of total US sales to the Community of $5,500 million.[9]

It has to be noted that individual national policies, particularly with respect to agriculture, would probably not have been so restrictive had not the EEC come into being. 'Without the prospect of a unified market in agricultural products, the rather powerful constraints operating on the individual countries would have forced them to take a more rational approach to agriculture.'[10]

Another example of the same tendency arises in the approach of the EEC to the recently completed Tokyo Round of tariff-cutting negotiations. As the average level of tariffs on the trade of the industrial countries prior to the new round stood at probably not more than 9 per cent, negotiations towards free trade (removal of tariffs) at least on industrial goods would have been a serious possibility. However, Cairncross notes, 'In its "overall" approach to the Tokyo Round of GATT negotiations the European Community agreed that *inter alia* the customs union "may not be called into question".'

This is a serious matter, for, as Cairncross says, Japan and the USA have in fact suggested the phased elimination of substantially all tariffs as a means of overcoming difficulties caused by existing preferential trading arrangements, particularly those of the EEC with the Mediterranean and Africa. Cairncross' conclusion is as follows[11]:

> Part of the trouble has been psychological in that the European Community's CET, its commercial agreements with 'outside' countries and also its CAP have come to be regarded as symbols of European unity.

In terms of the bargaining process discussed above, this latter observation taken alone is naive. Thus, the 'neo-functionalist' school of political integration theorists argues that the main source of 'integrative force' lies in the risk of loss of previous gains.[12] Loss of the CAP for instance may deprive the community of its forward momentum if the original national gains from membership are removed.

It seems very likely therefore that the substantial modifications of the CAP, and perhaps elimination of the CET, will have to await new initiatives towards integration, again by a linkage of major issues which render further integration appealing. Such possibilities probably lie in monetary and regional policy.

As stated previously, however, these are matters of economic union rather than customs union *per se*. For the present we concentrate on the pure trade effects of the union.

THE TRADE IMPACT OF THE CUSTOMS UNION OF THE 'SIX' AND THE 'NINE' IN PRINCIPLE AND IN PRACTICE

ATTEMPTS AT MEASUREMENT

Article XXIV of the GATT provides the general principles under which the establishment of a free trade area or customs union is acceptable under the Agreement. It will be recalled from Chapter 4 that the underlying principle of the GATT is that of multilateralism involving the MFN clause and the objection to preferential trading arrangements. Thus Article XXIV is a significant deviation from a general philosophy, although it may be explained as an expression of support for free trade between some countries, which is a step in the direction of freer trade worldwide. Given the exceptional nature of the provision however the question to be answered is as follows. In a tariff ridden world what will be the impact on trade flows of the creation of a customs union?

This section will attempt a quantitative answer to the question by reviewing some estimates for the original six countries and by offering some possibly suggestive calculations relating to trade of the 'Nine' in 1970 and 1977.

When examining the purely trading gains from a customs union it is usual to differentiate between *trade creation* and *trade diversion* and to assess the net result of the two. If one country, on forming a customs union with another, begins to import goods not previously imported this would be an example of trade creation. If, however, on forming the union the first country ceases to buy from a previously lowest cost supplier (due to a CET) and to buy instead from her union partner the result would be trade diversion. While trade creation is fully consistent with world welfare gains anticipated in the free trade model, the existence of trade diversion lends ambiguity to theoretical assessments of such gains from customs union. It should also be noted that, for the inhabitants of the country entering the union, trade diversion *itself* is ambiguous in welfare terms. The reason for this lies in the fact that the pre-existence of tariffs (before the union) means that although the union diverts import purchases from the low cost producer to the partner, tariffs on imports from the partner are abolished with the result that consumers in the first country are able to substitute *in the direction of the free trade optimum*,[13] away from their previous tariff ridden equilibrium.

In the present context, however, we are mainly interested in 'world' rather than 'community' welfare as implied in changes in the pattern of trade. We must therefore continue to regard trade diversion as an essentially negative effect of union.

An early estimate of trade effects covering the first five years of the EEC is given by Krause. His 'direct approach' to the estimate utilises the following three reference points concerning trade creation and trade diversion.

(1) If on establishment of the Community the CET was *on average* lower than previous national tariffs then we have a source of trade creation.
(2) Removal of all tariffs on member trade reduces the effective price of imports from member countries. It expands total 'intra' trade and can therefore be regarded as trade creating also.
(3) A loss of share of non-member country imports, however, must be taken to represent trade diversion.

Krause uses an equation which encapsulates these three components indicating the net proportional change in imports of each commodity. For (1) above the observed price elasticity of demand is multiplied by the proportional change in price implied by the new external tariff regime. To measure (2) the same elasticity is multiplied by the proportionate price fall associated with dismantling internal tariffs, and finally for (3) the share elasticity in a member country's imports is multiplied by the new CET, representing the price difference between member and non-member sources.[14]

On the basis of this equation Krause calculates that non-member countries could have expected to lose $975 million worth of manufactured exports to the EEC (at 1958 prices) in the transition period during which the new tariff regime would be put into effect. This is an estimate of trade diversion (net). On the same calculation the USA would have lost $275 million in sales of manufactured goods to the EEC and the UK would have been the second highest loser ($200m +) or about 24 per cent of both countries' 1958 sales level to the Community. The two countries mentioned would have taken half the total loss.

As an indication of the net effect of the Community, of course, these figures are misleading because strong economic growth took place at the same time in the EEC countries. We will return to this when considering dynamic effects, and will not pursue the matter here.

The above figures refer to the static effects with regard to manufactures. Krause finds it more difficult to estimate the impact of the EEC on agricultural trade. Essentially, there is the problem of what the situation *would have been* if the Community had not been established. He notes that in the ten years before the Community, 1948–58, there had been distinct trends towards self-sufficiency, at least in cereals, in the six countries. Possibly therefore the harmonisation provisions due for completion in 1968 would have little extra effect. Krause argues, however, that this is unlikely. He notes that 'pre-EEC constraints on irrational national policies were obviously at work in the member countries during the mid 1950s. Between 1953 and 1958, agricultural producer prices increased very little. Agricultural output expanded very much in line with the growth in consumption'.[15]

Nevertheless he concludes that early world losses were not high. He estimates that the USA lost an annual $200 million (not more) in 1965–66 on the assumption that without the Community the US share of the market would have stayed at its 1958–59 level. This sum represents half the loss to non-members occasioned by the CAP at this time.

Turning now to two interesting studies by Balassa, a technique is used which allows a separate estimate of trade creation and trade diversion on the basis of actual import data. Balassa's approach is to estimate *ex post income* elasticities of demand for various import categories from both members and non-members.

He suggests that comparing two periods (one before and one after) a rise in the elasticity measure for *intra-area* imports would represent gross trade creation. A rise for all sources of imports taken together would give expression to trade creation proper. A decline in the ratio for *extra-area* imports, however, would be representative of trade diversion. Generally, this is a similar interpretation to that of Krause.

The method, of course, has several obvious weaknesses. The first is the implicit assumption that the elasticity would have remained unchanged without the creation of the EEC, that is, that the union is the only major factor affecting the pattern of EEC imports. Again, the base period used has to be assumed to be in some sense 'normal'.[16]

In the first of his studies (in 1967) Balassa compares his base period, 1953–59, with the period 1959–65. The second study (1974), using the same base, extends the period to 1959–70. By comparing the elasticity measures for the two periods, the following broad conclusions emerge. The extension of the period increases the trade diversion effects and lessens those for trade creation; trade diversion, it appears, has taken longer to show through. Generally, though, the picture continues to be favourable with elasticities (income) for all imports from all sources increasing from 1·8 to 2 (some further trade creation). Elasticities for intra-area trade rose from 2·4 to 2·6 and remained unchanged at 1·6 for other area imports.

These broad figures, however, are consistent with considerable trade diversion in agriculture, none in raw materials and with definite trade creation in the case of most categories of manufactured goods. The exception is SITC groups 6–8 which include a variety of intermediate and non-durable consumers goods.

Thus, whereas Krause' results show in net terms trade diversion, albeit of relatively minor degree, Balassa's results show a mixed picture at the commodity level separated according to trade creation and trade diversion. In order, however, to look at the effect on individual countries reference must be made to Balassa's 'Common Market effect'. This is a growth related concept but can still be applied to gain a trade diversion/creation estimate. For each *commodity group* the Common Market effect is the difference between the actual imports from *all* extra-area sources since 1959 and the level of imports *predicted* by applying the rate of import growth ruling in 1953–59 to the 1959 magnitude. For each non-member *country* the effect is obtained by taking the 1959 levels of that country's sales to the Community and applying the *rates* of growth implied by the two calculations above, that is, from *all* sources, thus removing any 'competitive' effect for any one country. The Common Market effect is obtained by deducting from each other the two magnitudes implied.

Thus countries heavily represented by commodity groups in which there has been trade diversion will tend to suffer. Accordingly, Balassa finds that the USA and UK benefited in that the Common Market effect for their overall sales to the Community was positive, generally as a result of the rapid rise in sales to the Community of machinery and transport equipment. All other areas however[17] have suffered adverse effects of trade diversion in foodstuffs, chemicals, intermediate products and non-durable consumer goods which dominate their exports to the EEC. As a final observation, it is interesting to note that despite considerable trade diversion in agriculture the USA benefited overall from the CAP. As a result of high growth of meat production a rapid increase in imports of maize, feedstuffs and soya was required with the USA as the source.

Again, this need not have been the *actual* outcome for each country because the Common Market effect is designed to abstract from the country's actual sales growth to the Community. Through the competitive effect (i.e. changes in *shares* of the seven supplying regions in extra-area imports of the groups of commodities) a country or region can do better or worse than the Common market effect indicates. For instance the UK suffered competitively more than *three times* the gain from the Common Market effect due to actual loss of market share.

In terms of numerical magnitudes, Balassa suggests for 1970 overall trade creation of about $11·3 billion or about 13 per cent of total imports into the Community. About $11·4 billion came from manufactured goods (some trade diversion in agriculture) or about 21 per cent of manufactured imports into the Community.

Though there are several different approaches from that of Balassa, all but one agree that trade creation has exceeded trade diversion by about four times overall. The magnitudes are variable, however. As of 1970 the range of estimates lies between $8,000 million and $15,000 million, a margin of nearly 100 per cent.[18] Imprecise as this may seem the important fact to note is that even the maximum estimate amounts to not more than 1 per cent of the Community's GNP.[19]

Given, however, that several years have now passed since these studies were concluded (and certainly since the end of the time period studied), it is perhaps a useful exercise to apply Balassa's income elasticity approach to evidence for the present decade. There are two main reasons for so doing: first, to see if Balassa's generally sanguine conclusions (net trade creation) continue to be upheld, or whether the increased diversion of trade which he notes has become more serious; secondly, the study may cast some light on a question that has been raised on the overall *character* of the EEC. Johnson[20] argued powerfully that the EEC is fundamentally a mercantilist institution, being characterised by preferential trading arrangements and a general willingness to interfere in the free movement of goods internationally. *Prima facie*, Johnson's argument is a good one; the CAP, Generalised System of Preferences and the Associate status of the Lomé countries (all to be discussed presently) smack of a nervousness about the consequences of unconditional adherence to the GATT. Indeed, some political realities in support of this have already been produced above.

It is fair to ask therefore if, during the troubled years of the 1970s when mercantilist pressures have been on the increase worldwide, the EEC has begun to show its true colours as a protectionist institution. Certainly inflation and the fuel crisis have hit hard, reducing the freedom of governments to aim at full employment in view of potentially deteriorating trade balances. Perhaps the increased use of non-tariff barriers (NTBs), for instance, 'gentlemen's agreements' to limit exports, will during this period have begun to influence trade flows.

Some interest therefore attaches to whether the magnitude of the elasticities for the different commodity groups considered by Balassa have changed in a way to indicate developments in trade creation and diversion.

A comparable set of calculations has therefore been undertaken for the period 1970–77, the latest year in which the data were available. Caution must immediately be expressed over the figures. Our main interest is to compare the new figures with Balassa's estimate for the first eleven years (1959–70) of the Community; we are therefore not so much concerned with establishing the effect of the *creation* of the EEC, only of developments within it. However, as enlargement took place in 1973, we consider the 'Nine', which therefore involves three countries that were not members for the full period. Balassa of course considered only the 'Six', but worse distortion would have set in if we had considered the Six alone given the significance of their new free trading partners. Secondly, the 1970s have been much less stable in international monetary terms than the 1960s. It should be noted that Balassa's approach makes three basic assumptions in this regard.

(1) No autonomous changes in relative prices.
(2) No changes in exchange rates.
(3) No changes in extra-area trade flows caused by the dynamic effects of customs union.

As our comparison is mainly within the existence of the Community, we can probably disregard problems arising from the third assumption. Clearly, however, the second is relevant given exchange rate upheavals during and after the collapse of Smithsonian parities, and the first assumption is relevant with regard to the terms of trade effects of commodity price rises subsequent to OPEC. The, perhaps heroic, assumption we must make is that floating exchange rates during our period have broadly adjusted import prices to developments in domestic prices. This probably helps with developments in relative prices also, but we shall have occasion to note that it does not do so in all cases.

We take Balassa's commodity groups and compute respective Community elasticities for 'intra-area' imports and for total imports from the outside world. The calculations are based on changing Community imports and GNP both computed in real terms. As Balassa notes (1974) there are problems here due to possible relative price movements which, in principle, would require differing price indices for imports and GNP. Such indices for trade, however, are extremely unreliable so the GNP deflator has had to be used in both cases. Unfortunately inflation has been of a considerably higher magnitude than during the 1960s so any failure to remove commodity price rises will distort the elasticity measures more severely in our calculations than in Balassa's.

Table 8.1 shows import data taken from OECD 'International Trade Statistics' (Series B) and real GNP data from IMF 'International Financial Statistics'. Growth rates used in the elasticity calculations are annual averages for the period 1970–77. From these the income elasticity of import demand for each commodity group is:

% change in imports/% change in income.

The 1953–59 and 1959–65 estimates are included for interest although our main concern is with comparisons of the two later periods. Given the difficulties outlined above a cautious interpretation of the results is as follows.

Dominant in the commodity groups where continuing trade

155

Table 8.1   *Revealed Income Elasticities of Import Demand for Intra and Extra Area Trade for the 'Six' 1953–59, 1959–65, 1959–70 and for the 'Nine' 1970–77*

	The 'Six'						The 'Nine'	
SITC[a]	(1)		(2)		(3)		(4)	
Commodity	*1953–59*		*1959–65*		*1959–70*		*1970–77*	
Group	*Intra*	*Extra*	*Intra*	*Extra*	*Intra*	*Extra*	*Intra*	*Extra*
0 + 1 – 07	2·5	1·4	2·4	1·3	2·5	1·0	3·6	0·4
2 + 4	1·9	1·0	1·9	0·9	1·8	1·0	2·1	0·6
3	1·1	1·8	1·3	2·5	1·6	2·1	6·7	6·7
5	3·0	3·0	4·0	2·7	3·7	2·6	4·4	2·5
71 + 72	2·1	0·9	3·1	2·5	2·8	2·4	2·5	3·0
73	2·9	2·2	3·8	2·4	3·5	2·5	4·1	4·9
6 + 8	2·8	2·5	2·9	1·9	2·7	2·1	2·7	2·4

(a) Standard International Trade Classification.
Source: (1) (2) (3) Balassa (1967, 1974); (4) Author's own estimates.

diversion has been occurring is agriculture (SITC 0 + 1 – 07 = food, beverages and tobacco less tea and coffee-based beverages). While it is possible that rising prices (incompletely allowed for in deflation) account for the rise in 'intra' elasticities, it seems more likely that the rise is real representing increased reliance on Community sources for UK supplies following 1973. To some extent also the inclusion of Denmark (and, to a lesser extent, Ireland) as food producers *within* the Community rather than outside it as in the earlier periods will contribute. The decline in 'extra' elasticities between the two periods is certainly suggestive of quite major trade diversion, partly as a result of new membership and the expansion of the CAP.

There is some less convincing evidence that trade diversion has occurred in the materials group 2 + 4 which may possibly be explained by increased membership.

Elasticity estimates for the mineral fuels group (SITC 3) are absurdly high as a result of the failure of the GNP deflator to cover the rapid rise in fuel prices triggered by OPEC. A partial adjustment is suggested by using the OECD commodity price index over the period which would give income elasticity of 4·7 for intra and extra trade. This is no doubt still inadequate but it should be noted that this is not a group where trade diversion has taken place. The high elasticities in fact are reflecting the continuing import demand in the face of the rising cost of mineral energy sources. The similar figure for intra trade reflects natural gas sales, particularly from Holland to its continental neighbours.

SITC 5, the chemicals group, continues to reflect the high income elasticity of intra trade which, in the face of the might of the German industry, is not at all surprising. The addition of the British industry is also of considerable significance. Given this new membership it is notable that there is no real evidence of increased trade diversion indicated by the extra area value.

Turning to manufacturing industry proper, the important capital goods groups 71 and 82 (non-electrical and electrical machinery) perhaps show some tendency towards further trade creation on the external front. The general weakness of the British machine tool industry may be reflected here, but in that case it is surprising that there has not been a surge in *intra* trade with the country's substantial reliance on Germany and other continental partners.

Further evidence of trade creation is presented in the vehicles group (SITC 72). Dominated by road vehicles the elasticities associated with this group appear to have jumped on both fronts, but particularly on the extra-trade side. While price effects possibly account in part for this, the fairly modest change for both intra estimates suggests this is not serious. The jump for extra trade in all probability reflects the success of the Japanese car and motorcycle producers in countries where the industry is weak (the UK is a particularly good example) or non-existent (Benelux, Ireland, Denmark). Considerable growth in exports from this source to the big producers of Germany, France and Italy (though from a lowish base) is, however, evident. Those involved in the British industry may be excused for regarding this strong evidence of trade creation by the EEC with less than rapture, and it perhaps is an example of an area where major Community policy initiatives are going to be needed; that is, in industries and areas where livelihoods are threatened on a large scale by the readjustment pressures produced by a relatively free trade regime both internally (within the EEC) and, increasingly, from outside.

To complete the present task, however, we may note that in SITC groups 6 + 8 (miscellaneous intermediate and non-durable consumers goods) there is some small evidence of a reversal of Balassa's findings on trade diversion. It is difficult to generalise for such a diverse group but it is possible that it is a reflection of the relatively liberal British textile import regime, and perhaps increasing imports of iron and steel and metal manufactures from the Far East. Again, adjustment problems in these industries are of a serious magnitude.

With the conspicuous exception of agriculture, then, it is difficult to point to increased Community trade diversion notwithstanding the international troubles of the 1970s.[21] It is a moot point, however, whether or not this demonstrates the flaws in Johnson's argument referred to above. Together with the possible adjustment problems of the trade patterns shown, we may note the more frequent recourse to gentlemen's agreements, and the desire of the EEC to discriminate against Japan in the Tokyo Round. The final verdict must await the outcome of major policy (and political) decisions that the EEC will increasingly be under internal pressures to take. We will try to take up these themes in the conclusion to the present chapter.

At this juncture we have become familiar with the trade effects of the Community's CAP; and after frequent reference it is now necessary to describe that policy in more detail. This will also allow us to consider some related problems of the Community Budget and the way in which this, too, may have indirect implications for trade flows.

THE COMMON AGRICULTURAL POLICY AND THE COMMUNITY BUDGET

The underlying need for some sort of agricultural policy arises from the well documented tendency for farm incomes (particularly wages) to lag behind average earnings during the process of economic growth. In turn this tendency is largely explained by the existence of 'Engel's Law' which states that as family income increases, a smaller percentage of that income is spent on food; that is, the income elasticity of demand for food is less than unity.

Given these unfavourable demand conditions, it would only be possible to maintain agricultural incomes (at a given level of employment) if productivity and hence supply conditions in agriculture were also relatively unfavourable. Indeed productivity would have to grow more slowly than the demand for food itself for in these circumstances agricultural prices would rise, compensating for the slow growth in *quantity* of sales. Generally speaking, however, the circumstances of supply have not met these conditions and average labour productivity growth in agriculture has compared favourably with other sectors.[22]

Against this broad background the Treaty of Rome sought to establish a Common Market in agricultural goods (although the details were not spelled out as with the case of industrial goods). The objectives of this common agricultural policy were stated to be (Article 39):

(a) to increase agricultural productivity by promoting technical progress and by ensuring the rational development of agricultural production and the optimum utilisation of the factors of production, in particular labour;

(b) thus to ensure a fair standard of living for the agricultural community, in particular by increasing the individual earnings of persons engaged in agriculture.

158

Although laudable, these objectives contain the seeds of a major contradiction, the resolution of which was not set out in the Treaty. Thus, increased productivity, as suggested by (a) above, could only be compatible with increased earnings if drastic structural change were to take place in which the labour force in agriculture would be much reduced. The only alternative 'to ensure a fair standard of living' would be through the medium of market interventions to raise consumer prices and, to this extent, disregard consumer interests.[23]

As the Treaty did not set down the means for achieving the objectives it was for the Commission to propose in 1960 a comprehensive policy[24] covering not only immediate pricing and market organisation but also long-term structural reform. Political factors ensured however that, in January 1962, the Council of Ministers approved a CAP based only on the non-structural element of the Commission's report. Common agricultural prices were achieved by 1968.

The Commission continued to argue that a long-term analysis of the structural problem was required. In December 1968, therefore, it submitted a report 'Agriculture 1980' to the Council. After the Commission's Vice President, Sicco Mansholt, this became known as the second of the 'Mansholt Plans'. It envisaged two million of the Community's ten million farmers being retired or trained for other occupations and small inefficient farms being consolidated into large production units. The cost of these reforms was to be shared equally between the European Agricultural Guidance and Guarantee Fund and the individual member countries involved.

Only in March 1971, after fierce political debate, were the heavily renegotiated Commission proposals accepted by the Council of Ministers. Whereas France and Italy, as potential beneficiaries, favoured Community financed structural reform, Germany, as potential net contributor, objected, as did the Netherlands which had already financed its own structural reforms. The measures actually agreed on the structural side were modest with the Guidance Fund financing 25 per cent of the cost of structural reform projects with up to 65 per cent being available in backward areas.

The reason for such prolonged concentration, at least in Commission circles, on the need for structural reform is easily seen. Unsupported by such measures, the Community price policy must be increasingly costly, both for the Community as a whole and – of particular interest in the present context – for the world at large.

To explain the difficulties created it is well known that the Community agricultural policy depends on a series of negotiated prices for commodities, supported by import duties of various types. Thus, for grains, poultry, eggs, milk and sugar a variable import levy (on external supplies) is imposed representing the difference between a 'threshold' price and the most favourable c.i.f. import price for each commodity. The threshold price is technically related to the 'target' price for that commodity in the community. Thus, a basic target, as in the case of soft wheat, may be established for an area of greatest shortage with regional derivatives applied elsewhere. In these cases the threshold price is equal to the target less the cost of transport to the centre chosen.

Other commodities may simply be subject to a fixed tariff; for instance, in the case of beef, fruit and vegetables, but in each of these cases a variable levy may be applied to make up any difference between the duty paid import prices and threshold prices.

Obviously, however, the more attractive these prices are rendered the more likely it is that domestic (community) production will outstrip demand and surpluses emerge. Thus, a 'second string' of the CAP is required, provided by the existence since 1962 of the European Agricultural Guidance and Guarantee Fund. The 'Guarantee' side of this fund deals with support buying of produce to sustain high prices once surpluses emerge.

Under the arrangements described, of course, with support buying, *price* support is equivalent to *income* support, and it is clearly intended as such, 'to ensure a fair standard of living for the agricultural community'. There is, however, a very important corollary of such a roundabout means of income support, which emphasises that structural reform is crucial. If the intention is to keep farmers' incomes *growing* in line with incomes elsewhere, a constant level of protection (price support against low cost supplies) will not be adequate. Incomes will be raised at the time that prices rise due to the policy but they will only continue to do so if out-migration of labour from agriculture continues. The initial jump in living standards in agriculture, however, does nothing to encourage this trend. Income levels would stagnate and differentials with other sectors re-emerge. 'In the long run, it is the supply of farm labour and not the demand for the labour that has the major effect upon the return to farm labour. There is no escape from this simple but very important economic relationship.'[25]

In other words, structural change is vital if rising farm incomes are to be feasible without ever increasing protection against imports of cheap supplies from outside of the Community. For the Community as a whole, the rising cost, as predicted above, is now apparent. As Cairncross notes, 'The proportion of the Agricultural Guidance and Guarantee Fund devoted to guidance declined from one-sixth to one-twelfth.' That is, the 'guarantee' side support purchases increasingly dominated expenditures.[26]

The implications for EEC trade in agricultural commodities is, however, yet more serious than the implied commitment to increasingly severe import restrictions. Referred to here are the implications for agricultural output of the price rise induced increase in returns to the factors of production employed in agriculture. As the fixed factor, the return to land must increase, thus causing a rise in land values and in this way land rentals are permanently increased by a rise in agricultural product prices. The returns to labour also rise immediately but the effect will be to reduce the flow of out-migration from agriculture, thus dampening the initial wage rise. Similarly, the initial increase in wages will encourage the search for labour substitutes. If capital inputs like tractors and fertiliser are available at fairly constant cost, then these will be substituted for the more expensive labour, again reducing the pressure on wages. It is, incidentally, interesting to note that these adjustments imply that a high price policy is inefficient if the intention is to raise farm incomes. The rise in wages is eroded both by greater employment than there would otherwise have been, and by the increased use of other inputs, whose prices have not risen, as substitutes for labour. Land rents of course rise on a more permanent basis but large landowners, in all probability, have higher incomes than the national average. Farm workers are unlikely to benefit permanently.[27]

For present purposes, however, the adjustments referred to imply that farm *output* will rise in response to higher prices through the increased use of labour and other inputs. Demand within the Community however is unlikely to rise, given Engel's Law, to absorb this increase. The circle can only be squared by increased exports, and with high costs of production such exports are only feasible when heavily subsidised. Thus it has been reported that in 1977 nearly £2 billion was spent (approximately 27 per cent of total Community expenditure) unloading food surpluses on the world market.[28] Manifestly such a policy renders the world market price for many commodities artificially low, damaging the return to, and discouraging production by, efficient low cost producers in other continents. It has been argued in fact that the reduction in production so caused reduced the availability of foodstuffs artificially when weather conditions in 1972/73 induced famine in certain parts of the world.[29]

The estimates of trade diversion made previously have not taken these further effects on world markets into account, nor, finally, did they take into account the fact that higher food prices reduce demand unnecessarily, and thus reduce further the opportunity for non-Community suppliers to sell to Community consumers.

The discussion above implies that the budgetary costs of the CAP, due to support buying, will tend to rise over time as production responds to rising prices. In addition, however, there is the danger that these costs will be shared inequitably between members through the institution of 'own resources' financing. Thus, since 1978 the Community Budget has been financed as follows:

(1)   ninety per cent of all national Exchequer receipts from imposition of the variable levy on agricultural imports;

(2)   ninety per cent of customs duties received by member states through application of the CET (the 10 per cent remaining in 1 and 2 is allowable to cover collection costs);

(3)   up to 1 per cent of the proceeds of a general VAT.

Both the UK and, to a lesser degree, Italy pay relatively heavily through this procedure. The UK traditionally imports a substantial quantity of goods from outside the Community and hence (1) above is onerous. The UK is also at a disadvantage through its relatively high consumption of the 'VATable' goods in (3).[30] Predictably this has led to almost continuing 'renegotiations', the most recent being in May 1980 when the UK's net contribution was threatening to reach £1,200 million. The agreement negotiated held the 1980 contribution down to £371·5 million and in 1981 and 1982 the amount is to be held down to approximately £330 million. Without this agreement, and with UK government policy aimed at reducing the public sector's spending, the large growing contributions could only be made by further cuts in other areas which may in turn reduce the level of economic activity. This is an example of what Kaldor calls the 'resource costs' of membership.[31] As the CAP now accounts for nearly three-quarters of the Community Budget the question of finance is likely to prove increasingly divisive with little money available for *non-agricultural* programmes which may benefit countries like the UK. Thus, whereas the Regional Development Fund accounts for only 6 per cent of the EEC Budget, the support programmes for sugar and milk alone account for over 50 per cent.

DYNAMIC GAINS FROM THE FORMATION OF THE EEC

As was widely predicted, the 'static' gains from economic union have turned out to be small. It is the 'dynamic' gains from which the substantial benefits should arise. Following Scitovsky, we consider: (1) effects on the methods of production, and (2) effects on the volume and pattern of investment, the first a short-run effect, the latter long-term.[32] The first is mainly concerned with the benefit of intensified competition. Prior to union, cartels and oligopolies were prevalent at the national level and a major concern of the Rome Treaty was to prevent such practices being endorsed on a European scale.

Thus, Article 3(f) refers to the 'institution of a system ensuring that competition in the Common Market is not distorted' and 'Rules on Competition' are dealt with in Articles 85–94. Article 85 covers 'vertical' and 'horizontal' agreements liable 'to affect trade between member states and have as their object the prevention, restriction or distortion of competition within the Common Market'.

Articles 85 and 86, dealing with the private sector, have been successful as they generally are supportive of national policies aiming in the same direction. The Commission has also been free to interpret these Articles on its own and has been upheld when necessary by the Court of Justice. One major difference from national policies has been in the field of distribution where manufacturers establishing exclusive dealerships in other member countries have been outlawed – the Grundig – Consten case establishing the necessary case law.

Merger policy has been less successful, the Commission's only real power resting on Article 86. It is *not* granted the power of *prior approval* but only to prohibit the abuse of a position of market dominance. On the latter, the Continental Can decision was an attempt by the Commission to regard the acquisition of another firm by a dominant firm as abuse of position. Again the Court has been supportive of this interpretation.[33]

While this represents a useful advance, merger policy (as represented by the Colonna Memorandum which received qualified support at the 1972 Paris Summit) is somewhat confused, possibly due to the structure of the Commission.[34] Thus, the Commission's Directorate General 3 (for industry) is under a different Commissioner than DG 4 (for competition). While the former has advocated trans-European mergers, the latter has been proposing to bring them under close scrutiny.

Competition and merger policy are important in regard to trade between members as they relate to the 'freeing' of trade in the broad sense. There are other areas of industrial policy, however, which have some impact on trade flows. One concerns the question of adaptation of industries which are increasingly vulnerable to the pressures of intra- and extra-Community trade. Perhaps the British motor industry is an example of the former and the Community textile industry the latter. It is clearly in the interests of both the Community's income growth potential and the continuing freedom of international trade that such industries be successfully adapted or eliminated and resources moved to more promising activities.

By virtue of Articles 92–94 the Commission is able to issue Directives on State Aids (often to such industries) which have an adverse effect on the trade of other member states. Notwithstanding some successful orders to desist from unfair export promotion under the Articles, this has not prevented major national assistance being given to maintain in existence certain large and politically important enterprises.

The crucial distinction should be drawn between *appropriate* measures which aim to shift resources out of a declining industry, and *inappropriate* ones which seek to maintain resources in the industry.[35] The presently constituted CAP, of course, is an example of the latter.

There are perhaps two more areas of industrial policy that deserve mention in the context of trade as they both have to do with the elimination of increasingly important non-tariff barriers. Both were raised in the Colonna Memorandum on industrial policy – the first concerning 'national' policies of public sector procurement. The Memorandum wanted these to be thrown open to all Community firms, for although the Council had proscribed the reservation of such contracts after January 1970 the Memorandum noted 'a change of mental attitudes is essential to ensure compliance with legal provisions'. Apparently only 5 per cent of these contracts were being awarded to other member countries.[36] The general feeling in the Commission is that such contracts are important especially as many are in support of high technology industries such as aerospace and computers.

Such a policy goes beyond economics to the politics of European integration. On efficiency grounds it would be desirable to open such contracts to *all* bidders and not just those from the Community – perhaps by agreement on a reciprocal basis through the GATT.[37] That a 'European' industry in any of these fields is necessary is not easily defensible on purely economic grounds.

The final element of industrial policy which directly concerns the trading environment is that of 'harmonisation' of technical standards. If different national standards established in consumer, environmental or other legislation affect the conditions under which goods are marketed then an impediment to the free trade of goods takes place. This represents a major non-tariff barrier and it is an area in which the Community has made significant progress. An early start was made under general and specific provisions laid down by the Rome Treaty. Articles 100–102 of the Treaty confer a general power to harmonise various pieces of national legislation which directly affect the functioning of the Common Market and other, more specific, provisions relate directly to sectors of transport and agriculture.[38] Again the logic of the inclusion of such provisions is the desire to establish a non-distorting trading environment.

The Commission has taken a number of initiatives over the years aimed at removing technical obstacles to trade and by the early 1970s Council approval was being gained for a significant number of directives, with sixty adopted by the end of 1975.[39] In industries heavily engaged in intra-Community trade (e.g. motor vehicles) harmonisation is now advanced and this may in turn render agreement on these matters with *non*-member states easier to achieve.

The measures we have discussed so far in the present section have been concerned with the broad competitive environment (which should lead to rationalisation of the methods of production). We should also note Scitovsky's second class of dynamic advantage from union. This concerns the longer-run effect on the level and pattern of investment. Here, the argument is that the short-run competitive effects referred to above would reallocate output to the more efficient firms. Likewise one would expect investment funds increasingly to be allocated to such firms within or across national boundaries, thus increasing the average efficiency of new investment. Moreover, given confidence among entrepreneurs that the new free trade regimes would last over the life-span of the investment, investments would be planned for bigger markets and economies of scale could be more readily achieved. Two further points Scitovsky makes are worthy of mention. One major source of extra investment would be expected to come from the USA and secondly, the measurable effects of this greater investment would be small. Both predictions are probably true. US-owned investment through MNCs has been immensely stimulating, not only from the point of view of its amount (especially concentrated as it is in growth sectors) but for the emulative effects it has created. The European-owned motor industry must be an example of the latter; the American producing subsidiaries planned for Europe as one market and reaped major scale economies producing a limited model range. The European competitors were obliged first to rationalise production and very recently to internationalise production and the source of components. Such influences, arguably, have been more effective than any 'European' industrial strategy could have been.

On the question of the size of the effects, in annual terms, as Scitovsky suggests they must be small. Each year's new investment is a very small increment to the national capital stock as, for instance, Krause's calculations show.[40] The growth in capital stock is thereby slow, and multiplying this growth by Denison's estimates of capital stock as a share of national income, Krause duly finds that the annual impact of increased investment spending on income growth is small.[41]

In view of the comments about the stimulative effects of US investments just made, however, it must be stressed that the underlying assumption made by Krause of a fixed relationship between capital and output actually excludes such matters as economies of scale and organisation.[42]

We can probably conclude, therefore, that the establishment of the EEC, and its political permanence, have widened investment horizons. The effects on the level of output and hence on the intra-Community volume of trade, while small in any one year, are of a cumulative nature, as capital stock is gradually replaced.

CONCLUSION: HIGH POLITICS, LOW POLITICS AND FURTHER MOVES TOWARDS WEST EUROPEAN ECONOMIC INTEGRATION

We have seen two processes at work in the Community so far as economic integration is concerned. The first seemed to indicate a process where matters of high political significance between nations were negotiated into matters of low political import by a process of mutual concession; the role of the CAP and Euratom to counter the Common Market in industrial goods as a French–German 'bargain' has been mentioned. Once such crucial deals were struck, however, there appears, secondly, to have been some merit in the 'neo-functionalist' view that the process of integration acquires its own 'dynamic'. First, nations have been willing to compromise on quite major matters to safeguard the progress towards integration already made. In the case of the above narrative, perhaps the (limited) agreement on structural reforms in agriculture is a case in point. The other 'iterative' process at work though has been the response of the Community to problems thrown up by the process of integration itself, for instance the agreement to accelerate progress towards harmonisation following the removal of customs duties on internal trade in 1968.

With such processes, crucial 'deals' already struck may be difficult to unscramble unless they are no longer in anybody's interest, and the feeling that future progress *depends* on what has already been agreed probably means that fundamental reforms of the CAP (or, indeed, the elimination of the CET) must await new momentum towards economic union in another area.

Thus, the initiative towards monetary union (with the creation of the EMS) which emerged from the Bremen 'Summit' may be a case in point. Intended to stabilise the exchange rates between members' currencies (with the help of a revolving 'swap' facility between central banks denominated in 'ecus' and backed by one-fifth of members' gold and currency reserves) it could help to stabilise the trading environment. Indeed the German interest in this development seems to be to diffuse further upward pressure on the valuation of the deutschmark across the other currencies. In so far as trade flows are disturbed by the effect of speculative flows on exchange rates the EMS could be a positive development.[43]

However, the success so far achieved with stabilising exchange rates has been due to somewhat special circumstances[44] and continued success probably depends upon progress towards harmonisation of economic and monetary policies.

For 'inflation prone' countries, depreciation of the exchange rate is crucial for maintaining international competitiveness. Fixed exchange rates would require the inflation level to drop leading to the need for harmonisation of monetary policy. Moreover, if exchange rates cannot be altered, labour costs can only be made competitive by increased investment. In this way economic policy would need to include fiscal transfers to boost investment in lagging regions.

Thus, the potential 'linkages' for further economic integration in Europe are certainly present, and could substitute for the CAP and CET as cornerstones of integration. Given a successful outcome, not only would the Community have embarked on another important phase of integration but with more stable exchange rates and some relief of the economic constraints facing the less successful members, it would be able to make a substantial positive contribution to the expansion of world trade through the expansion of income both within and (after a lag) outside its own borders. With the present difficulties facing the dollar and the failure to agree on a multilateral initiative, a steady broad-based economic recovery within the world's most important trading group would have a widespread beneficial effect transmitted through the avenues of multilateral trade.

APPENDIX: THE EEC AND THE 'THIRD WORLD' – THE LOMÉ CONVENTION

Although four of the original six signatories to the Rome Treaty in 1957 still had colonial responsibilities, the elements of the Treaty which made provision for association of territories with the EEC (esp. Part IV, Articles 131–6) were essentially a concession to French demands. Italy expected to relinquish its trusteeship of Somaliland in 1960; Holland was in the final stages of negotiating withdrawal from Indonesia, and Belgium was beginning to experience the ultimately tragic end of its rule in the Congo. Only France had a long-term interest in continued relations with its overseas territories which, after the loss of Indochina, were concentrated in Africa. That country's continued close economic ties with the Francophone states perhaps help to explain the broader strategic value that France has always placed on close relations between Europe and Africa. The former African territories of France, Belgium and Italy therefore continued to be associated with the EEC after Independence under the provisions of the Yaoundé Conventions of 1963 and 1969. This somewhat anachronistic focus of the EEC's relations with the developing countries has been reinforced since the 1975 Lomé Convention added the non-Asian Commonwealth countries to those covered by Yaoundé. Notwithstanding significant additions in the West Indies the Lomé Convention essentially covers the whole of black Africa with the current exception of Angola, Mozambique, Namibia and Zimbabwe.

Of course, such a choice of members for association implies discrimination against other developing countries, a potentially serious distortion since the total population of the Lomé countries amounts to less than half that of India and only 6.7 per cent of Community imports from the Third World come from the signatories.

Fortunately, however, this potential danger has tended to be offset throughout the lifetime of the EEC by strong German and Dutch opposition to preferential treatment for countries that were no longer colonies. Therefore, although the Rome Treaty had established the principle that the same trading rules be applied for EEC – Associate trade as those for intra-EEC trade (leading to free access to EEC markets), the Germans and Dutch required compensation for this principle to be continued into the era of political independence. The compensation has essentially been the progressive dismantling of the CET, where applied, on competing goods imported from other developing countries.[45] The outcome of this process has been that the CET no longer provides much by way of favourable treatment for the signatories. Thus the CET on coffee declined from 16 per cent to 7 per cent and for cocoa from 9 per cent to 4 per cent during the Yaoundé regime. At these levels non-price factors such as delivery reliability and quality consistency probably have the major impact on determining market shares.

'Preference', therefore, was increasingly taken to mean financial concessions rather than trade concessions and when the Yaoundé signatories joined forces with the Commonwealth countries, prior to the signing of the first Lomé Convention in 1975, this theme was stressed. In this connection it may be noted that the Community's GSP scheme considerably reduced the value of preferential access to manufactured exports from the African countries, although safeguards restricting access under the GSP are easier to apply than for the Lomé countries.

The Lomé Convention, therefore, in addition to the now standard Yaoundé trade arrangement whereby signatories enjoyed free access to EEC markets for manufactured goods and tropical agricultural produce, also included a new scheme for compensating a shortfall in export earnings from certain commodities sold to the EEC – the Stabex scheme. The scheme operates by means of reference levels calculated in relation to each state's average sales to the EEC over the preceding four years. If during a calendar year exports of an eligible commodity fall below the reference level by a predetermined margin then the country concerned can request a transfer from the stabilistion fund to cover all or part of the gap in export earnings. The margin mentioned, when deducted from the reference level, establishes a trigger threshold which, when crossed, renders a country eligible under the scheme. Thus, for the least developed, land-locked and island states, a shortfall of more than 2.5 per cent below the reference level would permit compensation to be given. For the rest, the figure was 7.5 per cent. In the case of the poorest states the transfers are non-reimbursable and, for the remainder, they represent interest free loans repayable over five years.[46]

The Stabex finance was to come from a fourth European Development Fund (each Yaoundé convention had one as well as the first Fund in the immediate post-Rome Treaty period). In fact the total provisions under this fund, although absolutely larger than under Yaoundé II, did not compensate for the increased Lomé membership (in population numbers) and for the rapid inflation of the early 1970s. The same decline in real financial resources is evident under the provisions for Lomé II agreed in 1979 (see Table 8A.1).

Table 8A.1   *Aid and other EEC Finance under Lomé I and II: Current Prices (Eua millions)*[a]

EDF	Lomé I	Lomé II	Real % Increase Lomé II over I[b]	Annual % change per capita[c]
Grants	2155	2928		
Special Loans	444	504		
Risk Capital	94	280	−16%	−25%
Stabex	382	550		
Mineral facility	—	280		
Total EDF	3076	4542	−14%	−24%
EIB Loans	390	685		
	3466	5227		

[a] The eua is an accounting unit based on the values of the currencies of EEC member countries: 1975 = £0·42; 1980 = £0·66.
[b] The 'real percentage increase of column 3 takes account of the five-year coverage of Lomé II compared with the four years of Lomé I.
[c] The final column reflects the growth of population in the countries covered by the Lomé regime.
Source: ODI Briefing Paper No. 1, 1980

Notwithstanding the decline in real terms, aid under the EDF is regarded as 'high quality' by recipients and on the multilateral level the EEC/EDF is the principal source of grant aid outside the UN. Noteworthy also is the growth in provision for risk capital aimed at providing capital for industrial projects. Either share capital or loans would be involved here with the loans being of a 'second priority' nature or limited, with interest payable only after a certain degree of profitability had been achieved. Such finance, as distinct from loans with fixed terms, is clearly valuable given the uncertainties surrounding at least the initial returns from new industrial projects.

Two developments under Lomé II concern the Stabex scheme and the minerals facility. For Stabex, ten new products have been added, bringing the total to forty-four, and the dependence and trigger thresholds have been liberalised being reduced from 7·5 per cent to 6·5 per cent and from 2·5 per cent to 2 per cent for the least developed, landlocked and island states. A two-year grace period for loan repayment has also been incorporated for those countries not eligible for grants under the Stabex scheme.

Whereas Stabex covers primarily soft commodities a new minerals scheme ('Minex') is to be instituted which bears some resemblance to Stabex and is the second major change from Lomé I. Under this arrangement, a country may be eligible for a loan if the mineral normally accounts for 15 per cent (10 per cent for the least developed, land-locked or island group) of exports. In these circumstances the trigger is a 10 per cent drop in either export *capacity* or production and as such is not designed to compensate for loss of *earnings*. Moreover any such soft loan transfers are to be used for EEC approved projects in the mining sector. Five minerals (copper, phosphates, bauxite or alumina, manganese and tin) plus iron ore after 1984 (currently a Stabex item) are included. These arrangements clearly reflect an intention by the EEC to maintain production of minerals (and hence safeguard supplies) following major disturbances in producing countries.[47]

The arrangements for Minex, then, are clearly less generous than for Stabex, reflecting the EEC's fear that to extend Stabex to minerals would have been too expensive. Finally, regarding Stabex, it should be noted that the historical basis of the trigger mechanism mentioned above does *not* make provision for loss of *real* earnings. That is, continuing inflation in import prices is not taken into account.

The effectiveness of the Lomé regime, therefore, must increasingly be judged according to the development of the various financial schemes we have outlined above. The trade preferences, as we saw previously, are becoming increasingly ineffective, and indeed there has been a tendency for the Lomé countries to lose market shares in their exports to the EEC. A rather more substantial, trade affecting item, however, should be mentioned in conclusion. This is the Sugar Agreement negotiated under Lomé I to replace the Commonwealth Sugar Agreement which expired in 1974. Following transitional arrangements during 1975 the present situation is that the EEC has agreed to import 1·4 million tonnes of cane sugar from the Lomé countries (plus India) for the indefinite future at internal EEC related prices. As the latter are inflated to provide a 'satisfactory' return to the European beet industry, the Lomé countries receive (for their quota sales) a price well above that prevailing in the world market (depressed over the last few years of the 1970s). Although this must be welcome to the countries concerned, current EEC practice in unloading its surpluses on world markets actively contributes to the depressed sugar price. Moreover, the major world producers (e.g. Cuba, and some Central American Republics) are excluded. It is therefore difficult to raise a cheer for an arrangement which in its distorting features mirrors the worst aspects of the Common Agricultural Policy. The same comment applies to the trivial concessions (although greater than for other non-EEC countries) made to Lomé exporters of other products on which there is a CAP levy due to their competition with European agriculture. Perhaps the most significant of these is the beef quota, important to Botswana (and one or two other countries), which for the five years of Lomé II permits a reduced levy on 30,000 tonnes per year. Under Lomé I the quota had to be renegotiated annually, causing considerable uncertainty in the minds of producers.

In such cases, of course, it is the CAP and not the Lomé regime itself which is responsible for the trade distortions involved. In fact CAP exports by the Lomé countries represent only 9 per cent of their trade with the EEC.

NOTES: CHAPTER 8

1 J. Monnet, *Memoirs* (London: Collins, 1978), p. 222.
2 ibid., p. 419.
3 An abridged version of the Treaty, with main provisions, is available in: R. Vaughan, *Post War Integration in Europe* (London: Edward Arnold, 1976).
4 H. Wallace *et al.*, *Policy-making in the European Communities* (New York: Wiley, 1977), p. 51.
5 ibid., p. 59.
6 A. K. Cairncross, *Economic Policy for the European Community* (Kiel University Inst. für Weltwirtschaft, 1974), p. 8.
7 G. Sjostedt, *The External Role of the European Community* (London: Saxon House, 1977), p. 176.
8 L. B. Krause, *European Economic Integration and the United States* (Washington: Brookings Institution, 1968), p. 8.
9 D. Swann, *The Economics of the Common Market*, 4th edn (London: Penguin, 1978), p. 309.
10 Krause, op. cit., p. 87.
11 Cairncross, op. cit., p. 21.
12 Sjostedt, op. cit., p. 188.
13 R. G. Lipsey, 'The theory of customs unions: a general survey', *Economic Journal*, vol. 70 (1960).
14 Krause, op. cit., pp. 49–50.
15 ibid., p. 88.
16 The two studies are: B. Balassa, 'Trade creation and trade diversion in the European Common Market', *Economic Journal*, vol. 77 (March 1967), and 'Trade creation

and trade diversion in the European Common Market: an appraisal of the evidence', *The Manchester School,* vol. XLII, no. 2 (1974).

17 The areas are grouped by Balassa as follows: USA, UK, Continental EFTA, LDCs, centrally planned, other developed economies, EEC Associate states.

18 Much of this variation is accounted for by different assumptions covering what *would* have happened if the EEC had not been created – the *anti-monde* or construct for comparison with actual events. The *anti-monde* for Balassa, for instance, is that income elasticities would be unchanged without the EEC. Income elasticities for import demand, however, *do* tend to rise over time. Other writers have therefore *normalised* by reference to a *control* variable, for example, developments in income elasticities for US or other non-member country imports. A very useful survey of these difficulties is given in D. G. Mayes, 'The effects of economic integration on trade', *Journal of Common Market Studies*, vol. 17, no. 1 (September 1978).

19 See Mayes, op. cit.

20 H. G. Johnson, 'Mercantilism: past, present and future', *The Manchester School*, vol. XLII, no. 1, 1974.

21 A further influence for trade expansion after 1973 was the conclusion of industrial free trade agreements with the EFTA countries not joining the EEC. Although small economies some, notably Sweden, are significant industrial exporters.

22 D. G. Johnson, *World Agriculture in Disarray* (London: Fontana, 1973), p. 67.

23 Krause, op. cit., p. 89.

24 A plan sometimes referred to as 'Mansholt 1' to distinguish it from 'Mansholt 2', the plan of 1968.

25 Johnson, op. cit., p. 199.

26 Cairncross, op. cit., p. 97.

27 Johnson, op. cit., p. 184.

28 *Guardian*, 'The cuckoo in the Community nest', 14 November 1978.

29 Johnson, op. cit., pp. 17–64 and 205–25.

30 See 'The EEC Budget and the UK', *Midland Bank Review* (Summer 1980).

31 For a discussion of this concept see N. Kaldor, 'The dynamic effects of the Common Market' in D. Evans (ed), *Destiny or Delusion: Britain and the Common Market* (London: Gollancz, 1971).

32 T. Scitovsky, *Economic Theory and Western European Integration* (London: Allen & Unwin, 1967), p. 19.

33 See Allen in Wallace, op. cit., p. 103.

34 See Hodges in Wallace, op. cit., p. 121.

35 Cairncross, op. cit., p. 121.

36 Hodges in Wallace, op. cit., pp. 120, 126.

37 Cairncross, op. cit., p. 121.

38 Dashwood in Wallace, op. cit., p. 275.

39 ibid., pp. 277–80. The account given borrows heavily from this source.

40 Krause, op. cit., p. 243, Appendix B, Table B-1.

41 Even this, of course, assumes that *all* of the increase in the rate of investment spending is due to the formation of the EEC.

42 See Mayes, op. cit., for a discussion of this.

43 For a sympathetic view of the EMS see R. Triffin, 'The future of the international monetary system', *Banca Nazionale del Lavoro,* no. 132 (March 1980).

44 See 'International banking survey', *The Economist*, 22 March 1980, p. 37.

45 C. Cosgrove-Twitchett, *Europe and Africa: from Association to Partnership* (London: Saxon-House, 1978), pp. 82–91 and 117.

46 ibid., pp. 152–3. The account given here borrows heavily from this source.

47 ODI Briefing Paper No. 1 (Overseas Development Institute: 1980).

CHAPTER 9

Economic Integration in Less Developed Countries

Economic integration between groups of Third World countries has had continuing appeal as a means to promoting economic development and, in particular, industrial development. A number of such schemes have been initiated, and have experienced varying fortunes, raising questions both of the efficiency of existing schemes and soundness of the theoretical and policy arguments upon which they are based.

Thus the integration so far achieved has meant continuing interference with unfettered multilateral trade. While these arrangements may be argued to be a movement *towards* freer international trade,[1] it is fair to note that they have frequently been seen (at least in Latin America) as a *medium*-term alternative to the non-discriminatory dismantling of tariff barriers. With the underlying approach of the present volume, as set down in Chapter 2, it will be desirable to examine the theoretical reasoning behind this preference.

It will be seen from the following examination that much of the conflicting argument comes down to differing fundamental attitudes towards the ultimate effects of unimpeded trade between rich and poor countries irrespective of the immediate (and more tangible) advantages of allocative efficiency offered by free trade. Having presented the arguments it will be necessary to examine the actual experience of some major attempts at integration, giving due weight to identifiable dynamic effects. Our final concern will be to discern common themes from this disparate experience and to review the options for further integration programmes.

THE RATIONALE

As suggested by the theoretical discussion of Chapter 8, a preferential trading system between a group of countries can be interpreted as an acceptable movement towards the freeing of multilateral trade in a tariff ridden world. Provided 'trade creation' in a customs union outweighed 'trade diversion' then the union as a whole would experience gain. If the common external tariff (CET) were not higher than the

173

average of the pre-existing national tariffs, it would be difficult to argue that the rest of the world's loss exceeded this gain.

Given the indeterminacy of this theoretical argument, the final judgement must be empirical and this will be our first task in the next section. However, the theoretical argument for integration in the Third World context is not based on acceptability as a path towards free trade. Indeed, it has been pointed out elsewhere[2] that such analysis fails to show why a customs union should *ever* be preferred to a non-discriminatory tariff reduction which led to the same domestic price level. In the latter case consumers would obtain the same benefit and the government would suffer less loss of tariff revenue. The motivation must lie elsewhere, for economic integration in this context represents the choice of a halfway house between development based on autarky and development based on free trade.[3]

The preference, fundamentally, is based on the assertion of dynamic gains from integration, and particularly on the ability to establish industry more successfully than could be managed under conditions of either autarky or free trade. The cumulative benefits of some emphasis on industrialisation have been well rehearsed in the literature on economic development[4] and include the belief that here lies the source of high productivity employment for a growing labour force, and the less tangible, but important, 'learning by doing' effects on both labour and entrepreneurship. Just as the EEC has the explicit policy of creating a large market for the products of its high technology industries, the same 'infant industry' argument applies *a fortiori* to less developed countries.[5] A customs union could assist in achieving the dynamic gains of industrialisation by expanding the potential market, allowing industrialists to reap economies of scale in production, even allowing the establishment of certain industries totally non-viable at a lower level of output. Additionally, if the union proved trade creating, through dismantling the (commonly) high tariff barriers on member trade, there could be a stimulus from increased competition.[6]

Given the desire to establish an industrial base, therefore, it is argued that economic integration may allow member countries to achieve this objective at lower cost for each than could be realised alone.[7] Thus, on the assumption of a sharply rising marginal cost of protection and a given desire to achieve a certain level of industrial output a customs union can lower the cost by allowing concentration on least cost industries. That is, it would permit members to establish fewer but bigger industries serving the joint market which were more cost effective in producing a given total value of industrial output. Left indeterminate here is the question of the actual location within the union of the industries established, and as there will be fewer actual enterprises it is reasonable to suppose that their location will have a decisive effect on the *subjective* assessment by the participants of the gains from membership.

The authors of this approach suggest that it would therefore be consistent for integration, based on the industrialisation goal, to be in the form of a 'partial customs union', where the CET would not be accompanied by internal free trade. The members would decide on the number of industries necessary to achieve their industrial output goals, choosing the combination that would achieve them at lowest cost. These would then be allocated between the members on the grounds of comparative (not absolute) advantage. Thus, some industries may be established by one partner while protecting its home market and selling freely in its partners' markets, even though another partner may be able to produce this product more cheaply. The other partner(s) would have similar arrangements for industries in which they had a comparative advantage (or, in world terms, lowest comparative disadvantage).

The arrangement described would be compatible with eventual free trade if the comparative disadvantage with the rest of the world could be eliminated as a result of 'learning by doing'. It should be noticed, however, that on this reasoning countries whose economies were *complementary* would benefit most from integration, unlike the Vinerian trade creation/diversion model, where competitive countries might expect to gain.

Good as the Cooper–Massell argument is as a rationalisation of certain important trends in actual integration experiences (to be noted in the next section) it does not establish a theoretical case for customs unions as the most efficient means of establishing a given amount of industrialisation (as the authors themselves recognise). As Krause asserts, the given desire for industry, while achieved more cheaply through integration than through national protectionism, could in principle be achieved yet more cheaply (efficiently) through a policy of export subsidisation[8]: 'so long as governments have the option of granting and adjusting direct production subsidies, a customs union will not be the most efficient protective mechanism in the public goods case'.[9]

On the theoretical level this is a strong argument, as each country could concentrate its resources on expanding to an efficient scale those activities to which it was potentially best suited, and the market constraint which underlies the logic of the Cooper–Massell argument would disappear. It is the reasonableness or otherwise of the Krause assumption that developing countries *can* export manufactured articles (albeit subsidised) without limit to world markets that goes to the heart of the matter in terms of the case for integration. Indeed passionately held opinions are voiced on this topic, particularly from those who believe that trading relations between rich and poor countries have, in their nature, a built-in disadvantage for the latter in terms of numerous 'blocking' mechanisms which prevent the emergence of a balanced industrial structure.[10] Such writers have advocated integration among LDCs as a means of overcoming these alleged disadvantages, and the Latin American 'dependency' writers have undoubtedly been influential in the promotion of integration schemes in that continent.[11]

While the theoretical foundations and empirical verifiability of the dependency school have been questioned,[12] other writers in the 'mainstream' tradition have pointed to practical limitations on the manufactured export opportunities facing developing countries. First, it has been noted that the tariff structures of developed countries discriminate against the simpler manufactured exports that are of interest to the developing world. Often this is true in a systematic way with the export of processed primary products, where it is clear that tariffs escalate with the degree of processing actually carried out in the exporting country. Integration is partly a response to this tendency. Secondly, the opening up of export markets in the developed world is a highly specialised activity in itself. There is pronounced risk and uncertainty in assessing opportunities for exporting (and the risks of freer importing in the case of a trade liberalisation strategy). In this connection such problems are much reduced by integration with neighbouring countries. It is likely that more information will be available on prices and costs, lessening the uncertainty over the effects of trade liberalisation on domestic industry.[13]

It is also probably true, as Lizano suggests, that export subsidies are more likely to generate retaliation than is a CET, especially as the products concerned will tend to compete with those of 'sensitive' or declining industries in the developed countries. The same writer has also pointed out that, apart from industrialisation, developing countries want integration to provide an improved bargaining position. An instance of this, which will be further explored in the next section, is the question of the role of multinational firms (MNCs) in the development process. Thus, export subsidies could produce more distortions than a CET if they were to be awarded on a competitive basis by LDCs, in favour of MNCs, in order to induce them to establish export activities in one country rather than another.

Finally, before turning to the actual experience with regard to this and other aspects of integration, a very interesting suggestion for consideration in new integration schemes has recently been hinted at and again suggests that freer trade between rich and poor countries may place a 'block' on development rather than have the beneficial effects currently more widely recognised. This argument is that exchange between countries at a similar level of development (through integration) may be promoted to encourage the development of 'appropriate' economic exchange. By this is meant that highly labour intensive productive activities, emanating perhaps from the 'informal' sector in developing economies, may be encouraged to grow through provision of a protected trading environment within the integrated area. The development of a viable machinery producing industry based on 'appropriate' (relatively labour intensive) technology, perhaps using old designs, may need such a preferential market. Of course, if this technology is truly 'appropriate' to factor endowments, it may be objected that its introduction would not require interference in trade flows. It is increasingly argued, however, that the enormous difficulties faced by LDCs in the provision of employment for a rapidly expanding labour force may necessitate at least a temporary departure from economic efficiency. In the case of technology, for instance, it may be that time is needed to develop techniques from unsatisfactory beginnings, and to overcome the natural reluctance of entrepreneurs to take on untried techniques when schooled in the use of up-to-date, generally imported, plant and equipment. Similarly any attempt to rationalise the productive activities of the informal (or marginal) sector, and to develop the labour intensive techniques generally found there, may well need the pooling of research resources between countries. It would also probably require medium-term protection of the final product from the importation of competing and generally superior (and/or cheaper), varieties.[14]

There is of course a real resource cost in policy-making of this kind, suggesting that countries may be willing, increasingly, to sacrifice some national income (or at least its growth) in favour of a rapid expansion of employment per unit of capital invested. In so far as the protection provided a 'breathing space' for countries to diversify their economies in terms of products, and particularly of home produced appropriate machinery, the Cooper–Massell argument concerning the lower costs of market integration may be a powerful one indeed, and the departure from 'efficiency' need not be permanent.

THE EXPERIENCE

In view of the observations in the previous section, the examination of empirical evidence must seek to go beyond trade creation and diversion and examine the related matters of dynamic benefits and changes in industrial structure. Much of the dynamic gain is expected to arise from the process of industrialisation and individual partners may therefore be expected to correlate the benefit of membership with the amount of industry located in their own territory.

On the more conventional allocative side, data is mainly restricted to the Central American Common Market (CACM) as this is the only case where substantial integrative efforts have been made on the basis of internal free trade (and CET), and for which data for the pre-union period exist. It is the lack of the latter which rules out the use of the East African Community (EAC) in this respect, although the long experience of that serious attempt at integration will be utilised later in assessing the effects on the industrial structure of one of the participants.

The General Treaty on Central American Economic Integration was signed in Managua on 13 December 1960 by Costa Rica, El Salvador, Guatemala, Honduras and Nicaragua. This agreement incorporated two previous accords to which reference will be made: the Regime for Central American Integration Industries and a Multilateral Treaty on Free Trade and Central American Economic Integration.[15]

It was the latter that established the principle of immediate free trade in most products between the partners of the CACM and it is this feature which is of interest at present. This change seems to have had a major impact for while intra-regional trade constituted less than 5 per cent of total trade of Central America in 1961, by 1968 it constituted 25 per cent of total trade. Dependence on three traditional exports, coffee, bananas and cotton, decreased from about 80 per cent to a little over 50 per cent of total exports. This was accompanied by a rise in the share of manufactures in total Central American exports from 1 per cent to 20 per cent and the share of manufacturing in GDP rose from 11 per cent to 17 per cent.[16]

It is, of course, useful to be able to compare the magnitudes of trade creation and diversion, or to assess the net result, and as data on trade flows for the period prior to integration exists for these countries it is possible to conduct a similar exercise to that conducted for the EEC in Chapter 8 of the present volume. Nugent's calculations suggest that the gains from net trade creation in the CACM in terms of overall income were in fact of a similar order of magnitude to those quoted by Balassa for the EEC, namely, about 0.1 per cent added to the region's growth rate annually, as a result of the productivity gains due to the net increase in trade following integration.

Nugent also considers a separate allocative effect which concerns the effect of integration on the tariff structure of the participants. The point here concerns the negotiation of the CET which, in the CACM, seems to have followed the practice of the EEC, with the value chosen for each commodity representing the mean of the pre-existing country rates. If there is a substantial, non-systematic, historical accident in the level of tariffs on individual products in each country, the averaging process could well reduce the dispersion of rates across commodities in the CET compared with individual national schedules. Using the coefficient of variation (standard deviation divided by the mean) as a measure of the degree of dispersion of tariff rates, Nugent found a reduction in the dispersion for the CET compared with previous schedules for Costa Rica, Guatemala and Honduras. Quite clearly, the greater the dispersion of a set of tariff schedules across commodities the greater the distortion of both consumption and production decisions. With a reduction in the coefficient for the CACM as a whole of about 0·1, Nugent's calculations suggest that a gain of around 1 per cent of GNP may have resulted from the replacement of national tariffs by the CET.[17]

This result does not, of course, produce any general proposition for LDC integration schemes as it depends not on the high *level* of tariffs (common in LDCs) but on their *dispersion* with reference to the mean. Only if this is reduced in the CET schedules will the gain actually accrue.

There is a further effect with regard to pre- and post-union tariffs; however, that is more directly a problem for LDC integration and should warn against automatically regarding a gain from reduced variation in CET as an addition to the realisation of all potential gains from trade creation. The separate effect referred to here occurs when national tariff rates for each product vary considerably between potential partners in an integration scheme. If, for instance, the countries each produce a product with differing tariff rates applied to competing imports, and these individual rates are subsequently replaced by a CET with internal free trade, the partner with the lowest pre-union tariff will tend to have a major competitive advantage. It is likely therefore that intra-partner trade will continue to be regulated in integration schemes where the pre-union national tariffs are very different for the same classes of product.

If, therefore, a wide dispersion in national tariff schedules for different products implies wide variation in the actual rates applied to the same product in different partner countries, a gain of the kind Nugent identifies may be offset by a failure to realise, *ex-post*, the potential gains from trade creation, due to continuing intra-partner protection. This is, of course, an empirical matter for, in the case of the CACM, free intra-partner trade was actually realised. It has not been (despite intentions) in other cases, notably LAFTA.[18] Here the potential competitive effects of differing existing tariffs have been important in thwarting progress towards internal free trade.[19]

As suggested in the preceding section, it is really the supposed dynamic benefits arising from the allocative changes discussed above that are of major interest in the LDC context; for instance, economies of scale and 'learning by doing' at all levels. Yotopoulos and Nugent report two attempts to gauge the magnitude of some of the dynamic gains arising from the CACM. The first concentrates on export performance and seeks to account for the growth in exports of the participants, where participation in the integration scheme is only one of the explanatory variables used. This represents an attempt to separate the pure influence of integration from other influences that might be present in the calculations utilising the Balassa method adopted in Chapter 8. The methodology adopted is to attempt (by means of multiple regression techniques) to account for variations in the export performance of a sample of thirty-eight LDCs over the years 1947–61. Explanatory variables capturing demand and supply side influences are used, such as details of variation in real exchange rates (change in domestic prices relative to the domestic price of foreign exchange), changes in export prices, growth of GDP, growth of world demand for exports on both geographical and commodity bases, changes in export taxes and related levies on exporting. In addition to these a dummy variable is introduced into the equation representing participation (or not) in specific regional integration schemes. Hopefully, not only trade creation effects will be captured by the coefficient on this dummy, but also any dynamic or indirect effects of the integration scheme on export growth.

In the case of the CACM dummy, it was always significantly positive suggesting that the CACM added about 2 per cent to the annual growth rate of total exports in the Central American participants. This increase in export growth rate may then be multiplied by 0.276 (representing the coefficient of export growth in a regression explaining growth rate of GDP), to suggest that the direct and indirect effects of trade creation on income growth in the CACM were of the order of 0.55 per cent per annum. Notice that, due perhaps to dynamic influences, this is five times greater than the Balassa type estimate mentioned above.

This result is supported in the second approach reported by the authors in which, for the participating countries, and for the CACM as a whole, a modified Cobb-Douglas production function is fitted to times series data for 1950–66. Included in the function are two dummy variables to capture both the static, once for all effects, of integration (0 for all years prior and 1 for all years after the start of the CACM) and the continuing dynamic effects (0 for all prior years and 1, 2, 3, . . . subsequently). The coefficient on the first dummy suggests a single 5·2 per cent increase in per capita income for the CACM as a whole, indicating the allocative efficiency effects. The continuing dynamic influences captured by the coefficient on the second dummy suggest a 0.3 per cent additional increase in the annual growth rate as a result of integration and the latter may be compared with the 0.55 per cent quoted for the export performance estimate above. The magnitudes are broadly consistent, suggesting, at least for the CACM, that dynamic gains deriving from trade creation have been considerably greater than the allocative benefits of trade creation alone.

Notwithstanding the highly tentative nature of all such estimates a broadly favourable verdict on the operation of the CACM seems to be reasonable from the evidence so far. Indeed, it may be worth noting within these overall results that not all the so called 'dynamic' gains have necessarily come through industry as 90 per cent of intra trade in agricultural products was freed of restriction. Between 1960 and 1967 imports of agricultural commodities increased by 82.2 per cent but the growth of intra-regional imports was 187.7 per cent with imports from outside the region growing by only 38 per cent. It is probable that substantial improvements in specialisation (and efficiency) were attained in the production of 'fruit, vegetables, fibres, milk products and certain cereals (for example, rice)'.[20] The same writer notes that the expansion of the market enhanced the opportunities for investment and employment in agriculture, as evidenced by the growth of farm production serving the regional market. The achievement of integration in agricultural markets was a considerable one, it having played a negligible role in other schemes due in part to major but variable government interference in agricultural markets. Any such liberalisation in the LAFTA context would have led to major social disruption failing long-term policy co-ordination.

In view of the apparently successful operation of the CACM, therefore, it would be useful to understand the factors which led, in mid-1969, to the withdrawal of Honduras. Although ostensibly this was the result of a major border incident with El Salvador it is generally also believed to have been fundamentally due to dissatisfaction with the operation of the scheme from the point of view of Honduras. If so, it represents a clear, recurring, theme of integration experience to date, namely, the difficulty experienced in maintaining the acquiescence of all partners in the actual distribution of costs and benefits. Nations judge these subjectively, not necessarily agreeing on their assessment, and as Lizano has argued, it is more important for nations to *believe* that they are benefiting than to be able actually to demonstrate that they do so. In terms of the argument in the first section of this chapter, it seems likely that this perception is heavily based on the distribution of industrialisation projects directly linked to integration. Was this relevant to the withdrawal of Honduras from the CACM? The evolution of the scheme may help to answer this question and indicate possible solutions.

It will be recalled that one of the underlying accords behind the Managua Agreement founding the CACM was that on a Regime for Central American Integration Industries. The principle involved concerned the establishment, by mutual agreement, of plants requiring access to the CACM in order to operate at an efficient scale. Essentially the legislation was aiming at the establishment of industries not yet existing in the area as this would imply minimum disruption of existing businesses but would ensure rational allocation of new, scale sensitive, activities. The regime provided for certain benefits and protection for integration industries. Their products would enjoy immediate free access to all five member countries and firms producing similar products outside the agreement would only get such access after ten years (and then through successive tariff reductions of 10 per cent per year). Ample protection from foreign competition and preference in government procurement were also to be accorded to these integration industries.

In addition, the Central American Bank of Economic Integration and the Central American Agreement on Fiscal Incentives to Industrial Development were connected with the integration industry programme. The former was organised to meet the needs of long-term investent projects in industries of a regional character and other uses which would directly promote integration. As the name implies the Agreement on Fiscal Incentives was designed to work towards uniformity in incentives offered separately by each country to attract industry. The First Protocol under the latter agreement in fact dealt with the extra concessions that Honduras was to be allowed to grant in excess of those in the agreement itself.[21]

It is clear from this account of the machinery that considerable care was being taken over the allocation of the new industries and, with early concessions to Honduras, the relatively disadvantaged position of that country was being noted. The system of distributing industries (initially put forward for consideration by private interests) was to be by 'rounds' of negotiation. In this arrangement a second plant would not be allocated to a state unless all other members had been allocated one each, establishing firmly the notion of equality of benefit in the most tangible way.

In practice, however, only a handful of plants have been established under the regime and this seems to be partly due to a major inconsistency in the character of the integration exercise between the underlying Tegucigalpa accords of 1958 and the General Agreement in 1960. Thus, by committing themselves to overall internal free trade in 1960 the attractiveness of the integration industry regime was much reduced, as the positive incentive to agreement was free access for the products of those industries concerned. The concession was now to be available without a country being required to forgo establishing an industry as its part of the bargain.

The inconsistency referred to was accompanied (even, possibly caused) by very strong US opposition to the dirigiste, non-market character of the regime's principles, together with the possibility of political criteria entering into the selection of (especially foreign) investors in the new industries. The USA accordingly pressed for adherence to free market principles in intra-regional transactions, with the financing of this trade being conducted by the medium of convertible currencies.[22]

While this eventual, more conventional, choice of integrative scheme has been seen above to have generated significant gains, the failure to develop the integration industry aspect of the initial arrangement (the tangible demonstration of benefit to individual members) may well account for the disaffection of Honduras. The latter's disadvantages had been acknowledged but the effective abandonment of industrial allocation in favour of the market can be argued to have generated a growing apparent imbalance. First, Guatemala emerged as a major beneficiary from internal foreign direct investment and also enjoyed during 1966–68 a persistent positive balance in her trade with the partners which partly financed her deficit with the rest of the world. Honduras, in trade terms, was one of the countries experiencing the opposite, her surplus with the outside world financing her deficit with the CACM.[23] While rapidly expanding her exports outside the area she achieved only a slow growth in regional exports. While none of the foregoing suggests that Honduras was made worse off by the CACM, and Nugent's individual country calculations suggest the opposite, it seems very probable that Honduras' *subjective* assessment of the costs and benefits of membership was unfavourable. A more obviously equitable distribution of integration industries might have been more acceptable from the political standpoint.

Finally, in the CACM it was the original intention that the integration industries would be carefully chosen major additions to the productive capacity of the area concerned. State and private finance might have co-operated although private initiative would be the starting point for detailed official appraisal and continuing supervision. It is argued in some quarters that the devaluation of this aspect has led instead to the CACM merely encouraging, through internal free trade, the emergence of import substituting industrialisation with all the distortions observed elsewhere. Effective protection is highest on consumer goods, lowest on capital equipment, and dependence both on foreign technology and capital has become extreme. The standard experience with this type of industrialisation, eventual stagnation, has now appeared and without agreement on the location of industries individual countries are currently substituting for area imports by domestic production. A notable case is Guatemala whose GNP in 1975 was similar to the total Central American GNP in 1955, permitting significant substitution of this type.[24] Certainly politicisation of the 'rounds' of industry allocation has taken place, with countries competing for projects. This political development may have been exacerbated by the lack of a regional body to *propose* schemes for integration which perhaps might be acceptable as a 'package'.[25]

The difficulties of preserving continuing support for this, otherwise apparently successful, attempt at regional integration have been mirrored in a more extreme form by the experience of the Latin American Free Trade Area (LAFTA)[26] and, later, by the sub-group of LAFTA, known as the Andean Pact.

LAFTA was founded by the Montevideo Treaty of 18 February 1960. Although during the first eight years intra-group exports expanded at 7·4 per cent per year in comparison with the Association's total export annual growth rate of 4·4 per cent per year, it is generally recognised that this grouping has been rather unsuccessful. By 1968 intra-group trade still only accounted for 10·7 per cent of total trade. During the 1970s the entire arrangement (excluding the Andean Pact signatories) has been effectively moribund. None the less the developments which led up to the Andean Pact, and experience with the latter, are important in underlining the difficulties discussed in connection with the CACM.

A glance at the membership of LAFTA indicates the existence of a fundamental obstacle. While it is not possible, objectively, to define the optimum size of an integrated area, LAFTA is probably too big. The optimal grouping is most influenced by the need for wide acceptance of the goals of integration. As public goods are to be provided, notably including planned industrialisation, the ways and means must be generally agreed. Whereas the CACM and Andean Pact were reasonably placed in this regard (the latter not so clearly as will be seen below), LAFTA was not.[27] Thus, in the three larger countries (Argentina, Brazil and Mexico) there was little support for a larger Latin American market due to the presumed adequacy of the national ones. Industrial groups in the medium sized countries (Chile and Colombia) did not relish open competition with the previous three and the smaller, less developed countries (especially Bolivia, Ecuador and Paraguay) were only interested in limited, preferential treatment in the markets of the larger countries.[28] There was the additional widely held fear that LAFTA could grant a major competitive advantage to large international firms, both newly established and already based in the area, if free trade occurred. With this background it is noteworthy that[29]:

> The word *competition* does not appear even once in the Montevideo Treaty despite the fact that the key instrument formally characterising the LAFTA approach to integration is the allocation of resources through market forces.

In fact, the formal composition of LAFTA policy was a combination reminiscent of the CACM, with the same potential contradiction. Internal trade liberalisation was the cornerstone but two factors (apart from the matters mentioned above) meant that the CACM solution of immediate free trade was not feasible. The first has already been discussed and concerns the widely differing levels of external protection granted to the same industries in each country. Secondly, rates of inflation among the members differed widely and (under fixed exchange rates) this had the same implication as would varying differential tariffs and subsidies, granting firms in low inflation countries an advantage in competition among the members. Such a problem would either require unified monetary policy or floating exchange rates between the partners, neither of which was feasible at the time.

Instead of immediate free trade, annual multilateral negotiations took place on a product-by-product basis. As Balassa has pointed out, such a procedure invites political interference and obstinacy and a fixed timetable of tariff reductions would mean less chance of progress being blocked.[30] The result of this practice for LAFTA was that of 11,000 items negotiated for tariff reduction up to 1970 less than one-third registered any trade flows at all, and by the early 1970s intra-regional exports of manufactured goods (not all benefiting from LAFTA's trade liberalisation) amounted to less than 1 per cent of total industrial output.[31]

The other branch of LAFTA policy was to be the negotiation of 'complementarity agreements' with industrial sectors in the different countries co-ordinating their plans for expansion and specialisation. This was a provision to nurture horizontal and/or vertical industrial integration as in the CACM Regime. The annual 'sectoral meetings' where tariff concessions were negotiated were to be the forum for proposed complementarity agreements, the intention being to give private initiative a chance in solving the problems of negotiation involved in increasing trade in non-traditional commodities. Trade liberalisation would be an integral part of the complementarity agreements and, in fact, the extent to which they were used varied with their attractiveness as a tariff negotiating instrument. Initially, any tariff concessions negotiated by way of a complementarity agreement between the same sector in two or more partner states had to be included in their National Schedules for the benefit of the others. In 1964, however, it was decided to remove this requirement and the number of proposed complementarity agreements rose substantially as a consequence. Proposals for National Schedules declined accordingly.

Relatively few of these complementarity agreements have actually been ratified, however (sixteen as of 1971), and as an initiative towards 'integration industries', like the CACM experiment, the results have been disappointing. One of the most frequently cited reasons in the

LAFTA case is the dominant role of private initiative in deciding on sectors to be included. The result is that joint planning (a crucial feature of industrial integration) has been unimportant in practice and the mutual liberalisation of trade has dominated proceedings, the agreements becoming competitive in character rather than complementary. Since the effective reversal in 1965 of the exclusion of non-contracting partners from the concessions negotiated by way of complementary agreements between other partners, these agreements have become subordinated to the general trade liberalisation process, removing much of the incentive for industrial integration as observed in the CACM.[32]

The effect of this tendency has also been similar to the latter example; benefits in the sectors where effective trade liberalisation took place have tended to accrue unevenly, favouring the three largest countries. Thus Argentina, Brazil and Mexico accounted for 46 per cent of the total of Latin American inter-regional exports in 1961. In 1973 they accounted for 66 per cent, and these were largely manufactured items.

This tendency for integration to benefit the already more advanced partners is widely recognised and has dominated experience in the East African Community, an assessment of which will complete the present chapter. In fact it is perhaps this tendency which makes the crucial allocation of benefits and costs so difficult to resolve. It was certainly this issue, together with disappointment in progress on integration industries in LAFTA, that persuaded five members[33] to sign the Cartagena Agreement forming the Andean Pact in July 1968.

The approach of the five, based on the experiences indicated above, was the conviction that equality must be preserved in the integration process to the extent of impeding those market forces which, if left unchecked, would concentrate development in those areas of the pact that were already most developed. One of the most distinctive features of the pact is the special treatment accorded to Bolivia and Ecuador, as the least developed members. Again a two-pronged structure is involved with an Intra-Regional Trade Liberalisation Programme and an Industrial Programme, the latter based on joint programming. The focus of the industrial programming would be to gain the benefits of integration through scale economies and maximum use of available resources, but also to achieve an equitable distribution of the benefits. Sectoral Programmes of Industrial Development were created incorporating joint planning of investments, the CET for the products involved and the timetable of trade liberalisation. Location would be based on comparative advantage as far as possible but this would be weighed against the maintenance of balanced industrial development among the parties.

This desire for equality led to the establishment of a supra-national political organ (the Commission) and, most significantly, a technical body (the junta). The latter is empowered to propose *decisions* with the intent of maintaining equality in the distribution of costs and benefits. Such decisions have the secondary intent of avoiding politicisation of the integration process. One of the most celebrated of these, number 24, provides for common policy on foreign investment and illustrates another lesson of integration experience, not only in the pact.

For any comprehensive programme of integration to work, apart from finding an acceptable means of distributing costs and benefits, and avoiding undue politicisation of the process, it is necessary that countries share, at least in principle, common attitudes towards economic policy. Thus, in terms of Decision 24, at various times, different members have not followed the principles laid down. Ecuador and Bolivia sought to encourage multinational firms to invest in their territories as a means of catching up with the more advanced members. Chile withdrew from the pact in October 1976 due to a conflict between Decision 24 and her 'open door' policy to foreign investment. In fact post-coup Chile decided to follow economic policies totally counter to those implied by the pact.

The departure of Chile marked the most serious upheaval in a prolonged period of crisis in the pact between 1974 and 1976. Partners' increasing scepticism about the willingness of others actually to implement decisions as intended led to a general unwillingness to complete obligations. Thus, by 31 December 1975 obligations pertaining to the CET, the Programme for Intra-Regional Trade Liberalisation and the Sectoral Programmes had to be completed: 'The Andean Pact's failures would have become visible at other times if such had been chosen for the fulfilment of these obligations.'[34]

None the less, prior to this, the trade liberalisation programme, learning from the problems faced by LAFTA, was of an *automatic* nature being fairly extensive in coverage despite exceptions (such as reservations for industrial programming). Unfortunately, the emphasis given by the pact to equality of treatment epitomised by industrial programming, and indeed in the general operation of the scheme through junta decisions, has not prevented asymmetries emerging.

Thus in 1974 the most advanced member, Colombia, accounted for 51 per cent of all intra-Andean manufacturing exports. Shares of intra-Andean total exports were as shown in Table 9.1.

From our survey of Latin American integration experience altogether, it seems that, as suggested by Vargas-Hidalgo, three classes of problem have beset integration endeavours: first, the distribution of costs and benefits, especially when dynamic disequilibriating tendencies emerge seeming to benefit most those already better off. Secondly, the incipient politicisation of the integration process as in the CACM

Table 9.1 *National Shares in Total Intra-Andean Exports (Percent-age of Total)[a]*

		Bolivia	Chile	Colombia	Ecuador	Peru	Venezuela[b]
(1)	Goods with automatic tariff	1973	5·0	29·6	31·3	13·0	18·4	—
	reductions with no exceptions permitted	1974	2·4	17·6	47·9	8·9	10·8	
(2)	Total intra-regional flows	1973	4·2	12·6	37·5	16·2	23·7	5·8
		1974	2·3	18·1	43·8	12·3	18·6	4·9

[a] Energy products, sugar and meat are excluded.
[b] Joined after 1970.
  Source: Vaitsos (1978).

Regime's 'rounds' of integration industry selection; similarly with LAFTA's sectoral meetings, and that scheme's annual round of tariff negotiations. Thirdly, as emerged in considering the Andean Pact, underlying policy goals have to be agreed among the partners. The withdrawal of Chile is a clear example where national policies of 'outward looking' export-led growth were quite incompatible with the philosophy of the pact.

In our final case study, the East African Community, all three problems have been 'writ large' to the point of the collapse of the community in 1977. This institution, however, was a unique experience in LDC integration because the Community was based on a *pre-existing* free trade area originating in colonial times. In fact, the three economies concerned, Kenya, Tanzania and Uganda, had been more or less completely integrated within a customs union (with CET and internal free trade). Moreover, there were common customs and income tax administrations together with common transport and communications authorities and a common currency. The latter had, however, been replaced with national central banks and currencies by 1967.

The long established nature of the EAC allows consideration of the lasting effects of integration and, particularly, the long-run effects on industrial structure. First, however, the context is noteworthy for its similarities to what has gone before. The period following independence in the early 1960s marked the beginning of unease at the allegedly disproportionate benefits enjoyed by Kenya from the status quo. As the area of European settlement, Kenya had the most advanced economy and was the administrative centre. Industries had been established there to serve the three countries and, demonstrating the disequilibrating principle, the pre-existence of that industry, commerce and infrastructure tended to attract new investment aimed at servicing the East African market.

Consequently, by 1967 free trade was being inhibited by quantitative restrictions imposed from Tanzania. The problems being experienced led to the Treaty of East African Co-operation in June 1967 following on the deliberations of the Phillip Commission. The main feature of the treaty was the substitution of 'transfer taxes' in place of the quantitative restrictions against Kenya's exports, which the latter had found unacceptable in the proposed Kampala Agreement of 1964. The transfer taxes could be levied if (1) the country had an overall deficit in its trade in manufactures with its other two partners and (2) the value of imports from any one partner so taxed did not exceed the total of the deficit in the trade in manufactures with that state. Application was further limited to those manufactures produced in the deficit state or which *would* be within three months.

About one-third of Kenya's *total* visible exports went to Tanzania and Uganda during the 1960s and most were manufactures. This flow generally produced a trade surplus with the Community partners that partly financed a deficit with the rest of the world. Following 1967 Kenya's partner trade did recover, after quantitative restrictions were reduced, although not dramatically and the recovery was precarious. Between 1967 and 1968, 70 per cent of the recovery in exports to Tanzania was accounted for by six products. Two of these were 'new' enough to have avoided quantitative restrictions and were not produced in Tanzania and Uganda. The performance in more established products remained sluggish.

Another major provision of the 1967 Treaty was the establishment of an East African Development Bank. This was intended to provide finance for important industrial or related projects in the other two countries and was intended as one of the major redistributive organs. Likewise the transfer tax system was seen as a means of granting temporary protection to industries which would be viable in Tanzania and Uganda encouraging duplicate, but viable, capacity in those territories.[35]

Unfortunately neither of these major provisions of the 1967 Treaty was regarded by the beneficiaries as producing adequate compensation. Ten years later in 1977 the Tanzania border with Kenya was closed.

To what extent had Kenya's industrial structure actually benefited from this long period of territorial free trade? Some insight is gained by comparing Kenya's industrial structure with a 'norm' for that country's income level and population. The norm is provided after application of a famous technique developed by Chenery.[36] This author had conducted a regression analysis attempting to 'explain' sectoral value added for thirty-eight countries by income per capita and size of population. The latter was a proxy for scale economies.

Given the standard equation so developed it is possible to insert Kenya's income per capita and population to obtain a predicted value-added figure for each sector. It produces a 'norm' based on world experience, for a country of Kenya's size and income level. Using estimated equations from a later UN study, based on a greater number of countries, one of the present authors conducted the exercise for five broad (two-digit ISIC) groupings of Kenyan industrial production in 1967. The 'predicted' and actual values added are shown in Table 9.2.

Table 9.2 *Comparison of Actual and Predicted Value Added in Kenyan Manufacturing.*

	(1) Predicted V.A ($m.)	(2) Actual V.A ($m.)	(1) as % Total	(2) as % Manufacturing
(1) Food, Beverages and Tobacco	39·18	30·86	38·5	27·2
(2) Textiles	9·54	4·37	9·4	5·0
(3) Chemicals and Petroleum	7·25	13·23	7·1	12·9
(4) Non-metallic minerals	8·44	5·95	8·3	5·7
(5) Metal Products	8·84	30·46	8·7	29·9

Source: Snowden (1974).[37]

The five categories accounted for 80 per cent of actual manufacturing value-added in Kenya and the actual value of production in both chemicals and petroleum and metal products are well in excess of predicted values, the latter grouping accounting for nearly 30 per cent of the total value-added in Kenyan manufacturing. The apparent excess of Kenyan production in groups (3) and (5) is substantially accounted for by the existence of intra-community trade. The result for chemicals and petroleum products is largely explained by Kenya's oil refining industry, which catered for Uganda's needs at the time as well as some of those of Tanzania. Also the chemical industry, dominated by soaps and edible oils, was a major exporter to the two partner states.

The major discrepancy for the very broadly defined metal products is partly accounted for by the location in Kenya of the workshops of the East African Railways and Harbour Authority along with the then joint airline. Taking more precisely defined 'metal products' (ISIC 35), exports in 1967 to Tanzania and Uganda represented approximately 20 per cent of the value of these products. Interestingly, both chemicals and petroleum, on the one hand, and metal products, on the other, have relatively large 'population' elasticities in the UN equations, suggesting scale economies working in Kenya's favour.

Alternatively, whereas the food group appears to have a value added below the predicted level in Kenya, this is partly accounted for by the exclusion of coffee and tea processing in Kenya's data. On the other hand, Kenya's under-production of textiles almost certainly demonstrates a 'Community' effect resulting from the substantial imports of cotton piece goods from Uganda, reflecting the comparative advantage of the domestic production of raw cotton in that country. A similar analysis for Uganda revealed the above 'normal' size of this sector which is consistent with the explanation given.[38]

Concluding this examination, then, the results suggest that Kenya's long history of free trade in East Africa had allowed the realisation, at least in some industrial sectors, of significant scale economies. Given this initial structural adaptation the 1967 reforms, it appears, were inadequate to provide compensation for the now independent partner states. Additionally, of course, matters were made less easy to resolve as fundamental differences began to appear in the economic ideology of Kenya and Tanzania. Kenya's welcome to foreign investment was not applied in Tanzania with a result that any dynamic benefits enjoyed by Kenya in attracting new investment through her early start were compounded. Indeed political factors entered on another level with the advent of the Amin regime in Uganda in 1971. Meetings between all three heads of state were precluded by animosity between the Presidents of Tanzania and Uganda rendering further political initiative towards integration difficult if not impossible.

CONCLUDING COMMENTS

We have reviewed at some length the experiences of the major 'Third World' attempts at integration, and the first conclusion is strikingly obvious. The alleged difficulties faced by developing countries in expanding their non-traditional trade with the developed world are at least matched in their attempts to expand such trade between themselves. The uncertainty of world conditions has surely been matched by uncertainty attached to progress with integration and even to its continuance. Further integration, at least on a broad front, can probably only be regarded as reasonable given either: (1) well justified pessimism concerning the ability of the country to expand exports of a non-traditional nature on world markets or (2) the emergence of political and social conditions in a number of countries which rendered their aims and philosophies concerning the goals of economic development very close indeed, and securely so over the foreseeable future. In the first six years of the Andean Pact there were seventeen changes of government, sometimes of a drastic nature, which rendered agreement over allocation of costs and benefits difficult to maintain.

Without these rather stringent conditions a minimal strategy would be of the 'integration industry' variety, without any parallel attempt at general trade liberalisation. The early CACM or Andean Pact approach might be mentioned in this regard, concentrating on absolute fairness in allocation between partners. To make the scheme worthwhile to the partners the projects concerned could be chosen because their scale or complexity requires the pooling of markets and/or resources, and where considerable technological or 'learning by doing' spin-offs are anticipated. Perhaps the obvious candidates here would be major developments in the machinery producing and general capital goods industry (or in the joint financing of major technical institutes and research programmes). If, following the line of thought articulated at the close of the first section of this chapter, the intent was to develop appropriate technology, the costs of so doing, and getting the products accepted, may be more readily met with a protected regional market.

This would be one example of the need to assess potential integration industries on a cost–benefit basis taking account of scale economies and the non-marginal effects of large development projects. As Robson concludes: 'The new emphasis gives pride of place to co-operation for production on a regional basis. It is now widely accepted that integration of this kind has an important role to play.'[39]

If, finally, enough of (1) and (2) above are felt to be present to warrant a further attempt at internal free trade in an integration scheme, the experience of East Africa may be relevant. Apart from the tangible location of industry, countries seem to be sensitive to trends in their trade balance with integration partners even if their overall world trade is balanced. Perhaps, therefore, there is a case for a regional development bank to allocate funds to industrial projects in countries experiencing negative effects from trade expansion. The East African Development Bank did manage to allocate funds in the manner intended to Uganda and Tanzania but these were not adequate, and thought is needed about an objective basis for national contributions to, and receipts from, such a fund. It would be desirable for the base to reflect approximate gains of each from the community, perhaps by a scale related to the change in industrial production. Balance in intrapartner trade over time could be an explicit objective and could form the basis for allocations from the fund. The scale of financing would be important and would have to exceed by far the annual 4 per cent of investment in the partner states represented by the EADB disbursements in the years of its operation.[40] If the potential partners are unwilling to contemplate major financial transfers through such a mechanism, it is likely that sufficient common ground does not exist to warrant a comprehensive undertaking in the direction of regional free trade.

The validity of the integration industry argument, and the reasoning outlined at the end of the first section of this chapter, should form the foundation of further attempts at integration. As our case studies above have tended to show, failure to produce real structural change by way of integration has meant that trade liberalisation within these schemes merely prolongs the misallocation of resources now widely recognised to accompany 'excessive' exercises in import substitution. The Latin American exercises as well as the East African Community have tended in that direction. Industrial stagnation has followed and it is perhaps notable that Brazil, a country adopting a vigorous 'outward looking' policy, has sustained a far more rapid pace of industrial expansion than almost any other country in the continent.

Equally substantial is the issue of equality of share in benefit. It is ironic that the supposed dynamic gains of integration, in the form of industrial growth, have not strengthened the integration process. Unfortunately, the industrial growth that has occurred has shown a tendency to become concentrated in one member state affecting fundamentally the perception of benefit. Some form of sectoral planning and allocation seems to be an essential prerequisite to a successful integration programme.

NOTES: CHAPTER 9

1 The reasoning behind the GATT acceptance of such discriminatory arrangements.
2 C. A. Cooper and B. F. Massell, 'A new look at customs union theory', *Economic Journal*, vol. 75 (1965).
3 E. Lizano, 'Integration of less developed areas and of areas on different levels of development', in F. Machlup (ed.), *Economic Integration, Worldwide, Regional, Sectoral* (London: Macmillan, 1976), p. 276.
4 For a good review, see R. B. Sutcliffe, *Industry and Underdevelopment* (New York: Addison Wesley, 1971), Ch. 3.
5 B. Balassa and A. Stoutjesdijk, 'Economic integration among developing countries', *Journal of Common Market Studies*, vol. 14 (1975/6).
6 ibid.
7 See Cooper and Massell, op. cit., and C. A. Cooper and B. F. Massell, 'Towards a general theory of customs unions for developing countries', *Journal of Political Economy*, vol. 73 (1975).
8 L. B. Krause, 'Recent developments in customs union theory: an interpretative survey', *Journal of Economic Literature*, vol. 10, no. 2 (June 1972), p. 428.
9 The benefits of industrialisation are seen as so substantial in the case we are discussing as to warrant industry being regarded as a public good.
10 S. Amin, *Accumulation on a World Scale*, Vol. 1 (New York: Monthly Review,

Press 1974) discusses several alleged 'blocking' mechanisms. See especially the notion of 'unequal exchange' (pp. 54–62) and slow growth of primary exports (pp. 88–9).

11 For a review see C. V. Vaitsos, 'Crisis in regional economic cooperation in (integration) among developing countries: a survey', *World Development*, vol. 6 (1978).

12 See B. Cohen, *'The Question of Imperialism'* (New York: Macmillan, 1974).

13 Balassa and Stoutjesdijk, op. cit.

14 J. B. Nugent and P. A. Yotopoulos, 'What has orthodox development economics learned from recent experience?', *World Development*, vol. 7, no. 6 (June 1979).

15 Both signed in Tegucigalpa on 10 June 1958.

16 J. B. Nugent and P. A. Yotopoulos, *Economics of Development: Empirical Investigations* (New York: Harper & Row, 1976), p. 359.

17 ibid., pp. 354ff.

18 Latin American Free Trade Association, to be referred to below.

19 F. Pazos, 'Regional integration of trade among less developed countries', *World Development*, vol. 1., no. 7 (July 1973).

20 J. Mario Ponce in *Current Problems of Economic Integration* (New York: UN, 1971), p. 18.

21 This account draws heavily from H. Brewster, 'Industrial integration systems' in *Current Problems of Economic Integration* (New York: UN, 1971).

22 See Pazos, op. cit.

23 See Pazos, op. cit.

24 For a strong argument on these lines see Vaitsos, op. cit.

25 Advocated in Balassa and Stoutjesdijk, op. cit.

26 Membership comprises: Argentina, Bolivia, Brazil, Chile, Colombia, Ecuador, Mexico, Paraguay, Peru, Uruguay and Venezuela.

27 R. N. Cooper, 'Worldwide *versus* regional integration: is there an optimum size of the integrated area?', in F. Machlup (ed.), *Economic Integration, Worldwide, Regional, Sectoral* (London: Macmillan, 1976).

28 Vaitsos, op. cit.

29 ibid.

30 Balassa and Stoutjesdijk, op. cit.

31 Vaitsos, op. cit.

32 See Brewster, op. cit.

33 Bolivia, Colombia, Chile, Ecuador and Peru.

34 R. Vargas-Hidalgo, 'The crisis of the Andean Pact: lessons for integration among developing countries', *Journal of Common Market Studies*, vol. 17, no. 3 (March 1979).

35 A. Hazlewood, 'The end of the East African Community: what are the lessons for regional integration schemes?' *Journal of Common Market Studies*, vol. 18, no. 1 (September 1979).

36 H. B. Chenery, 'Patterns of industrial growth', *American Economic Review*, vol. 50 (1960).

37 P. N. Snowden, 'Company finance in Kenya's manufacturing sector 1963–70', unpublished PhD thesis, University of Leeds, 1974, p. 33.

38 E. J. Stoutjesdijk, *Uganda's Manufacturing Sector* (Nairobi: East African Publishing House, 1967), p. 89.

39 P. Robson, 'Regional economic cooperation among developing countries: some further considerations', *World Development*, vol. 6 (1978).

40 Hazlewood, op. cit.

CHAPTER 10

The Council for Mutual Economic Assistance (CMEA [COMECON])

As with economic integration in less developed countries (Chapter 9), an assessment of the CMEA as an economic grouping of socialist states poses an immediate problem in terms of the framework provided in Chapter 2 of this volume. This framework emphasised free trade as an ideal towards which an institution may or may not contribute, whereas the integration schemes discussed in Chapter 9 were seen by their proponents as an *alternative* to the free trade path. A more fundamental divide exists when consideration is given to socialist economic integration. The more fundamentalist planners in some of these countries, far from viewing free trade as a goal, regard essential imports, in the words of one writer, as a disgusting fact of life.[1] Autarky, at least within the bloc, is seen by certain members (notably the USSR) as a positive good.

While political factors provide a substantial rationalisation for this hostility to free international exchange, the CMEA shares with the LDC groupings discussed in Chapter 9 a fundamental bias towards industrialisation. The control of international transactions is designed to render trade subservient to the overriding goal of comprehensive, planned, industrial growth.

The parallel with LDCs becomes stronger when it is recalled that the postwar division of Europe was such that of the original sixteen members of the OEEC[2] only five had a per capita national income less than that of the richest member of the CMEA (Czechoslovakia) in 1949.[3] Only the triangle encompassing Western Czechoslovakia and Southern Poland (Bohemia–Silesia) could be described as a significant area of industrial development.[4] Thus the membership of the CMEA had in its number some of Europe's most backward and devastated areas.

In the following examination, therefore, due weight is given to the goal of industrialisation and the extent to which the CMEA has, through the international links it established, conduced to that goal. It should be emphasised that the merits of socialist central planning are not directly at issue; the assessment is of the CMEA on the assumption that, without it, the countries concerned would follow a socialist

195

development path. This assumption is justified by the geo-political position of the USSR. It is also the case that the institutional arrangements of the CMEA emerged partly as a *result* of political integration movements in western Europe, not as an inevitable consequence of central planning.

Institutional evolution is discussed in the first section below and sources of strain in the movement towards integration will be noted. Distinct parallels with the LDC experience are evident here and, given the concentration in this case of economic power in the hands of the state, perhaps attest to the strength of difficulty facing attempted planned industrialisation on the basis of autarkic groupings. The following section discusses the emphasis on growth by planning in the CMEA states and the implications of the various planning philosophies for trade flows. This will provide the context for the subsequent discussion of the trade experience, in particular, pricing, bilateralism and the *efficiency* of trade. Trade diversion, discrimination and the issue of dumping in East–West trade will also be touched upon. The concluding section will examine the possibilities of freer trade between centrally planned economies given the CMEA developments discussed.

INSTITUTIONAL DEVELOPMENT

The emergence of the CMEA ostensibly resulted from Russian allegations that the Marshall Plan and the body established to facilitate the distribution of its funds, the OEEC, represented a threat to national sovereignty. This precipitated the withdrawal of the two East European nations that had accepted the Marshall Programme, and the founding of the CMEA (marked by a communique published on 22 January 1949) signalled the withdrawal of the eastern states from participation in 'pan-European' organisations (e.g. the UN Economic Commission for Europe). The 1949 communique was the only document stating CMEA aims to appear for the next decade. It voiced hostility to the Marshall Plan and stressed the principle of national 'equality'. The participants 'did not consider it appropriate that they should submit themselves to the dictatorship of the Marshall Plan, which would have violated their sovereignty and the interests of their national economies'.[5]

Whether or not justified in fact, this stress on sovereignty in the earliest document of the CMEA has been vitally important in the way that the institution has evolved. Whereas in the early years it helped the USSR to undermine plans for Balkan federation and Polish–Czechoslovak economic integration, it was used by Rumania in later years to hold back plans for CMEA-wide integration under Soviet domination.[6]

The participants in the 1949 Moscow conference were Bulgaria, Czechoslovakia, Hungary, Poland, Rumania and the Soviet Union. Albania joined a month later (only to leave in 1962 during the Sino-Soviet rift), and East Germany was accepted during 1950 after the Federal Republic had (from October 1949) been allowed a delegation to the OEEC. Whereas other socialist states were to become members later (Mongolia in 1962, Cuba in 1972 and Vietnam in 1979) the focus of this chapter is on the European CMEA. The only organ of the CMEA to be foreshadowed at the Moscow conference was the Session of the Soviet (Council) which would meet 'periodically', each country sending delegations in turn to a rotation of members' capital cities.[7] The host country would have the chairmanship. Only in the 1960 Charter, however, did this body have its powers and duties specified.

Between 1949 and the coming into effect of the Constitution in 1960 the CMEA was largely dormant. Unlike in Western Europe, with multilateral clearing at the BIS, only very limited progress towards multilateralisation of trade was made by the CMEA membership. The signing of a number of trilateral deals (in which each country achieved balance) were concluded but more progress was made in establishing permanent arrangements for technical assistance. Thus, the Second Session of the Council meeting in Sofia (August 1949) made arrangements for scientific and technical co-operation, including the establishment of bilateral agencies for these exchanges. Such technical and scientific transfers have, over the following years, been the most conspicuous success of the CMEA with industrial blueprints and technological processes provided free to other members. Joint testing of capital goods and production decisions based upon those tests were to be developed later.[8]

The Seventh Council Session in May 1956 formalised the emergence of technical committees comprised of experts who, during 1954–5, had made recommendations on bilateral specialisation in different industries. In 1956 these became twelve standing commissions each allocated to a member country. Reflecting the then distribution of activity are the Agricultural Commission established in Sofia, Oil and Gas in Bucharest, Chemicals in Berlin, Coal in Warsaw, Non-Ferrous Metals in Budapest, Electric Power, Ferrous Metals and Foreign Trade in Moscow, Engineering in Prague. This allocation, based on existing endowment, reflects an attitude towards specialisation which was to be the source of increasing conflict in the early 1960s. The committees, however, soon became the chief fora for continuing contact between members.

The remainder of the 1950s saw some expansion of product specialisation being incorporated into trade plans, the emergence of joint investments, and some multilateral projects such as the 'Friendship' (Oil) pipeline.

By 1960, however, pressures were growing for a more formal basis to the CMEA. These pressures derived from the signing of the Rome Treaty creating the EEC, in 1957, and the fear that Western markets would be lost as a result of the common external tariff. Further CMEA integration was seen as a necessary response and the adoption of the CMEA Charter in 1960 was the result. It specified the duties of the organs mentioned above as well as those of a Conference of Representatives. The latter body was transformed into an Executive Committee in 1962.

The chief formal body was to be the Session meeting at least once a year with delegates of each country's choosing. Binding decisions could be made only on procedural and organisational matters. It had only the power of recommendation on economic and scientific–technical collaboration. Such recommendations had to be agreed on by the countries involved, reflecting again the 'sovereignty' issue. The new Executive Committee was designed to supervise the implementation of Session decisions and recommendations adopted by affected governments.[9] It was also charged with Plan co-ordination and, since the ninth Session in Bucharest (1958), its role has been to draw up and co-ordinate trade plans before production plans rather than vice versa. Not all members are equally keen on this policy, and on such potentially important matters it is clearly national agreement that is crucial in achieving progress (in a community which emphasises national 'equality'). National agreement, therefore, is sought within a 'pseudo-CMEA' organ, the *conference* of party leaders.[10] Here party and government leaders try to achieve agreements which can be worked upon by the Session.

The need for national government agreement on major issues became clear in 1961 when Polish and Czech fears over the emergence of the EEC encouraged the Soviet Union to press for the co-ordination of development plans up to 1980 with agreement on guidelines for the 'international division of labour' (country specialisation). The more developed states tended to regard the greatest gains from specialisation as accruing if each country specialised in producing outputs that used intensively factors they had in abundance – the traditional Heckscher–Ohlin doctrine. Rumania, intent on an industrialisation programme of her own, objected strongly to this principle as she could not predict what her costs would be over such a time scale; 'this would tend to perpetuate the backwardness of the underdeveloped countries and to conserve the old economic structure inherited from the domination of monopolistic trust'.[11]

This position was firmly adhered to by Rumania and the eventual document, 'Basic Principles of International Socialist Division of Labour', adopted at the fifteenth Session in Warsaw (December 1961) reflected the division of interest. Thus one of the principles of the 'international socialist division of labour' is stated to be: 'combination of international specialisation of production *with all-round, comprehensive development of the economies of the individual socialist countries* with a view to the fullest and most rational utilisation in all the countries of natural and economic resources, including manpower'[12] (italics supplied).

Much is made of the need for balanced development and fairness echoing the hopes of members of LDC integration schemes discussed in Chapter 9. However an implicit criticism of Rumania's iron and steel plans at the time is contained in the recommendation that: 'Iron and steel centres should preferably be set up in countries that are fully, or nearly fully, provided with ore and processed fuel, or at least possess one of the two'.[13]

These Rumanian fears were heightened particularly by continued pressure (after the Basic Principles were published) for more formal joint planning. Given the external development referred to above the Poles, particularly, were keen on increasing the efficiency of use of investment resources through the joint programming of heavy investment projects. There had previously been some marginal successes in specialisation *within* and then *between* products on a bilateral level outside of the CMEA itself. Additionally, there had been some joint investment projects in which, again on a bilateral planning basis, one country provided capital for a project in another country and would receive payment in the form of the products produced. East Germany had financed a Polish coal mine on this arrangement and Poland was perhaps the most active in developing the joint project idea.

None of these bilateral arrangements could substitute, in the Polish view, for CMEA-wide joint investment programming as a means of maximising growth of production. Thus, in 1960 Gomulka had told the Polish Central Committee: 'There is no co-operation whatsoever in the important sector of investment: everyone peels his own turnip – and loses by it'.[14]

The Polish view was adopted by Khrushchev in 1962 when he published an article in which, using EEC developments as a justification, he proposed 'a unified planning organ, empowered to compile common plans and to decide organisational matters'.[15] In this regime large projects would be designed to serve the area as a whole. Even the USSR, previously intent on establishing the full range of industry at home, was now willing to participate in this specialisation. Rumanian intransigence however was total. Such super-national organs would 'turn sovereignty into a notion without any content'.[16]

A partial way out of this *impasse* was to be found in the creation of a number of parallel bodies, not actually part of the CMEA but having protocols with it. One writer has referred to such bodies as 'super' standing commissions, having the powers of the CMEA standing commissions but which are capable of making binding agreements without further authority.[17] There are a number of these bodies covering ferrous metals, chemicals, atomic energy related apparatus, the bearing industry and trade in non-ferrous metal products.

Each encourages exchange of products in its own area to ensure full utilisation of existing capacity and undertakes co-ordination of the construction of new capacity. Membership usually comprises the European CMEA countries, excluding Rumania, with each sending three representatives, one each from the Ministry of Foreign Trade, the national planning office, and, in the case of Intermetall (ferrous metals), the metallurgical industry. They meet quarterly, exchanging information on excess capacity and demand in individual products. Detailed quarterly plans are constructed on this basis and delivery contracts negotiated. Hewett concludes that such arrangements are the most promising source of further progress towards integration. 'They consist of technicians who are directed to improve the allocation of resources on a branch level, both in terms of current capacity and future capacity, and who have the authority necessary to accomplish their assigned task.'[18]

A potential drawback of these organisations, however, has been mentioned elsewhere. These specialised agreements seem to be more readily concluded between the more advanced CMEA countries to the exclusion not only of Rumania, but also of the other relatively underdeveloped member, Bulgaria. This seems to have increased pressure on both to undertake joint development projects of their own.[19] While part of this difficulty is directly attributable to Rumania's own preference it remains arguable that allocation decisions, being substantially based on current costs, would tend to favour existing rather than aspiring producers.

The 1960s were to be characterised by increasing pressures within the CMEA. Polish, Hungarian and, until 1967, Czech doubts were being expressed over the ability of the CMEA, as then constituted, to make a major contribution to the increased efficiency of resource use that these advanced members believed was necessary. The Polish arguments over investment allocation were only one aspect of this and the three countries named were instituting, or proposing, substantial changes in their internal planning which were more or less incompatible with CMEA arrangements.

The following section therefore comprises a brief overview of planning practice in the CMEA countries. The aim is to illuminate the role of international trade in the planning context and the extent to which such trade may contribute to economic efficiency.

CMEA NATIONAL PLANNING AND ITS IMPLICATIONS FOR TRADE

As Kaser points out, when the Soviet Union attained political pre-eminence in Eastern Europe it was, in effect, exporting politico-economic management for the first time.[20] The easiest approach, there-fore, was to export Soviet industrial and planning practice in its totality. At the time, of course, this reflected Stalin's preference for industrialisation based on the capital goods industries. The achieve-ment of these aims was to be through the practice of planning through material balances, a form of planning which seeks only consistency, not optimality. It can be envisaged in Leontieff terms as the planner having a desired *vector* of final demands and an input–output matrix which would project the gross outputs by sector consistent with those final demands. If it is found that the gross outputs implied are inconsistent with capacity in one or more industrial sectors, the desired final demands will have to be adjusted.

With this procedure the term 'material balances' is meant literally. The units of measurement are physical, not monetary, and prices have no role to play. No yardsticks of efficiency are available. It is also evident that the approach is more obviously relevant to a large, crude and self-contained economy laying the foundations of industrialisation than it is to an already fairly sophisticated and non-self-sufficient economy. Notwithstanding this observation the model was transferred to Eastern Europe at the expense of indigenous efforts. The necessary adaptation is that some foreign trade is inevitable given the 'unbalanced' nature of such economies. This 'imbalance' is the result of past international specialisation which has left a structure where full employment of all domestic resources can only be achieved in all sectors with the help of imported inputs in at least one sector. For the less well endowed economy, of course, some raw materials must be imported but so, inescapably, will supplies be needed of specialised products traditionally imported.

The natural reaction of the Soviet type planner in this new situation would be to construct his desired final demand vector as previously. The gross sectoral outputs now implied, however, will include neces-sary material imports. The estimated imports will have to be met by whatever are the traditional exports that country has produced so that part of final output will have to include provision for these exports. Taking into account this necessary 'hard-core' trade and the original desired final demands it is likely, given input–output coefficients, that some sectors will have excess or deficient supplies. That is, the implied need for domestic production of certain products for final and inter-mediate use may well exceed domestic production plus 'hard-core' imports. If so it is to be hoped that the excess supplies emanating from other sectors can be released for export to finance the further implied imports. If this is not possible it will again be necessary to adjust (depress) the original final demands, most probably in the consumer goods area.

Relevant to our assessment of this trade-modified procedure is that it is the estimated level of necessary imports that determines the level of exports; trade is being effectively minimised. If, for instance, the terms of trade happen to be sufficiently favourable to permit the necessary imports without commitment of *all* the surplus material balances, the remainder can be distributed within the internal economy either to final demand or to stocks. Prices have no allocational role whatsoever (collectively they merely determine the terms of trade), and as such there is little point in building up surplus reserves with other centrally planned, trade averse, economies. As will be discussed in the next section, the foreign trade prices that emerge are essentially the outcome of a bargaining process in which it is the *overall terms of trade* that have real significance for each party.

While a planning procedure with something like the above characteristics was adopted in Eastern Europe during the 1950s, it is clear that by the definitions used in Western economics the process is inefficient. With prices playing no allocative role there is no way to test the optimality of the planner's choice of final demands or of the chosen exports in terms of their resource costs.

During the late 1950s, however, the inability to judge the resource cost of goods exported induced the more advanced economies, East Germany, Czechoslovakia, Hungary and Poland to seek indicators of cost, at least for the foreign trade sector. The result was the use of *foreign trade efficiency indicators* to gauge the cost effectiveness of exports. Difficulties arose in this area, however, because the most easily available indicator (the ratio of domestic cost to price available in foreign trade) depended on prices actually reflecting costs. Given the planning system then in use domestic prices were set administratively with different profit levels arbitrarily added for different sectors and prices often set for administrative convenience.

Various means of getting round these problems were tried but logical solutions such as computation of direct and indirect labour cost for each product meant ever greater data difficulties. It appears that the indicators could not be systematically used other than to point out those exports that had very high domestic resource costs.

While these efforts aimed at improving the basic Soviet planning model apparently persisted in East Germany, Czechoslovakia, Hungary and Poland until the later 1960s, the latter two were, in greater or lesser degree, to abandon the material balance approach.

The essence of the new (post-1966) Polish approach in the foreign trade sector was to minimise the resource cost of producing a predetermined vector of final outputs while maintaining an acceptable trade balance with different trade partners. An advantage of the planning model adopted is that a fairly simple decision rule for enterprises is implied. Assuming the availability of accurate estimates of the real cost to the economy of earning foreign exchange (a shadow exchange rate), and a similar estimate for the cost of raw materials, the enterprise can simply be instructed to maximise the difference between the shadow value of exports and the total of labour, capital and raw materials used to produce them. Presumably, raw materials rather than general inputs are singled out because world markets provide a ready yardstick by which to establish shadow prices. Other intermediate inputs are accounted for by dividing the economy into 'blocks' of interrelated activities, each 'block' assumed to be independent of the others. One enterprise is put in charge of each block and is charged with achieving the optimum position.

This procedure reduces the difficulties arising from irrational internal prices, and improves the real returns from international trade. It should be noted, however, that it is still not a system for *maximising* the gains from trade. The planner, in choosing the pattern of final demands, may well pre-empt cost-effective exports which have to be compensated by export of less suitable items. Only in the long run, when foreign trade shadow prices begin to influence investment decisions will the efficiency gains from trade begin to be realised. The second observation, relevant to the following section, is that the shadow prices have to coexist, rather uneasily, with actual, generally irrational, prices. While incentive payments to enterprises are based on the shadow price mechanism, the administered prices are still applied to actual transactions, seriously affecting flexibility. Unfortunately the resultant decision to move towards 'rational' internal prices, which would obviate the need for separate accounts, led to the riots of December 1970 and a partial retreat back to the dual system.

Inefficiencies resulting from the interaction of two different price mechanisms also threaten the gains from international trade within the CMEA. Pricing matters will be examined in the following section but the discussion above has sought to illuminate the nature of trade in planned economies.[21] Its role in these circumstances is as a 'shock absorber', and only in the long run, given new style planning, will the full potential gains be realised. Equally evidently, those gains will only accrue if prices ruling in trade between the countries of the CMEA are rationally related to real cost.

INTERNATIONAL TRADE, PRICE SETTING AND EFFICIENCY

As a result of the type of planning procedure discussed above it has been argued that the CMEA countries have an anti-trade bias relative to comparable capitalist countries; that they follow an autarkic path.[22] If this is so, almost by definition the CMEA will be incapable of promoting efficiency through a significant expansion of trade. On the basis of the argument in Chapter 2, a grouping of states which actively seeks to avoid trade is not likely to promote the efficient use of resources. However, although it is probably necessary that autarky be avoided it is certainly not sufficient for trade to be conducive to economic efficiency. The trade itself can be organised in such a way as to be inefficient.

In this section, therefore, we assess the autarky thesis before proceeding to another characteristic of CMEA trade which does derive from the planning process – the tendency to bilateralism. This bilateralism has strong implications for the process of price-setting in trade agreements and this in turn suggests the possibility of maldistribution of the gains from trade. The issue here is whether the USSR has 'exploited' Eastern Europe through the terms of trade. Further, the way in which prices are set seems to have longer-term implications for the efficiency of the growth path being followed in the CMEA states, particularly those seeking to follow more optimal policies at home.

Examining first the thesis that CMEA development paths are autarkic, superficial comparison with similar capitalist economies would seem to be supportive. What such comparisons neglect, however, is that the countries concerned had comparatively low values of per capita trade in the interwar years, no doubt as a result of their low level of development.[23] The postwar years in which central planning was applied were in fact characterised by very rapid growth in the values of per capita trade for these countries; rates comparable in fact to those of the EEC states. These fast rates of expansion seem to have persisted in the most recent decade. In explaining them it is probably the case, as Broner suggests, that any tendency to autarky deriving from the planning mechanism has been overridden by the need for raw materials and industrial inputs arising from a very high rate of industrial growth.[24] The figures presented in Table 10.1 with West Germany and Japan included for comparison may be illustrative.

While the accuracy of these data are perhaps open to more debate than usual, it is not unreasonable to believe that a fairly substantial trade expansion has taken place as industrialisation drew in imported inputs. Broner's own research in fact suggests that when due allowance is made for income levels in trading partners, population, distance,

Table 10.1 *Real Annual Growth of GDP and Exports 1960–70 and 1970–78 (per cent)*

	GDP		Exports	
	1960–70	*1970–78*	*1960–70*	*1970–78*
W. Germany	4·4	2·4	10·2	6·9
Japan	10·5	5·0	17·5	9·7
Rumania	9·0	10·6	9·9	—
Bulgaria	5·9	6·3	14·5	10·7
Hungary	3·8	5·4	9·7	13·0
Poland	4·3	7·0	10·0	9·3
USSR	5·2	5·3	—	7·8
Czechoslovakia	3·1	4·9	6·6	6·0
E. Germany	3·1	4·7	8·3	7·9

Source: World Development Report, 1980 (Washington DC: The World Bank, Tables 2 and 8.

complementarity of national economies and preferential trading arrangements, the *trade potential* of the CMEA countries (based on *West* European data) is *in fact* substantially realised. His predicted trade values for 1970 appear in Table 10.2.

Table 10.2 *Estimates of exports based on a trade-flow model for CMEA countries and for CMEA without the USSR: 1970 (US$m. at current prices)*

	Total CMEA			Eastern Europe without USSR		
	Fitted	*Actual*	*Ratio A/F*	*Fitted*	*Actual*	*Ratio A/F*
Total	45,268	30,892	0·68	12,065	18,095	0·95
Intra CMEA	19,103	18,507	0·97	10,270	11,551	1·12
Rest of the World	26,165	12,385	0·47	8,795	6,544	0·74

Source: Broner, Table 5, p. 54.

While the magnitude of CMEA trade, when correctly compared, is not low (and growth rates have evidently been impressive), this does not suggest, as Broner appreciates, that the trade is *efficient*. The preceding discussion of planning arrangements seems likely to ensure that it is not. Moreover, the ratios shown in Table 10.2 are evidence of fairly substantial trade diversion. Although intra-trade is close to predicted values, that with the rest of the world tends to be below. To support the trade diversion impression, intra-bloc trade today accounts for approximately three-quarters of the total for CMEA nations. Before the

Second World War, however, this mutual trade was less than one quarter of the total.[25]

Having established the overwhelming contribution of intra-trade to overall trade growth, it is necessary to note one of its major characteristics – that of bilateralism. The planning discussion highlighted the obsession with material balances in the predominant model where trade is a 'residual' sector. Surplus balances are used as exports exchanging for supplies of items in domestic deficit. Balance of trade is secured by the tendency to supply only enough exports to pay for necessary imports. This preference for balance on the trade account does not need to imply bilateral balancing, but it usually does so in practice. Again the prices agreed for the items in exchange set the bilateral terms of trade, and hence the distribution by country of gains from the transaction. Overall balance could, of course, be achieved by one country, A, running a surplus with another, B, while at the same time managing an offsetting deficit with a third, C. The surplus C has with A would be offset (in a three-country system) by a deficit with B. In these circumstances, however, as Holzman points out, C has little inducement to run a surplus with A.[26] Under planning it is not certain what goods A has that she will be willing to export. Thus a nation running a surplus with another runs the risk of not being able to buy more than it can sell to third countries.[27] This uncertainty regarding the availability of goods in exchange for money is a form of 'commodity inconvertibility'.

The CMEA countries are aware of the inflexibility that this implies and have made efforts to multilateralise transactions. The first serious attempt was in 1964 when operations commenced of the International Bank for Economic Cooperation (IBEC). A new trade currency, the transferable ruble, was also introduced permitting surpluses and deficits between members. Although each member is required to keep *overall* balance, this is not required for trade with each state. For the reasons outlined immediately above, however, the system has not really worked. One estimate suggests that only 2 per cent of intra-CMEA turnover was cleared multilaterally during 1964–68.[28]

For such reasons therefore the major part of intra-CMEA trade remains bilateral. How then are the prices for these bilateral exchanges set? As price levels in each partner state are administratively fixed, and hence not comparable, a common yardstick had to be found. The obvious one to use was world market prices and base negotiations on them. For the planning process it is inconvenient if these fluctuate widely and for this reason there have been various attempts at stabilisation for purposes of intra-trade. Indeed there has been a continuing desire, at least in some quarters, for an independent price basis. Instability caused by the Korean conflict, for instance, led the CMEA to freeze contractual prices between themselves at the average of their 1949–50 levels, for the period 1951–56. Apparently, this did not prevent the main features of world price changes during the period feeding through into CMEA trade prices. However, this gradual undermining process *did* lead to widely differing prices for similar products in different bilateral trade agreements. An attempt to introduce more uniformity in price-setting was made with the 'price clause' following 1958, although the various permissible adjustments still left individual deals somewhat at the mercy of the bargaining strength of individual negotiators.[29] The Varna Conference in 1962 was an unsuccessful attempt to introduce a single CMEA price on the basis of the price clause.

Instead policy seems to have been to use an average of world market prices, for example, for 1960–64, as the base and hold to them until they have grown too far out of line with current circumstances. The 1960–64 base, for instance, seems to have survived until 1970. Although base changes can be expected to affect prices negotiated in the bargaining process, they are *only* the basis of negotiation. As the process determines the terms of trade these negotiations are prolonged. From this outline it seems reasonable to suppose that political factors enter into the bargaining, probably to the advantage of the least trade dependent participant. That this possibility exists is illustrated by one estimate covering the period between 1945 and 1953 (the year of Stalin's death). It is suggested that the transfer of economic resources from Eastern Europe to the Soviet Union in that period amounted to $14 billion or equivalent to the Marshall Plan funds received by Western Europe from the USA.[30] Some have continued to argue that the terms of trade mechanism continues to be wielded to similar effect.

Menderhausen, for instance, compared prices paid by the USSR for roughly similar imports from CMEA partners and from the rest of the world. Prices paid to CMEA producers appeared lower, and when a similar comparison was run for Soviet exports to both the CMEA and the outside world, the bloc appeared to pay more. It seemed therefore that the bargaining process we have discussed *was* used to the advantage of the least trade dependent member.

More recent evidence, however, suggests that this is not so. Holzman provides a theoretical refutation by pointing out that all that is needed to generate Menderhausen's results is to view the CMEA as a strongly trade diverting customs union.[31] If the bloc countries aim at 'collective' autarky, as their trade flows seem to suggest,[32] prices in the bloc will not tend towards equality with the rest of the world. Direct controls rather than tariffs ensure this result and the peripheral nature of bloc 'foreign' trade. In these circumstances, if the bloc members trade between themselves on the basis of comparative advantage, and adjust 'world' prices for the purposes of this trade to *equalise* the rate of profit between the parties the Menderhausen results can easily be generated. Of course, if this analysis is correct, there should be evidence of the USSR paying *more* for bloc imports than for imports from the rest of the world. There is, indeed, evidence that this is the case.[33] Moreover, in a later paper Holzman demonstrates that the Western countries have tended to discriminate *against* the CMEA in trade charging higher prices for bloc exports than for similar exports in trade outside the bloc.[34] There are a number of reasons for this discrimination, sometimes political, sometimes economic. In the latter category falls the greater perceived uncertainty in trade with the CMEA and the lack of full commercial links.

Further empirical evidence that the USSR does not systematically discriminate against its partners is provided by Hewett's recent study of price trends in intra-CMEA trade. In fact he shows that the price level of total Soviet exports to the European CMEA members *fell steadily throughout the 1955–70 period*. This was fairly uniform for exports to individual members. On the other hand, Soviet imports of manufactured goods from the CMEA became more expensive. In particular, imports of consumer goods showed a price rise of about 20 per cent between 1960 and 1970. Consumer goods were an increasingly important Soviet import representing 29 per cent of total trade in 1970. Overall, if Soviet terms of trade with the CMEA represented 100 in 1960, they had fallen to 79 by 1970.[35]

The background to these figures is that, in the late 1960s, the USSR was primarily a supplier of raw materials providing over 90 per cent of European CMEA crude oil, pig-iron and iron ore and more than 60 per cent of cotton, coal, manganese and wheat. On the other hand, the USSR took the major share of East European machinery manufactures, the figures ranging from 60 per cent for Bulgaria to 33 per cent for Rumania.[36]

With traditional planners' preferences for the capital goods sector the machinery producers of Eastern Europe were able to secure higher prices for their products even in times of officially agreed price freeze. As further evidence that European CMEA members have been able to extract concessions from the USSR, Bulgaria's overall terms of trade with the USSR have been favourable *despite* their raw material bias.

Of course, it would be wrong to attribute these figures to Soviet benevolence. In fact it seems to have been a *quid pro quo* for maintenance of an autarkic grouping when the natural trading partners of certain members of the bloc almost certainly lie outside it.

CONCLUSIONS

The attitude of the USSR in fact provides the essential background for an assessment of the present state of the CMEA. While it is probably true that the existence of the CMEA has assisted central planning in the member states to establish industrialisation on a larger scale than could have been achieved alone, present circumstances demand change. The USSR has been showing increasing dissatisfaction at the mounting opportunity cost of its exports to the CMEA. As primary goods they would be readily convertible into foreign exchange which in turn could be used to purchase high quality goods in the West. Following the 1974 oil crisis, intra-CMEA price changes in 1975 favoured primary commodities with a doubling of the oil price and a 52 per cent rise in raw material prices.[37] This represented a major terms of trade loss for the European members.

Such influences, together with increasing Soviet raw material supply difficulties, are combining with the completion of 'extensive' industrialisation to force East European states to think about allocative economic efficiency. If living standards are to continue to improve – and the regimes are at least sensitive to this requirement – increased productivity is vital. The Polish and Hungarian reforms in planning recognise this but will the continued existence of the CMEA be conducive to these reforms? Clearly the attitude of the USSR is crucial. They, together with primitive Bulgaria, are in favour of multilateral plan integration as a means of raising output. The Comprehensive Reform programme of 1971 indicated as much and events since then have moved towards more Russian control.[38] There is continuing support in the same quarter for *a separate basis for intra-CMEA trade pricing*. All such developments seem diametrically opposed to the interests of the advanced states whose new plan attempts at optimisation require sensible trade prices as an input into production allocation decisions. Their interests now favour *world prices* rather than prices which reflect the preferences of planners dealing with economies at an altogether earlier stage of evolution.

Such interests coincide with those who favour expanded East–West trade. No centrally planned economy would dare to liberalise trade unless it had already rendered domestic prices consistent with world prices.[39] Otherwise exchange would tend to be to its own disadvantage.

On the other hand, if regimes continue with traditional planning, 'necessary' Western imports will be financed by bilateral deals in which planners release whatever exports they can in payment. Given currency inconvertibility (another result of such planning) these exports will tend to be sold for whatever hard currency can be gained. 'Dumping' (prices well below real production costs) will readily and disruptively occur.

It is hard to escape the conclusion that the CMEA has outlived the limited economic usefulness that it might have had in the period of early postwar industrialisation.

NOTES: CHAPTER 10

1 E. A. Hewett, *Foreign Trade Prices in the CMEA* (Cambridge: Cambridge University Press, 1974), p. 124.
2 See note 6 to Chapter 7 of this volume. The five were Austria, Greece, Italy, Portugal and Turkey.
3 M. Kaser, *Comecon* (London: Oxford University Press, 1965), p. 10.
4 ibid., p. 16.
5 Communique quoted in Kaser, op. cit., p. 12.
6 ibid., p. 14.
7 A permanent secretariat also emerged by 1955. See Kaser, op. cit., p. 41.
8 M. A. G. van Meerhaeghe, *International Economic Institutions* (London: Longman, 1971), p. 224.
9 ibid., pp. 218–220, and Kaser, op. cit., Appendix 4 for Charter extracts.
10 Hewett, op. cit., p. 7.
11 Quote cited in Hewett, op. cit., p. 4.
12 'Basic Principles . . . ', part 2, reproduced in Kaser, op. cit., Appendix 6.
13 ibid., part 3.
14 Kaser, op. cit., p. 93.
15 ibid.
16 ibid., p. 94.
17 See Hewett, op. cit., pp. 10–14, from which this account borrows heavily.
18 ibid., p. 13.
19 C. M. Friesen, *The Political Economy of East – West Trade* (New York: Praeger, 1976), p. 76.
20 Kaser, op. cit., p. 17.
21 This account of planning practice draws upon the illuminating discussion in Hewett, op. cit., Ch. 4.
22 F. D. Holzman, *Foreign Trade under Central Planning* (Cambridge, Mass: Harvard University Press, 1974), p. 140.
23 A. Broner, 'Autarky in centrally planned economies', *Journal of Common Market Studies*, vol. 15 (1976–77), Table 2.
24 ibid., p. 45.
25 See Holzman, op. cit., note 34, p. 397.
26 ibid., p. 149.
27 ibid.
28 Hewett, op. cit., p. 15.
29 ibid., p. 31.
30 Friesen, op. cit., p. 61.
31 Holzman, op. cit., p. 271.
32 See Table 2 above.
33 See Holzman's Bulgarian data, op. cit., p. 280 and below.
34 Holzman, op. cit., p. 301.
35 Hewett, op. cit., Table 3.5, pp. 78–9.
36 Friesen, op. cit., p. 62.
37 ibid., pp. 64 and 68.
38 ibid., p. 63.
39 Holzman, op. cit., p. 141–8.

CHAPTER 11

The World Bank (IBRD), International Development Association (IDA) and the International Finance Corporation (IFC)

The World Bank group, including IDA and IFC, forms the major multilateral agency for chanelling financial resources to the developing countries. In doing so the Bank also directly and indirectly influences the flow of international trade. Since it insists on competitive bidding for all tenders on World Bank-aided projects, it encourages free international trade directly. It has also through its influence and exhortation urged the adoption of lower levels of protection and freer exchange rate policies upon developing countries. The Bank Group has also been heavily involved directly and indirectly in technical assistance. Thus the Bank and its associate institutions have influenced flows of capital, transfers of skill and know-how and have also had some influence upon the flows of goods through international trade. Have these activities of the Bank Group improved world economic welfare? If so, have they achieved as much as they might have done given different objectives and policies? These are extremely difficult questions to answer and probably all that we can do is to survey some of the relevant evidence and present some qualitative and rather tentative answers.

OBJECTIVES

Although, on the basis of the Bretton Woods Agreements, the first task of the IBRD was to be to assist with the reconstruction of the productive capacity of Europe and most of its initial loans were made to countries in Western Europe, it soon turned to the other long-term task of aiding the development of the less developed members of the IBRD.

In the development task the Bank's main objectives are to stimulate, support and provide from its own resources flows of capital into worthwhile projects and programmes in the developing countries. In addition the Bank Group aims to improve the quality of project planning and in some cases to improve the general economic policies of recipient

211

countries. This has drawn the Bank into technical assistance mainly in the form of project evaluation teams and survey missions. But it has also led it into dialogues with the governments of some less developed countries in which the Bank on its own, or in association with the IMF and some bilateral donors, has sought to persuade these governments to adopt policies considered by the Bank to be more favourable to economic development. This is one of the most controversial aspects of the Bank's operations and one which we shall return to below. Article 1, III of the Bank's Charter enjoins it to promote the expansion of international trade and balance-of-payments equilibrium and may also lead it into using its influence or even leverage to support these objectives.

Emphasis on the various objectives of Bank policy has changed over time. This has been partly due to the growth of experience, and partly in response to criticism or to changes in contemporary theories on how to promote economic development. This has been particularly true of the subsidiary aims and policies of the Bank undertaken to achieve the general objective of improving the lot of the Third World, and can be observed in the changes that have occurred in the composition of its investments and other activities in the various sectors of the economies of LDCs.

POLITICS AND PERSONNEL

Other factors which have influenced the attitudes and policies of the Bank are of a political and financial nature. The Bank is a specialised agency of the United Nations, but its membership is not identical with that of the UN. The Soviet Union, mainland China and the Communist countries of Eastern Europe are conspicuous by their absence. Unlike the UN but like its fellow Bretton Woods institution, the IMF, the power structure is heavily weighted in favour of the rich Western economies. Votes are based on the size of subscriptions, which means that the United States alone has over a quarter of the votes. The US with France, West Germany, Canada, Australia and Great Britain have over 50 per cent of the total votes. The upper echelons of the Bank's professional staff also tend to be rather heavily dominated by American, British and West European personnel. The president up to now has always been a citizen of the USA. This inevitably leads to suspicion that policies will be influenced by the political and economic philosophies which hold sway in these countries. In particular the Bank has been accused of being over-concerned with fostering private enterprise and promoting laissez-faire policies in client nations.

Since the rich countries are necessarily in a creditor position *vis-à-vis* the LDCs it is also alleged that under their influence the Bank has been too concerned with the rights of creditors to repayment and has set its face strongly against any repudiation of foreign debt by poor countries with balance-of-payments crises.

In its first development loan, to Chile in 1948, the Bank insisted on Chile reaching a settlement on its outstanding previous debts. The Bank adhered strictly to this policy in its dealings with all countries as its charter requires it to do, but it aroused particular and understandable indignation in Latin America where few felt much responsibility for the sins of their predecessors in defaulting on debts in the stress of the World's greatest depression.[1]

The Bank is also alleged to be hostile to the nationalisation of industries, particularly where they are foreign owned. In financial matters the Bank is alleged to share the hostility of the IMF to domestic inflation, heavy subsidies to nationalised undertakings, high levels of protection, budget deficits and over-valued exchange rates. These are all policies to which many, especially Latin American, developing countries are prone. The Bank is also accused of having a paramount interest in political stability which means that it may be led into providing aid to regimes which are extremely reactionary and have little or no interest in social reform or in promoting any real improvement in the standard of living of the majority of their citizens. Some such countries may have no prospects of genuine social and economic development without radical changes in policies which may only be achieved by a social revolution whether by violence or through the ballot box.

It can be argued that such conservative attitudes are likely to be forced upon the Bank by its dependence on the main capitalist democracies for finance through their subscriptions to the Bank and access to their capital markets. The Articles of Agreement of the IBRD require it 'to promote private foreign investment by means of guarantees or participations in loans and other investments made by private investors'. Only if these are not forthcoming on reasonable terms should the Bank provide 'finances for productive purposes out of its own capital, funds raised by it and its other resources'. In fact the Bank chose not to operate by guaranteeing loans raised by its members from private investors. This arose from the practical consideration that different members would be assessed by the market as different credit risks and despite the Bank's guarantee this might well be reflected in differential interest charges. This would have been embarrassing to the Bank and might have damaged its credit standing. Instead the Bank chose to issue its own bonds rather than guarantee those of member governments. Inevitably in this situation the Bank had to earn a reputation for solid conservative policies to attract funds from Wall Street and subsequently from European capital markets. This forced the Bank into fairly conservative lending policies and into making loans with rather high interest rates, lower than would have been required if the LDCs had attempted to borrow directly, but higher than the concessional terms which have now become common in bilateral lending from rich to poor countries. Loans were made at rates around 4–6 per cent with repayment schedules of six to thirty-five years, the average length being about twenty years.

The Bank initially took a very 'banker-like' attitude to loans, financing only specific projects that promised to generate sufficient profits to enable repayment of the loan. It concentrated on public utility investments in power and transportation and limited its contribution to the foreign exchange costs of the project. For reasons which we shall consider below these possibly weakened the Bank's contribution to the overall development of the LDCs and may in some cases have actually been counter-productive.

However, even in its early years the Bank did increase the flow of financial resources from the rich countries to the poor. As Richard N. Gardner says,[2]

> After the disastrous experience of defaults in international bond issues during the interwar period it is doubtful that the capital market of the United States could have once again been tapped on such a large scale, particularly for the less developed countries, without the International Bank as intermediary.

To the potential investor in the USA or later in Europe, World Bank bonds represented a diversified package of investments selected and supervised by an experienced and prudent management, backed by guarantees of borrowing governments and by the vast reserves in the capital subscriptions of the member nations which could be called on if required. As such World Bank bonds soon came to be regarded as a first class investment. Undoubtedly this increased the flow of finance to the LDCs.

Given the constraints imposed upon it by reliance on borrowing from the private sector capital markets of the USA, Switzerland, West Germany, Britain and other West European countries the Bank probably succeeded in promoting flows of finance from rich to poor countries as well as could be expected. The staff of the Bank also took the view that shortage of capital in the early years of its operations was not the main obstacle to extending its aid to LDCs. In their view the difficulty was to find sufficient, well-designed projects whose economic returns would justify Bank finance. This was inherently likely. Few of the emergent nations had the engineering, economic and managerial expertise required to identify, design, implement and manage large projects in power, transportation and industry.

The Bank tried to overcome these difficulties through survey missions of Bank staff and consultants. By working along with local officials they helped to implant the ideas and techniques necessary for the generation of worthwhile projects. The Bank also set up its own Economic Development Institute in 1955 to train top administrators in underdeveloped countries. Over the years, partly as a result of the efforts of the Bank and partly from the vastly increased numbers of graduates and professionally trained staff now available in many LDCs as a result of the combined efforts of UN and bilateral technical assistance programmes, a shortage of well-planned projects has become a less inhibiting factor.

THE LENDING OPERATIONS OF THE BANK

The first loans of the Bank were for reconstruction in Europe. In June 1948 the total loans stood at just under $500m. – $250m. to France, $195m to the Netherlands, $40m. to Denmark and $12m. to Luxembourg (IBRD, *Annual Report*, 1947/48). In the 1950s Bank lending ran at an average level of $400m. gross of cancellations and repayments. Most of these loans, especially in the later years, were for development in countries that would be classed as underdeveloped. With the major exception of the loans to assist the development of southern Italy they were largely to non-European countries and Southeast Asia was becoming the main recipient. The current geographical distribution of Bank and IDA lending is shown in Table 11.1.

Table 11.1 *Bank and IDA Lending by Geographical Region in 1979 ($USm.)*

	1979	%
E. Africa	646	6·4
W. Africa	556	5·6
E. Asia and Pacific	2,130	21·0
S. Asia	2,077	21·0
Europe, Mid-East and N. Africa	2,336	23·0
Latin America and Caribbean	2,265	23·0
	10,010	100·0

Source: World Bank, *Annual Report* (1979).

Over the whole period of the Bank's operations, as Table 11.2 shows, Asia and Latin America have been the main beneficiaries of loans from the Bank group. India has received by far the largest share. Given its vast population and immense problems of poverty this is hardly surprising and would appear only just.

Table 11.2   *Bank and IDA Cumulative Lending Operations Up to 30 June 1979: The Top Ten Borrowers*

	Bank Loans (US$m.)	IDA Credits (US$m.)	Total (US$m.)	Population (m.)	Finance per capita ($)
India	2,646	6,750	9,396	596	15·8
Brazil	4,619	—	4,619	104	44·4
Mexico	3,814	—	3,814	58	65·8
Indonesia	2,476	758	3,234	128	25·3
Korea, Republic of	2,405	111	2,516	15	167·7
Jugoslavia	2,337	—	2,337	21	111·3
Colombia	2,243	20	2,263	23	98·4
Philippines	1,978	122	2,100	41	51·2
Turkey	1,807	179	1,986	39	50·9
Pakistan	884	1,080	1,964	67	29·3
Total IBRD loans and credits	51,697	16,732	68,430		

Sources: World Bank, *Annual Report* (1979) and *World Bank Atlas* (1976).

This juxtaposition of India with Brazil, Mexico or Korea throws into sharp relief one dilemma with which all major aid agencies are faced. Given a desire to promote economic development in the underdeveloped countries should aid be allocated to the poorest and least fortunate of the poor nations or to those where growth is likely to take place rapidly? These will seldom be the same. The arguments for the latter policy stem partly from a Rostovian view of the development process.[3] This sees countries as at various stages in the process of economic growth. Some have reached a point of 'take-off' where a relatively small extra push will accelerate them into self-sustained growth. Then savings and investment rates will be high enough to lead to constant accumulation of capital and growth of income. This theory leads to the optimistic view that it is not too difficult to identify such countries, concentrate aid resources on them, give them vital aid injection for a limited number of years and then just leave them to get on with it. Once they are on the virtuous path the aid donors can switch their attention to the next group which by now will, hopefully, have made necessary institutional changes, acquired the managers and entrepreneurs and the economic dynamism to benefit in the same way as their precedessors.

216

This argument for concentrating aid on those most likely to show a quick and high return is reinforced by a desire to reward success and, even, punish failure. The idea is that aid should be known to be more readily available to those countries and governments who have demonstrated by sensible policies and past achievements their ability to increase growth or at least to make changes in policies and institutions which seem likely to conduce to rapid growth. Aid can then act as a bribe to persuade governments to conform to the agencies' views of what is required to promote growth.

These arguments gain strength from the obvious paucity of aid resources in total let alone from one agency. Spread thinly over the two-thirds of humankind who live in the LDCs such funds may have no significant impact whatsoever. Concentrated on a few promising nations, however, aid loans may have a powerful reinforcing effect on domestic measures and enable rapid growth to take place. This general philosophy was at one time very influential with the US Agency for International Development, and has had some effect in aid organisations in most donor nations. It would be surprising if it had not also had some effect on the Washington based IBRD.

A Bank pamphlet, *Some Aspects of the Economic Philosophy of the World Bank* (September 1968) contains evidence on the IBRD's own thinking in the 1960s on this matter in a paper by Andrew M. Kamarck on 'Appraisal of Country Economic Performance' (pp. 7–19 of the pamphlet). He writes[4]:

> One of the principal lessons that the World Bank Group has learned from 20 years of experience is that the economic development or growth of the country depends primarily on a continuing improvement in the effectiveness with which that country uses its economic resources . . .
>
> Fundamentally, improvement of economic performance is something that can be carried out only by the government and the people of the country concerned. It cannot be imposed from abroad. But capital from the outside can be used as an incentive to the government to take action to improve the country's economic performance . . .
>
> The present position, therefore, is that in all of its lending the Bank Group (a) directly attempts – by attaching conditions to its loans – to improve the use of resources in those projects or sectors or institutions where its finance is directly involved; and (b) also tries to make a basic analysis of the economic problems and prospects of a country in cooperation with the government, what is holding up faster growth and what action the government is capable of taking to correct this situation, (c) what steps the Bank Group can reasonably

expect from the government toward attaining improved economic performance, concurrently with the extension of Bank Group assistance.

Despite its concentration on project-tied aid it appears that the Bank has always been interested in the overall economic performance of its clients. In part this can be explained by its concern with repayment of loans. Since these are guaranteed by the host government any bank would have to reassure itself about the likely capacity of the recipient country to pay the interest and amortisation of a loan. But the interest of the World Bank Group necessarily extends beyond the mere financial considerations. It is, after all, charged with the duty of aiding development. This would force it to consider projects in the light of the whole policies of the government. A project to supply irrigation, justified as an investment to increase agricultural productivity, could be frustrated by government policies on the prices of agricultural products or by weaknesses in its policies to produce and distribute chemical fertilisers and pesticides. It is a fairly natural extension from this position to concern with the government's policies in finance, balance of payments and population, especially when the Bank Group's commitments involve several projects of support for specific programmes. Examples cited by Teresa Hayter and in the monumental study by Mason and Asher show the Bank involved in matters of general economic policy from quite early days. In 1949 the Bank was urging Chile to curb inflation as a prerequisite for Bank lending. In the 1950s Peru was persuaded not to accept more short-term suppliers' credits. In Hayter's words, 'Sometimes the Bank succeeded in persuading a government to raise the rates charged by, or to reduce the number of people employed in, railways or power companies, even when no particular Bank project was involved.'[5] The Bank stopped making new commitments for loans to several Latin American governments of whose policies the Bank disapproved. In Brazil, for example, Bank lending ceased from 1960 to 1965 because the Brazilian government repudiated a stabilisation programme agreed with the IMF.[6]

There are two major issues involved in this discussion. The first is the question of the allocation of aid between countries. The second is, how far should an international aid agency seek to use its control over finance to influence the internal policies of the governments of LDCs?

Humanitarian considerations would suggest that limited aid resources should be used to assist the countries whose populations have the lowest standards of living. But while this should certainly apply to emergency relief it is not so clear that it should apply to development aid. The purpose of one is to raise current standards of consumption. The purpose of the other is to raise the capacity of a country to generate a future flow of goods and services which will enable raised standards of living to be enjoyed by its citizens in five, ten, twenty or more years hence. In the long run the second purpose is likely to bring greater benefits to the community than would subsidising current consumption by a similar sum of money. The only exceptions are likely to be situations of emergency such as flood disasters or famine following a drought.[7]

The Bank was set up to provide development funds, other agencies exist to provide emergency relief. Since the Bank has to promote development it must consider the efficiency with which borrowers can use funds to earn high economic and social returns. If a country has a weak central government, a relatively corrupt and incompetent civil service, few trained engineers and managers and a recent history of low growth rates, it is unlikely that it would be able to make effective developmental use of capital funds lent to it. Its 'absorptive capacity' for aid is likely to be limited. The Bank would rightly consider such a country a poor risk for capital aid and would choose to lend elsewhere, to countries that displayed more promising characteristics. The main difficulty that arises in using simply a rate of return criterion for the allocation of aid is that it can end up with the biblical situation – 'to him that hath shall be given'. Frequently the countries which can be shown to have good prospects of earning high economic returns on capital are among the better-off developing countries and already enjoying rising per capita incomes. Very poor African and Asian countries may have desperate needs for assistance but be rather poor prospects for development.

If one agrees with the value judgement that aid priorities should be to improve the prospects of the poorest communities in the world, one must adopt a criterion which weights any improvement in their lot more heavily than a similar absolute increase in the per capita income of a group whose relative poverty is less desperate. In other words, one should apply a cost–benefit analysis to project evaluation which has a built-in factor to allow for an assumed diminishing marginal utility of income. Given similar economic rates of return after allowing for distortions of market prices, external costs and benefits, the project whose net benefits accrue to the community with the lower standard of living should rank higher than one whose benefits accrue to a less disadvantaged community. In the 1970s Bank policy has moved closer to this approach, stressing the importance of raising employment, improving the distribution of income, meeting 'basic needs' and alleviating 'absolute poverty' while also recognising that increasing production is a must.[8]

THE ROLE OF IDA

Richard Gardner uses the appealing phrase, 'The Banker develops a heart', to describe the shift in the orientation of Bank lending from reconstruction in Europe to aiding the developing countries, but perhaps that sentiment should have been reserved for the setting up of the International Development Association (IDA). The IBRD is constrained in its aid policies by its need to satisfy private lenders and to charge near commercial rates of interest. This necessarily led to emphasis first upon the financial, then, with increasing sophistication, upon the economic, rates of return on projects, and scrutiny of the financial prospects of the borrowing country as the main determinants of whether a loan would be forthcoming. The Bank's staff became increasingly aware of this bias and of the growing indebtedness of some developing countries which threatened to reduce the number of countries eligible for Bank loans. This, plus international criticism of the conservative policies of the Bank led to the setting up of the IDA in 1962. Formally this was a new and separate institution. In practice it was, and is, simply the Bank under a different hat. IDA is the 'soft' loan division of the Bank. IDA loans uniformly bear a service charge of only 0·75 per cent, are for fifty years and have a grace period of ten years.

Clearly this widened the scope for aid to LDCs at the lower end of the per capita income scale. It did this in two ways: first it reduced the problems of repayment for countries where low income made it difficult to generate savings or where structural rigidities made it difficult to convert savings into foreign exchange. Secondly, by easing the problem of debt servicing it permitted the Bank to pay more attention to investments where the payoff was more social than economic, or where the economic returns would be very long term: for example, investment in education, family planning and housing. Over the years the Bank Group's loans have become much more diversified. From the original concentration on power and transport the Bank has spread its activities over a much wider range of activities, some of them with a social emphasis. Table 11.3 illustrates the recent range of loans and how the distribution by sector has changed over time. Up to 1963 power and transportation absorbed over 70 per cent of the Bank's loans. Recent years have seen this drop to 30 per cent and a vast expansion in lending to agriculture, industry, through development finance companies, and socially oriented activities such as education, population, urbanisation and water-supply have begun to figure prominently.

The IDA window for lending has had two further aspects. It enabled the Bank to make loans to countries which could not have afforded the harder terms of IBRD loans, so extending assistance to many of the poorer nations. Also, without IDA the net transfer of resources from the Bank Group to LDCs would now be very small in relation to total ODA of about $20 billion in 1978. The net flows from the Bank and IDA are shown in Table 11.4.

Table 11.3   *Sectoral Composition of World Bank Lending (Fiscal years, percentage shares)*

	Up to 1963	FY 1967	1977	1979
Infrastructure				
Communications	0·9	3·6	2·0	1
Power	34·5	29·7	13·5	14
Transportation	38·3	21·2	14·8	19
Subtotal	73·7	54·5	30·3	34
Economic Sectors				
Agriculture	8·6	7·7	32·7	25
(of which rural development)	—	—	(20·6)	
Industry	14·2	11·9	21·1	16
Tourism	—	—	1·4	1
Subtotal	22·8	19·6	55·2	42
Social Sectors				
Education	0·1	4·6	4·1	5
Population	—	—	0·5	1
Urbanisation	—	—	2·2	3
Water Supply and Sewerage	0·2	0·1	4·3	10
Nutrition	—	—	0·2	
Subtotal	0·3	4·7	11·2	19
Others (including programme loans	3·2	21·2	3·3	5
	100	100	100	100

Sources: World Bank/IDA, *Annual Report* (1979), and earlier issues; M. ul Haq, 'Changing emphasis of the Bank's lending policies', *Finance and Development* (June 1978).

Table 11.4   *Net Disbursements from the World Bank and IDA to LDCs, Fiscal years 1962–77 ($m.)*

Source	1962	1965	1970	1977
Bank	124	165	508	1,872
IDA	12	220	163	1,132
Total	136	385	671	3,004

Source: Mason and Asher, op. cit., Table 12.2 for 1962 and 1965; OECD, *1978 Review, Development Co-operation* (1978), Table C.3 in Statistical annex.

The addition of IDA, however, was in no way intended to reduce the stringency of Bank conditions as far as efficiency in design and management of projects was concerned. In principle the criteria for loans from

IDA are the same as for World Bank loans. The repayment terms are lower only because the country as a whole cannot afford the hard loan terms of the Bank. It is difficult to believe though that the institution of soft lending did not assist the Bank to take a more sympathetic attitude to projects in the social welfare sphere.

INVESTMENT IN THE PRIVATE SECTOR

The sectoral distribution of World Bank lending had also been constrained in other ways by its charter. The role of the Bank was intended to be supplementary to private flows of investment. This inhibited the Bank from direct investment in industrial and agricultural activities for these were areas where private foreign direct investment might be expected to play a role. Moreover the Bank could not invest without a government guarantee and many governments in developing countries were unwilling to guarantee loans to private firms on grounds of ideology or for fear of accusations of favouritism. This would not have prevented Bank loans to nationalised industries, but at least in the first ten years of its life the Bank showed hostility to public enterprise in manufacturing industry. This hostility, in part ideological, probably arose as much from the Bank's observation of the actual performance of public enterprises in many developing countries.

To get round the difficulty implicit in its charter the Bank adopted two strategems to increase its aid to the private sector. One was the creation in 1956 of the International Finance Corporation (IFC), the other was to lend to investment banks and development finance companies in the LDCs for on-lending to private enterprises for industrial and agricultural development. IFC was set up with the objectives of providing capital for private enterprises, encouraging the development of local capital markets and promoting foreign private investment in developing countries. IFC does not require a government guarantee. Its functions are like those of any investment bank. It can participate directly in private ventures, providing up to 25 per cent of the capital. Originally it was not permitted to make equity investments but, since 1961, when the Corporation's articles were amended to permit equity investments, IFC normally does buy equity shares as well as providing long-term loans. Like any investment bank its criteria for lending includes the financial soundness of the project but the IFC is also supposed to concern itself with the contribution of the project to the broader economic development of the nation. In practice the former criterion has been clearly dominant. At least up until 1969 IFC made no use of shadow pricing or other techniques of cost—benefit analysis to distinguish the economic from the financial rate of return. However, it seems to have avoided investing in enterprises whose profits depended on excessive protection.

In the total aid and foreign investment flows, the activities of IFC are very minor. Its initial capital was under $100 million in 1957 and during its first five years it committed only $58 million in investments. In the following five years about $20 million a year was the average investment. Since then the investment rate has risen rapidly, with net disbursements in 1976 of $193 million and in 1977 of $198 million, but still remains small in comparison with other resource flows to LDCs.[9]

Normally IFC's investments fall in the range of $1 million to $20 million. The lower limit is set by the costs of appraisal of schemes while the upper limit is to prevent undue concentration. IFC tries to sell off to private enterprise its shares in an enterprise as soon as this is commercially feasible so that it can 'roll-over' its capital frequently and increase its overall impact. Initially IFC was intended only to supply capital where private enterprise was unwilling to venture on reasonable terms, but the difficulty of finding projects which were both profitable and unattractive to private capital has led to a shift in IFC's position. The criterion now seems to be that the presence of IFC should be required for its success. For example a need for IFC's special abilities in negotiating with governments.[10]

Much more capital, however, was channelled to the private sector through development finance companies (DFCs) in LDCs than through the direct activities of IFC. The funds which the Bank Group has channelled through DFCs have probably had a large indirect impact in aiding private enterprises throughout the developing world. The Bank Group contribution is normally only a small part of the funds of any DFC. In turn the DFCs' contribution to enterprises is usually only a part of their total capital. In this way the initial capital supplied by the Bank Group, along with the technical expertise which they provided, has had multiple effects on industrialisation in developing countries.

The Bank Group has been rather less successful in fostering the development of local capital markets to help increase local savings and channel them into worthwhile industrial and agricultural development. The Bank itself has supplied technical assistance in this field but IFC and Bank Group financed DFCs have been the main instruments for this purpose. IFC offers 'stand-by and other underwriting arrangements in support of public offerings or private placement of shares, debentures and other corporate securities'.[11] It has introduced new types of securities and in putting together new forms and expanding old ones it has created opportunities for local investment. IFC has also helped to develop local markets by selling off its own holdings in companies after they have proved their viability.

The DFCs' performance in this last task has been disappointing.

They are often reluctant to sell off either their successes or their failures, tending rather to subsidise the latter and publicise the former.

The Bank Group has encouraged foreign private investment in LDCs in a number of ways. First, its actions in insisting on settlements of outstanding debts helped to restore confidence in foreign investment in LDCs. Secondly, its intervention and offers of its good offices in helping to settle disputes over nationalisation of foreign owned assets also helped to improve the atmosphere for overseas investment. This assistance has now been institutionalised in the creation of The International Centre for Settlement of Investment Disputes (ICSID) in 1966 within the Bank Group. Thirdly, in its support for the creation of infrastructure in many LDCs it has opened the way for profitable private investments whether locally or foreign financed. Fourthly, in its use of influence it has tended to support conditions conducive to private investment in LDCs.

AID CO-ORDINATION

The Bank has led the way in forming consortia and consultative groups of aid donors and specific recipient countries. These enable the exchange of ideas and information and help to improve the rationality of aid allocation. The work of these fora is especially valuable to smaller donor nations who cannot afford or do not wish to devote resources to elaborate country and project analysis of their own. The Bank usually provides the technical services for such meetings including commentary on the statements and documents provided by the recipient nation. Their activities have probably increased the flow of aid to the LDC members by a combination of exhortation; for example, joint financing and donor confidence in Bank appraisals of projects and programmes. They have probably also helped a little to improve the matching up of recipient needs and individual donors' capacity to meet them. However, their performance has been very variable and opinions both inside and outside of the Bank on the value of consortia and consultative groups is mixed. 'Despite this divergence of views (and the modest list of achievements attributable to co-ordinating groups), consortia and consultative groups represent important half-way houses in the effort to rationalize the administration of development assistance at the country level.'[12]

OVERALL ASSESSMENT OF THE BANK GROUP

In the foregoing outline of the activities of the Bank Group many areas of controversy were raised briefly. In this section some overall assessment of what appear to be the more important controversies is attempted.

It has often been alleged that the Bank is too conservative to fulfil its tasks in aiding development, that this shows in its lending policies and in its attitudes to recipients' economic policies, and that its conservatism stems from the fact that its power structure ensures the dominance of the major capitalist nations.

LENDING POLICIES

The Bank's lending policies have certain characteristics which give some support to the accusation of conservatism. The stress on creditworthiness by the Bank, including a demonstration that a defaulting country was willing to make a reasonable settlement, could be considered evidence that the Bank was more interested in the welfare of bond holders than in the development of poor countries. This is particularly irksome when the default has been by governments long gone, in the face of economic disasters beyond their control, such as the 1930s Depression, and sometimes involving debts for services of questionable value or for bonds now in the hands of speculators. Similarly, the past refusal of the Bank to lend to nations which nationalised foreign owned enterprises without 'reasonable compensation' can be represented as excessive concern for the capitalist enterprises of the rich Western nations. However, at least during the first five to ten years of its life the Bank had to take such positions in order to establish its own credit in major capital markets and especially on Wall Street. As long as it was dependent on private investors' willingness to buy its bonds for its major source of funds to lend to LDCs this was essential. But, in addition, the Bank had a charter obligation to encourage private investment. Even without such an obligation it could well be argued that given the world as it existed in the 1950s the only large source of capital for the LDCs was bound to be from foreign private investment. In every year since 1972 non-concessional flows of finance have exceeded the official development assistance. During 1975–77 ODA from multilateral agencies was only 8·5 per cent of the net resource receipts of non-oil developing countries.[13]

In more recent years, the Bank has been more liberal in both these areas. In 1970 Bolivia and in 1971 Guyana nationalised foreign companies. Despite the opposition of the USA the executive directors of the Bank took the view that negotiations, with reasonable prospects, were underway between the disputants and approved loans to both of these countries.[14] The Bank has also taken an active part in debt-rescheduling operations for some countries with repayment difficulties. Such operations come very close to condoning default.

Since Bank loans have to be repaid the Bank has to be concerned with both the willingness and ability of governments to meet their obligations. When a nation builds up a very large debt in comparison with its foreign earnings and any likely inflow of new loans, the temptation to default becomes very great. Defaulting on interest and amortisation payments frees resources which are entirely untied and can be used for whatever purposes the government cares. Some debtor nations can probably improve their own growth prospects by simply defaulting on past debt, but the effects are more widespread and the repercussions on the flows of international capital from a few such actions could be damaging to the LDCs as a whole.

The Bank's lending policies have also been criticised for their project orientation, for confining finance to foreign exchange costs of projects, for excessive concern with growth, as expressed in rates of increase of GNP, and with over-concentration of its activities in the transport and power sectors while neglecting agriculture, industry and social sectors such as education and housing. The charge of conservatism has come up again over the Bank's reluctance to lend to public sector industry.

Most of these criticisms can be refuted quite simply by an appeal to the facts. The Bank Group has lent to a minor extent for programmes as well as projects.[15] It has for long been aware of the need to consider projects in the context of sectoral and macroeconomic analysis. In the last ten years it has swung heavily towards support for agricultural developments, education and population control. It has stressed distributional objectives. This has been expressed in the speeches of the President, Mr. McNamara, for example, in his address to the Board of Governors in Nairobi (24 September 1973), in the policies he has laid down for the Bank, in the research and policy documents emanating from the Bank in recent years and is now reflected in both commitments and disbursements of funds (see Table 10.3). The *Annual Report* for 1973 (pp. 14–15) stated that:

> Greater attention has been given to types of projects that can help spread the benefits of development more widely, especially among the poorer sections of society... In no sector has the volume of lending increased more rapidly than in agriculture. The sharp increase has been accompanied by a marked diversification in patterns of lending. In the Bank's early years, the emphasis was on basic irrigation infrastructure, such as dams and canals. But, over the years, there has been a shift toward financing on-farm activities such as provision of credit and technical services.

The Bank has also increasingly directed its efforts to smaller farmers. 'Between 1968 and 1972, the proportion of agriculture projects in which some participating farmers owned less than five hectares of land has risen from 17% to 50%' (p. 15). Unfortunately, the word 'some' could be very few, but there seems little doubt that the leadership of the Bank is anxious to move quickly forward towards helping the poorest sections of the world community. Intentions, however, take time to realise. It is difficult to develop, control and evaluate projects designed to help the poor. The Bank's greatest expertise has been built up in the transport and power sectors. The specialisation of the Bank in its early years in these fields can be justified by the great lack of good road and rail communications and the need for power to develop industries in most of the emerging nations. Their sustained commitment to these sectors up to the mid-1960s and beyond can also be defended on the grounds that they had the greatest experience and the best technicians for working in these areas. Other bilateral donors by the mid-1960s were providing nearly ten times as much aid overall as the Bank, and the Bank could well argue that these other donors could look after programme lending and agriculture. US AID in particular was heavily engaged in training agricultural extension workers and providing finance and technology for agricultural development. The Rockefeller and Ford Foundations were also heavily involved – especially in research.

Now that the Bank seems to be recognised as the leading agency in the development field it has to evolve a broader approach and this it has done. Most of the bilateral donors, especially those without the vast resources of US AID, look to the Bank for both intellectual leadership and practical guidance. Partly to meet these needs and partly because this is the general direction of trends in economic thinking on development, the Bank has broadened its horizons and moved into fields whch it would never previously have considered such as population control, urban planning, tourism and environmental planning. Examples of loans in these fields in the early 1970s are given in the *Annual Report* (1973), pp. 18–23.

The Bank has not simply responded to criticism, though of course that has been part of the explanation, it has contributed to most of these discussions through internal documents and published papers by its staff. The Bank's own research has greatly expanded in recent years in response to the basic questions of how to spread the benefits of development to the poorer sections of the communities, how to assist small farmers in non-irrigated lands and how to use the Bank's loans to influence development to achieve distributional goals and meet 'basic needs'. The titles of some recent Bank or Bank sponsored studies may serve to illustrate the range of focus of Bank research: *Redistribution with Growth*, 'Population, Environment, and National Resources', 'Study of the Substitution of Labor and Equipment in Civil

Construction', 'Iron Deficiency Anemia and the Productivity of Adult Males in Indonesia', 'Potential Distributive Effects of Nationalisation Policies: The Economic Aspects', *Prospects for Partnership: Industrialisation and Trade Policies in the 1970s*.

As to the charge of denying aid to publicly owned industry the Bank in fact made its first such loan in 1967. Out of the twenty-one specific industrial projects financed in 1969–73 only four were privately owned (*Annual Report* (1973), p. 18).

ATTITUDES TO RECIPIENTS' POLICIES AND 'LEVERAGE' OR INFLUENCE

The Bank Group have an overriding interest in the ability of a potential recipient of loans to be able to repay. This leads the Bank into concern with the general financial state of the economy as well as the prospects for the projects being financed. In order to ensure the success of its venture in any nation the Bank invariably attaches conditions to its project loans. These normally are concerned with issues directly affecting the projects; for example, methods of putting out contracts to ensure competitive bidding, control over use of funds to avoid corruption, concern with pricing policies and management methods. However, sometimes these affect general government policy. Many nations subsidise national corporations in power and transport. The Bank has been anxious that this should not distort the allocation of resources. Generally the Bank has wanted these activities to be paid for by the consumer and to be independent of subsidies. Nor has this necessarily been contrary to distributive equity. Transport, telephones and electric power are generally consumed by the relatively well-to-do in most LDCs so that subsidies which keep down charges to consumers tend to redistribute income from the poor to the rich.

However, Bank interest sometimes goes beyond even these, still project related issues, to the very sensitive areas of fiscal and monetary policies, means to control inflation and measures to cure balance-of-payments deficits. Does this constitute unwarranted interference with the internal affairs of LDCs? Clearly it involves infringement of their sovereignty if they are induced to take actions which they would otherwise not have adopted.

This is bound to be a matter of judgement. Normally, the Bank is not opposing a unified government policy in trying to use leverage. The typical case is that there are groups within government who want to adopt the policies recommended. Indeed where this is not the case leverage is very unlikely to succeed. Countries usually have the option of turning down the loan from the Bank and going it alone or with help from other donors.

228

The Bank's influence on its own with the relatively small resources it has to offer will seldom be sufficient to sway the decision where there is strong opposition within the country. Obviously the Bank's influence becomes much greater if other agencies such as the IMF and bilateral donors share its views.

Were the Bank simply being doctrinaire in its imposition of conditions on loans condemnation would be deserved. But if, as seems more likely, it is imposing conditions because these are seen, on the basis of honest, pragmatic study, to be necessary to success for the projects it clearly has some justification. The Bank cannot be expected to make loans which it feels will be misused. In general the aspects of a country's performance which have attracted Bank interest and use of leverage have been closely related to creditworthiness – a very legitimate matter of concern to the Bank.[16] The Bank's diagnosis and remedies advocated may have been incorrect, but that is the penalty of being human, not necessarily evidence of original sin.

THE POWER STRUCTURE IN THE BANK

It has been and still is a legitimate grievance of developing countries that the leadership of the Bank is heavily dominated by Western nations. The Bank has moved some way to meet this in staff appointments. Although the Bank has no national quota system such as have most UN agencies it has been increasing its recruitment of citizens of LDCs and trying to reduce its dependence on American and European staff. One would expect this trend to continue as more well-trained and experienced economists, engineers and administrators become available in LDCs. The danger of attracting too many away from posts in their own countries is, however, very real. It may be met to some extent by taking such staff on contract for a limited number of years with the understanding that they return to their own nations.

At the top level of administration it is unrealistic to envisage the rich countries allowing control over the money they provide to fall into the hands of the debtor nations. As long as the Bank Group is dependent on contributions and loans from the Western nations one can expect these creditor nations to insist on retention of the majority of votes, and key administrative positions in the Bank. Nevertheless, there is scope for increased representation of the developing countries short of their having majority control. It is also anomalous that Russia, China and several other Communist nations should not belong to the Bank Group. If they were to join this could increase the power of the developing countries directly through the accession of the largest developing country, China, and by increasing divisions among the industrial nations. However, to join the IBRD requires also joining the IMF and this they are reluctant to do because that involves annual consultations.

NOTES: CHAPTER 11

1 Edward H. Mason and R. E. Asher, *The World Bank Since Bretton Woods* (Washington, DC: Brookings Institution, 1973), p. 168.
2 R. N. Gardner, *Sterling-Dollar Diplomacy*, 2nd edn (New York: McGraw-Hill, 1969), p. XXXI.
3 W. W. Rostow, *Stages of Economic Growth*, 2nd edn (Cambridge: Cambridge University Press, 1971).
4 A much fuller set of quotations from this article can be found in Teresa Hayter, *Aid as Imperialism* (London: Pelican, 1971), pp. 58–63.
5 Hayter, op. cit., p. 65.
6 Mason and Asher, op. cit., p. 198.
7 There may be situations where raising consumption standards of certain groups will raise their productivity and can be a form of investment, for example, workers whose normal diet is inadequate to sustain a full day's work. Also provision of food of the right kind may avoid damage of a permanent and debilitating type to children, and so is an investment.
8 See Mahbub ul Haq, 'Changing emphasis of the Bank's lending policies', *Finance and Development* (June 1978), pp. 12–14.
9 OECD, *Annual Review* (Paris: OECD, 1978), Annex Table C.3.A.
10 Mason and Asher, op. cit., p. 352.
11 IFC, *General Policies* (1971), p. 81.
12 Mason and Asher, op. cit., p. 536.
13 OECD, *1978 Review, Development Co-operation* (Paris: OECD, 1978), Table VI.I.
14 Mason and Asher, op. cit., p. 338.
15 Both the IBRD and IDA are permitted by their articles to make programme loans, but in the period 1974–78 less than 5 per cent of Bank resources actually went to programme loans. Generally the Bank has felt IMF financing was more appropriate. See Gerald M. Alter, 'World Bank goals in project lending', *Finance and Development* (June 1978), pp. 23–5.
16 Mason and Asher, op. cit., p. 456.

CHAPTER 12

Changing Needs and New Roles

THE ECONOMIC PROBLEMS OF THE 1980s

Growth has slowed, inflation is high and economic disparities within and between nations remain large and are increasing. There are risks of recurrent famines in poor nations, international trade is sluggish and payments imbalances are huge. These are the economic characteristics of the early 1980s. They contrast with the unprecedented, rapid and relatively stable expansion of trade throughout the 1950s and 1960s up to 1973. These two decades, after Bretton Woods, established the main international economic institutions, saw outstanding growth and prosperity, not only among the industrial nations but also in many of the nations of the Third World. It is true that income disparities increased and that the standard of living of the bottom 40 per cent of the populations in LDCs may have improved little. In some cases it even deteriorated, but for most people in rich and poor countries there appeared to be steady and fairly rapid progress.[1] This was brought to an end by the 1973 oil crisis and by the inflationary effects of workers' expectations of continually rising real wages in the face of a situation which required that the energy importing countries accept a fall in relative living standards as the terms of trade shifted drastically against them.

Governments' attempts to control inflation and correct balance-of-payments deficits by restricting domestic demand have produced the worldwide recessions and high unemployment rates which plague us today. Continuing inflation inhibits governments from adopting Keynesian policies to reduce unemployment. Continuing unemployment increases trade union resistance to technological change and to job-displacing imports from the newly industrialising countries. Pressures from unions and employers in threatened industries; textiles, clothing, shoes and leather goods, shipbuilding, steel, electrical consumer goods, paper and paper products lead governments to take protectionist measures of one sort or another.[2] These in turn slow structural adjustment and growth in both rich and poor countries. While temporarily preserving jobs in those threatened industries in the developed nations such protectionist actions increase unemployment in the LDCs, cut their foreign exchange earnings, their ability to pay for imports and so feed back into unemployment in OECD nations' export industries. Saving jobs in senile industries denies other opportunities of more productive work in more skill-intensive export industries.

OBJECTIVES FOR THE 1980s

Most governments and most people seem to want to return to high rates of growth and higher levels of employment with with low rates of inflation. Few seem particularly worried that higher growth could lead to exhaustion of non-renewable natural resources or to excessive pollution and environmental disasters. Implicitly it is assumed that recent fears of these kind were exaggerated and that a combination of market forces, government intervention and advancing technology can overcome the technical problems if only we can sort out the political and economic obstacles to economic progress. Nevertheless, the debate in the 1970s on conflicts between growth, the availability of resources in the future and the preservation of a pleasant environment have made governments and people more conscious of the risks that certain developments carry unacceptable costs in terms of pollution and other hazards to health and amenities. There also remain worries over natural or politically induced scarcities of specific minerals and foods.

Most societies seem to want higher incomes and less unemployment. Constraints upon their achievement of the objectives are seen in the industrially developed nations as mainly inflation and balance-of-payments difficulties. While in the poorer nations lack of resources, especially foreign exchange, is generally highlighted and many of them argue that the existing international economic order discriminates against them. For the oil surplus countries the problems are seen as a need for safe outlets for the investment of their surplus revenues and of maintenance of the real value of their assets and the purchasing power over imports of their oil revenues. These egocentric views of the problems and constraints lead to exaggeration of conflicts of interests. Some conflict is inevitable, but there are also important mutual interests, worthy of emphasis, which could permit joint action for progress for all. All nations would gain from expanded world trade and such an expansion would be achieved by reforms in both the rules governing the commercial policies of nations through the GATT and the flows of credit and finance through international financial arrangements.

One major political and economic problem is to find ways in which the surpluses of the oil-exporting nations can be recycled to help the net oil-importing LDCs to pay for the imports of capital goods and technology needed for their development. This calls for action within the IMF and the World Bank to create financial assets which would be attractive to the OPEC nations and attract funds which could be lent to LDCs.

Another major problem is to enable LDCs to increase their exports to developed countries so as to earn more foreign exchange to be spent on imports from the industrial nations. This involves pushing back the growth of protectionism and promoting structural adjustment in industrial countries, so that their resources move out of unskilled labour-intensive manufacturing into the skill-intensive manufactures in which their comparative advantages lie. These tasks fall within the brief of the GATT.

Success in both these areas would bring great gains in terms of raising employment and growth worldwide, raising income and employment in LDCs, particularly. Although such policies could stimulate inflation they will also provide some counter-inflationary pressures in the industrial countries by reducing prices of many consumer goods. Institutional reform could never be a sufficient condition for the attainment of these goals but it may well be a necessary one.

Unfortunately, while economists and groups of experts such as the Brandt Commission do stress these mutual interests of the nations it would be naive to suppose that either governments or the workers and businessmen in threatened industries in the OECD will be willing to recognise and act upon such motives. The gains from liberal trading policies are always diffuse and the gainers – consumers and exporters – can seldom notice the benefits or attribute them to trade liberalisation. But the costs of adjustment bear heavily upon the few in the industries which have to shrink. Moreover, the costs come fairly quickly while the full benefits from freer trade take time to accrue. Democratic governments with elections to be faced at fairly brief intervals tend to have limited horizons and implicitly discount heavily long-run gains. The lobbies on agriculture and vulnerable industries tend to be well organised, vocal and often concentrated in marginal constituencies. These factors make it very difficult for individual governments to follow enlightened trade policies despite the considerable weight of evidence that reducing barriers to imports would probably increase net employment in the OECD nations, raise consumer incomes, stimulate growth and reduce cost-push inflation.[3]

If developing countries place more stress on raising their absolute standards of living than on reducing the income gap between rich and poor countries, they have a strong interest in the restoration of high growth in the industrial countries. Although trade among LDCs is now large, 22 per cent of total exports in 1976, and grew faster than exports to DCs in the early 1970s, the industrial nations will remain their major markets for the next decade. Faster growth in the OECD nations would expand these markets directly, but would also ease their problems of structural adjustment. It is much easier for the governments in the industrial nations to cease propping up senile industries if the demand for labour is generally buoyant as newer industries expand. This would reduce the pressure for protectionism.

But it is also true that reduced protection would itself stimulate growth. It would raise incomes of LDC exporters, and hence their demands for OECD products, by encouraging structural adjustment so that industries moved to their most efficient locations and labour in the OECD nations shifted from low productivity labour-intensive to the skill- and capital-intensive industries in which these countries' comparative advantage lies.

Developing countries could directly reduce the pressures for protectionism by offering to cut their own barriers to imports. As both the OECD and the Brookings studies have clearly shown, the level of effective protection in most developing countries is absurdly high and inflicts significant damage upon their own current living standards and their prospects for growth in exports, income and employment.[4] Their export industries are generally either agricultural or labour-intensive manufactured products. But their import substituting industries are generally relatively capital intensive. As a result their systems of protection not only encourage inefficiency but also raise the incomes of the relatively better-off sections of their communities at the expense of the poor and provide corrupt politicians and bureaucrats with illicit fortunes.

Reduced levels of protection in LDCs would also encourage trade among developing countries. Most organised attempts to do this up to now have been through attempts at regional groupings, but these attempts have to date with few exceptions been attended with little success. General liberalisation could do much more.[5]

The decisions involved are all entirely in the hands of national governments in both rich and poor countries, but there are various ways in which reform of the rules of international institutions, especially in the IMF and the GATT, could help to discourage the growth of protectionism and foster both the growth and efficiency of trade.

MONETARY REFORM IN THE 1980s

In choosing to consider prospective developments in the global economy from the points of view identified above, recognition is being given to the diffusion of economic power which has taken place since the foundations of the postwar order were laid. The developing nations, the oil producers and the industrial nations each have some interest in reforming that order but preferences and priorities vary.

Within the OECD nations the shift of influence away from the USA, chronicled in Chapter 3, further complicates the picture.

This context is particularly crucial when consideration is given to the prospects for international monetary reform. Thus, Chapter 3 suggested that world trade would be enhanced by (1) greater stability (or predictability) in foreign exchange markets and (2) the recognition that, especially for LDCs, the process of 'adjustment' should be seen in a growth context. Relevant to the former, considerable discussion has taken place on the merits of a Substitution Account within the IMF and it is generally believed that agreement on such a scheme is politically feasible. More recently, and relevant to the second issue above, the Brandt Commission has advocated a new multilateral institution specialising in concessional, 'programme' lending.

These, of course, are substantial matters upon which to reach international agreement, particularly given the development of diffused influence in the economic sphere discussed above. It must be asked, therefore, if sufficient common ground exists for significant monetary reform to be possible. For example, the proposed Substitution Account within the IMF, while it has enjoyed varying degrees of support within OECD and OPEC circles, has been fairly consistently opposed by the LDCs. Similarly, novel schemes for channelling funds to LDCs have met with a mixed reception in the OECD nations, as, for instance, with the SDR – Aid 'link', at the same time as LDC demands for a 'new international economic order' have been growing.

In presenting the 'line-up' in this way it is recognised that there is no reason in principle for the Substitution Account to be linked to the question of concessional finance. However, the varying interests to which we have referred could imply that such a linkage of issues would facilitate progress in both directions.

Support for the Substitution Account arises, in part, from the fear that disenchantment with the US dollar as a reserve asset is hastening the emergence of a multi-reserve system. As more trade comes to be denominated, for instance, in marks or yen, reserve demands for these increase, raising the possibility of destabilising speculation between the major currencies. Such arguments have concerned some elements of the US administration and there has been both German and Japanese anxiety at the emergence of those countries as reserve currency centres.

The second source of support for the Substitution Account has come from the oil producing nations and, in particular, from Saudi Arabia. Concern here is with the security of foreign currency denominated assets both from the point of view of real return, where exchange rate risk is important, and in the sense of possible seizure, as in the case of Iranian assets in the USA.

Concern over the Substitution Account in LDCs can best be

understood by looking at the proposed operation of the account. It will be remembered from Chapter 3 that the aim is to permit countries holding reserves of national currencies (especially US dollars) to exchange a quantity of them for SDR denominated assets on a voluntary basis. The fundamental problem here is the current and capital account solvency of the scheme. If the account were ever to be terminated, any depreciation of dollar assets against SDR liabilities would either have to be made good by the account (if its assets had remained denominated in dollar terms) or by the USA (if that country's liabilities held by the account were denominated in SDRs).

Similarly, in current account terms, how would the interest payable on the account's assets relate to that paid on its SDR liabilities? Again, either the account or the reserve centre (the USA) would have to ensure that any decline in the SDR/dollar rate did not affect the return to the ultimate holder.

Understandably, the USA has been wary of offering guarantees far more general in scope than under the various bilateral arrangements (e.g. 'swap' facilities) negotiated in the past. If the USA is not to cover the exchange risks implied it would probably be necessary to 'back' the account with the remaining gold reserve in the possession of the IMF. This would seem contrary to the interests of LDCs as beneficiaries, through the Trust Fund, of any further IMF gold sales. Additionally, some LDCs, notably India during the Committee of Twenty proceedings, objected that a Substitution Account might reduce the pressure (or the inclination) to make further straightforward issues of SDRs.[6] As LDCs would benefit from such issues, especially if a 'link' were to be introduced, their interests would be further jeopardised.

With such conflicts of interest on reform issues, therefore, it seems reasonable to suppose that a *package* of measures, offering something to each of our three categories of country, would stand the best chance of success. It would be appropriate if the package contributed towards resolution of the 'reserves' and 'adjustment' issues to which reference has been made.

The following, therefore, represents a tentative sketch of how such a package might be formulated. The approach reflects the observation made in Chapter 3 that the IMF has evolved, in certain respects (notably with the creation of the SDR and the oil facilities), towards the type of institution envisaged in the Keynes Plan. The fundamental idea behind that plan rested on a domestic banking analogy. Countries in surplus within an international Clearing Union would accumulate 'bancor' balances which would be exactly matched by the deficit balances of the remaining member countries. These 'overdrafts' in the union would thereby receive *automatic* financing and, as Keynes recognised, the beauty of the scheme was that the 'credit' would be both impersonal and costless to the lender. This lack of cost needs to be explained. In Keynes' view, surplus countries were, voluntarily, holding idle funds and would therefore not object if these were used to finance the payments deficits of other members of the union. As with the domestic banking analogue they could 'spend' their idle funds at any time, the 'burden' of finance being passed on to the next country running a surplus. *There could be no threat of illiquidity for the union, and the time period over which each country could run its 'overdraft' need not be constrained by the fear of withdrawal of finance.*

While it would be desirable to capture this feature in a proposed reform there are two difficulties in terms of the issues we have been discussing. First, the world has not standardised its reserve assets and, probably more than Keynes could have predicted, international capital markets and central bank participation in them, have afforded an unprecedented degree of choice over reserve portfolio composition. Hence an institution based on a new reserve asset could still face illiquidity if surplus accounts were withdrawn in favour of some other asset. The principles of financial intermediation would therefore require that the liabilities of this new institution (the reserve asset) would have to carry a competitive return in comparison with the readily available alternatives.

The second difficulty arises from this last observation. If the institution must pay a competitive rate of return to holders of its liabilities, the scope for *concessional* 'overdrafts' to LDCs would depend on the availability of a source of interest subsidy. It should be noted, however, that if the new reserve asset were willingly held, and the institution's liquidity therefore not threatened, the advantage of being able to provide long-term finance to borrowing countries would remain and this could be useful in the context of debt rescheduling. The *service burden*, however, would still depend on the degree of interest subsidy available.

Indeed it is the need for *concessional* finance to which attention has recently been drawn by the Brandt Commission which purports to identify a financing gap: 'a bridge between long term project financing available from such institutions as the World Bank and the short term adjustment finance available from the IMF'.[7] Their preference in filling this gap is for long-term *programme* (balance-of-payments support) lending on a concessional basis. This concessional element is important in alleviating the debt service burdens that LDCs currently face.

Of interest from our present point of view, therefore, is the Commission's review of a number of novel sources of concessional finance, including sale of the remaining IMF gold stocks and a small levy on world trade. While one critic has suggested that a superior development tax could be based on world sales of consumer durables,[8] the trade tax has one advantage that will be made clear shortly. The Brandt Commission suggest that a 0.5 per cent trade levy would realise approximately $7 billion annually. For comparison, sale of the gold stocks and investment of the proceeds could yield an annual $2.4–3.2 billion. Revenues from these sources would be channelled through a new institution providing a source of concessional programme funds.

Could such sources of concessional finance be utilised in the 'Keynesian' arrangement we have been discussing? The question here is whether, instead of channelling these funds directly to developing countries in need, more objectives might not be met by using the funds to subsidise the rate of interest charged on 'overdrafts' in our proposed scheme. There is reason to believe that political agreement would be facilitated by this approach because advantages could be offered to each of the three groups of international 'actors' we have identified.

The scheme would operate as follows. Consistent with Keynes' original idea, the Substitution Account could offer special SDR denominated, 'Development Bonds' in exchange for an equal value of national currency reserves, and these bonds would serve as a substitute reserve asset. As the bonds (unlike 'bancor') would not be the predominant reserve asset it would be crucial that they be very attractive to hold. Thus, while not 'redeemable' directly for dollars from the account they could be freely used in intra-central bank transactions whether for portfolio or settlement purposes. They would offer an SDR denominated interest rate set at, or above, a basket of world market rates. In this way they would carry an indexation element against inflation (the SDR base) and the setting of their nominal interest rate would ensure no long-term loss in comparison with other available assets. Such attractive conditions should mean that any holder need not fear for the acceptability of the asset in international settlement, and, as a consequence, the account would not face illiquidity despite the 'liquid' nature of its liabilities.

While it is crucial to maintain the attractiveness of this asset it may be possible to engineer a reduction in the interest rate which would guarantee this by making acceptance of the bond in settlement of payments deficits mandatory, with countries being designated to receive specified quantities of the bonds as has been the case with the standard SDR. Thought could also be given to making the bond an instrument that could be bought and sold freely in world capital markets, increasing its liquidity yet further. A possible objection to this, however, would be that it would facilitate speculation against the dollar. Thus, during periods of incipient dollar weakness countries could buy the SDR denominated asset, wait for the dollar/SDR rate to decline and make a capital gain. The prospect of adverse speculation against the dollar has, in fact, been one of the main US concerns in the

Substitution Account debate.[9] The problem would be particularly acute if SDR denominated assets were to be continuously available from the account allowing purchase at the discretion of dollar holders. Such an arrangement combined with capital market quotation could have severe implications. Accordingly, the present scheme envisages a discrete issue of Development Bonds followed only after a period of years by a further issue.

Thus, following the issue, the account would receive a quantity of (largely) dollar denominated assets, and the intention would be that these funds should be transferred over, say, four years to LDCs for agreed purposes, notably programme lending and/or debt adjustment. The degree of concessionality provided for in these loans would depend on the total of 'automatic revenues' which could be negotiated to underwrite the system. This would indeed be the limit to the magnitude of substitution that the account could undertake. In the process of maintaining a worthwhile concessional element the revenues would have to finance a return to the bond holders that ensured the 'marketability' of their asset.

None the less, the sums involved could be quite large. If for instance the gold sale and a small levy on trade could realise $9 billion in annual income for the account, this could finance a 20 per cent return on $45 billion of transferred dollar reserves. This represents a significant fraction of total outstanding official currency reserves (roughly $300 billion). There are a number of advantages to this scheme which we can list in terms of the three groups of interests we have discussed.

First, the LDCs would receive a large quantity of concessional finance which, while not grants, would be attractive in terms of interest and duration. Indeed, the amounts would qualify as 'massive transfers' and would certainly be available in the case of acute debt service crisis feared by some commentators. Programme lending under a modified-charter World Bank would be the other main use.

Secondly, the OPEC countries would have at their disposal a secure, multilaterally controlled reserve asset which had inflation protection, and presumably portfolio diversification must be assisted to this degree. 'Solidarity' with LDCs would also be demonstrated.

Finally, for the OECD countries, two benefits should be highlighted. The first is that the beginnings would have been made in removing some of the 'overhang' of dollars; a source of 'nervousness' in foreign exchange markets. This would be achieved while at the same time *not* requiring the USA to offer exchange rate guarantees to all SDR holders against the eventuality of dollar depreciation. The subsidy element discussed above would be used to cover the difference between LDC concessional interest payments and the SDR denominated interest rate required by the bond holders. Indeed, the USA would only start to amortise its liabilities to the account when repayments of principal by LDCs began to be received by the account. Thus, in the initial years of the scheme world reserves would *rise* by the cumulative total of the transfers, but as *asset settlement* took place a similar quantity of dollars in the system would gradually be replaced by the SDR bonds.

The second advantage for the OECD countries concerns the 'cost' of the scheme as embodied in the trade levy. As we have just noted, the net effect of the scheme would be a *temporary* increase in world reserves and some significant expansionary influence on world trade could be expected as the funds were expended.

The ramifications would be twofold. First it would increase the 'automatic revenues' going to the account, opening the possibility of a further substitution exercise. Secondly, through the muliplier operating in the OECD countries resources could be generated that would easily outweigh the cost of the levy. The bigger the scheme, and the faster the transfers could be made, the greater would this effect be.

This instance of mutual gain resulting from resource transfers to the 'South' has been recently popularised by the Brandt Commission, but the logic has been questioned in other quarters.[10] It is objected that if the OECD nations wish to expand their economies they can do so directly, in concert, and achieve the same effect. Apart from moral and humanitarian reasons for favouring further resource transfers to LDCs, additional points can be made in favour of the arrangements discussed above. A major banking dislocation associated with LDC debt default could have serious implications for world trade. It would be highly desirable to have alternative financing available to avoid this risk. Additionally, the present climate of opinion in the OECD nations is against expanding budget deficits for the sake of achieving fuller employment. One reason for this concerns political fears over inflation (especially in West Germany) which may well be exaggerated. The 'back door' method of expansion through exports may be a more acceptable device.

Moreover, and perhaps of greater importance, most OECD nations now seem to believe that their (oil induced) current account deficits are in need of 'correction' given long-term savings-investment goals.[11] Notably, for instance, West Germany and Japan are experiencing atypical deficits either on current account or on the overall balance of payments, respectively, for which 'current account' solutions are sought.

Given the views outlined it is unlikely that an explicit, concerted programme of expansion would be acceptable due to the tendency for the oil deficit to increase. The scheme suggested above has the advantage that OECD expansion is *incidental* to a world monetary reform desirable on its own terms (as are resource transfers to the poor).

A more concrete advantage is that although OPEC surpluses would increase, the concomitant crises in world currency markets, as safe assets are sought, would be directly ameliorated, improving the climate for expansion in the OECD. In so far, finally, as the transfer permitted the LDCs to persist in their payments deficits the strain on OECD accounts would be further eased.

REFORM OF THE GATT

The Tokyo Round left several issues unsettled. Among these were issues of great importance to the maintenance of free and non-discriminatory trade: the need to reform emergency safeguard measures; the need to either outlaw voluntary export restrictions (VERs) and orderly marketing arrangements (OMAs) or to bring them formally into the GATT both with accompanying measures to ensure that they become subject to multilateral surveillance; the need to improve methods of ensuring compliance with the GATT rules and to improve procedures for settling disputes between members; the need to gradually dismantle or liberalise the Multi-Fibre Arrangement which has severely restricted LDC exports of textiles and clothing to developed country markets and generally to reduce the tendency for countries to seek to 'organise', that is, restrict trade; and finally the need to bring trade in agricultural products more in line with GATT principles of non-discrimination and freedom from non-tariff barriers.

SAFEGUARDS

It is clearly reasonable and humane that countries should be able to slow the rate of growth of imports to give respite to a hard-pressed industry. It takes time to shift workers, some of whom may require retraining, to alternative jobs. But countries must be prevented from making use of emergency safeguards (Article XIX of the GATT, VERs and OMAs) to restrict imports indefinitely. It is desirable that any restrictions should be non-discriminatory, for reasons argued in Chapter 4, and temporary. To facilitate this it is best that the restrictions be imposed openly, be degressive over time and subject to multilateral surveillance. They should also be linked to policies of 'positive adjustment' in the affected industries. Help to the industry involved should not be designed to bolster it up but to aid the movement of factors of production out of the sectors which can no longer compete with imports and into activities where they can be used more efficiently. If governments can be persuaded to agree to accept an Article XIX reformed in this way they would be in a stronger position to resist pressures from special interests for increased protection.[12]

Such a reformed Article XIX should gain the support of Japan and the NICs for they are the countries which have suffered most from the discriminatory applications of VERs and OMAs in the recent past. Developing countries in general should welcome such reform. Already more than thirty LDCs are significant exporters of manufactures and they will be joined by many more as long as a liberal trading regime can be maintained. It would increase their respect for the GATT and their willingness to support and adhere to it, which is very much in their interests so to do. Large powerful countries have much less need of a rule of law than have small, economically weak ones.

The evidence of the studies of the effects on employment in specific industries of imports from LDCs shows that in most cases the amounts from LDCs are in general too small a proportion of internal consumption for even quite rapid increases to displace many workers.[13] Often natural wastage through retirement and normal labour turnover will easily take care of the problem. But where this is not so, for example, in textiles, clothing and leathergoods, where centrally planned economies' exports to OECD nations have also been rising rapidly, positive adjustment policies and measures to alleviate hardship to workers are necessary both on humanitarian grounds and to reduce resistance to trade liberation.

The evidence suggests that, to date, few of the official adjustment schemes in operation in the OECD nations have been effective in speeding the movement of import-displaced workers into new jobs. Mostly, they have been aimed at compensating workers for job losses by unemployment benefits and redundancy payments. Retraining schemes have also figured, but unfortunately have not been very successful in placing workers in new jobs relevant to their acquired skills.[14] US labour unions have been particularly critical of US policies. Adjustment assistance has been derisively labelled by them – 'burial assistance'.

In an earlier study one of the present authors made a number of suggestions for improving adjustment assistance. The following section reproduces these (with permission of the British – North American Committee).

TYPES OF ASSISTANCE

TO WORKERS

Workers made redundant most of all need income support. In most

OECD nations unemployment insurance benefit and redundancy payments may already be adequate but to make adjustment more acceptable it is probably advisable to pay additional compensation to workers where import competition has been a factor in their loss of employment. Older workers who may be confronted with greater difficulties in finding alternative employment and suffer more shock from sudden redundancy are a special case for additional cash grants.

Secondly, they need opportunities to learn new skills. This need not be through formal training programmes though those may also be valuable. Grants enabling workers to finance their own retraining may work as well. Such survey evidence as there is does not show very high returns from government training programmes. They may be too inflexible or trainees may merely take jobs from others.[15] Relocation costs could also be met from adjustment assistance if other sources do not provide this.

TO FIRMS

The objective is to encourage enterprises which have long-term viability and to help firms to move out of activities which are already, or soon will be, uneconomic. This does not always mean moving out of the industry. A great deal of the growth in trade nowadays is intra-industry rather than inter-industry. This is partly because industry labels are rather broad and encompass within them many very different activities. Product differentiation, economies of scale, fashion and variety in the available production technologies, among other factors, make it quite common for countries to export and import rather similar goods at the same time.

Where firms are non-viable the need is to eliminate them from the industry as painlessly as possible. The generally accepted method is to subsidise the scraping of plant.

Re-equipment is a more difficult issue. Where firms can be viable with a little help, equipment grants or loans can be justified, for even good firms may find it difficult to attract capital in a declining industry which has a 'bad name'. But it is difficult to discriminate in advance between those firms which have a good future and those which have not. There is a risk that the wrong ones will gain resources and that the adjustment problem is merely prolonged. There are always arguments ready to hand which can be used to gain government aid to prop up sections of industries which should have been encouraged to adjust. Examples from shipbuilding, steel, motorcycles and automobiles in the UK are not hard to find.

One can try to safeguard against this by ensuring objective scrutiny by an independent body. Caroline Miles recommends an investment bank type of institution for this purpose.[16]

SOME POLICY SUGGESTIONS

There is a need to develop an early warning system so that industries at risk can be identified and measures set afoot so that costs of adjustment can be minimised and protectionist forces do not have time to build up.

Adjustment policies should be linked to safeguard procedures. When a country seeks permission to use emergency restrictions it should be required to show that it is taking action to promote structural adjustment.

Adjustment assistance with respect to imports cannot be considered in isolation from the whole complex of general, regional, sectoral and social policies. They have to be harmonised lest they work against adjustment.

There may be a need in some cases to set up special government agencies to carry out the policies. Government departments each have their own axes to grind and may be too close to the short-term whims of their political masters. Semi-autonomous bodies could take a broader and longer view of the nations' interests in structural adjustment without the same pressure from politicians with import-sensitive constituencies. However, the issues are probably too politically sensitive for governments ever to let them out of their direct control.[17]

In a more recent contribution to this debate George R. Neumann of Chicago University has argued for a wage-subsidy programme combined with regular unemployment insurance benefits as an alternative approach. The argument is that if subsidies are given to firms that take on workers who have a card certifying that they had lost their jobs as a result of imports the number of jobs open to the workers would be increased, leading to shorter duration of unemployment and higher expected earnings upon re-employment. A substantial advantage of this, as compared with the mere income-maintenance programmes of the past, is that it provides direct incentives for job creation and should help to compensate workers for the loss of 'job-specific skill earnings' when they accept jobs in different activities.[18]

The developing countries, through UNCTAD and the GATT, should press for research and action on improving trade adjustment assistance and the linking of such action to the use of emergency safeguard restrictions of imports by OECD nations.

PROCEDURES FOR SETTLING DISPUTES AND ENSURING COMPLIANCE WITH GATT RULES

Another area in which reform of GATT rules and procedures could contribute to the maintenance of liberal trading regimes is in the methods of ensuring compliance with GATT rules and settling disputes between members. It may be said that what really matters here is the willingness of governments to adhere to rules and listen to behests which curtail their freedom of action, rather than the details of procedures. But as both Jan Tumlir and Robert Baldwin have recently argued, 'Rules and procedures help fend off some of the short-run pressures that obviously are not in a country's long-run interest and also act as a means to co-ordinate the conflicting objectives of various groups.'[19] Baldwin's main recommendation for change here is to require that the GATT panels, which issue 'non-binding' decisions on whether a violation has occurred and recommend appropriate actions, should no longer be made up from officials of government delegations, but instead should consist of independent experts who have no axes to grind or conflicts of interest to interfere with their objectivity. He also suggests that the GATT secretariat should themselves be permitted to monitor compliance with the codes and to initiate panel investigations when they believe that powerful countries may have exerted pressure on weaker ones to refrain from complaining about violations. He believes that this would increase the credibility of the GATT and help to 'correct the growing tendency of government leaders to thwart trade liberalisation by colluding among themselves to introduce trade distorting measures'.[20]

THE MULTI-FIBRE ARRANGEMENT

This, is the most important 'orderly marketing arrangement' (OMA) affecting the largest quantity of exports from developing countries. It imposes quantitative restrictions on trade and discriminates between suppliers in violation of the basic principles of the GATT. It came into being in its original form of the Long-Term Arrangement on Cotton Textiles (1962) as an attempt to deal with the effects of a surge in exports from Japan. It was intended to be temporary, to allow imports to expand and in no way to be accepted as a precedent. Observers saw it as at least an improvement over the chaotic *ad hoc* restrictions being imposed by individual nations. It was intended to be fairly liberal. Over time, in its successive forms, it has become more restrictive and now covers wool and man-made fibres. As a result the overall growth of exports of such textiles from LDCs has fallen significantly. Moreover the MFA is being quoted as a model for further OMAs to cover such products as steel. This trend would be most dangerous to the growth of world trade and would particularly threaten the NICs and other potential NICs whose bargaining power is low.

Textiles and clothing represent the archetypal labour-intensive product for the earlier stages of industrialisation in developing countries. To stultify the early growth of such exports is to inhibit economic development very seriously for many poor and densely populated countries. It is crucial that the members of the GATT think deeply about these issues once more when the MFA comes up for renegotiation in 1981.

AGRICULTURAL PROTECTION

The GATT has almost totally failed to apply to agricultural trade the basic principles for which it stands. Most trade in agriculture is controlled by non-tariff barriers and in a most discriminatory manner. Subsidies to domestic farming in Western Europe not only prevent imports but result in significant dumping of several products, most importantly sugar, in world markets. A recent study by the UN Food and Agriculture Organisation (FAO) in 1979 has estimated that a 50 per cent cut in the developed countries' protection on food and animal feed commodities would yield a $3 billion increase in total foreign exchange earnings on exports from fifty-seven of the more populous developing countries.[21] The effects upon the exports of the developed country exporters of grains, meat, wool and dairy products are even greater. As a result the consumers and tax payers in the OECD countries suffer in paying high prices and taxes to pay for subsidies to domestic agricultural producers. Income is transferred from poor consumers, who tend to spend a large proportion of their income upon food, to relatively rich farmers. These charges are particularly valid for the Common Agricultural Policy of the EEC.

Further and more determined efforts are required in the GATT to liberalise agricultural trade. But how to do it in the face of the entrenched agricultural lobbies in Europe, Japan and the USA is a question of extreme complexity. Practically all experts acknowledge the total irrationality of the CAP. The few defences mounted are very weak in that their claimed objectives could usually be obtained in much less costly ways.[22] Despite its indefensibility on economic welfare grounds the political reality appears to be that a frontal attack on the CAP and other agricultural protection in developed countries is unlikely to achieve success. All that can be hoped for is that the increasing budgetary costs upon countries like Germany and Britain, together with the absurdities of frequent surpluses of commodities subject to domestic price supports, will gradually undermine the EEC's commitment to this costly and inefficient system of agricultural protection. Then joint pressure from both developed and developing country exporters of agricultural products may obtain some reductions in the levels of protection given by the CAP. Governments in the EEC should also recognise that easier entry for food products would play a useful role in lowering food prices and dampening inflation. The spotlight of international opinion should be focused upon the damage inflicted upon LDCs by agricultural protectionism, and pressure should be kept up within the GATT for reform of the CAP and other agricultural protection in developed countries.

OTHER ISSUES

There are many other issues in the economic relations between nations which could be the subject of proposals for action within the existing institutions: trade relations between the market economies and the centrally planned economies; the issues of subsidies and countervailing; the future of aid; the relations between nations and the multinational corporations between whose branches so much of world trade now takes place; the issues of transfer of technology between nations; stabilisation of primary commodity prices and developing countries' export earnings. All of these are important, but in our view the dominating issues of the next few years are going to be the macroeconomic problem of restoring growth and lowering unemployment together with the micro problems of increasing efficiency and dynamism through altering the structure of trade in line with the current and prospective comparative advantage of nations. For that reason we have chosen to concentrate in this last chapter on these crucial issues.

NOTES: CHAPTER 12

1 See David Morawetz, *Twenty-Five Years of Economic Development 1950–1975* (Baltimore, Md.: Johns Hopkins University Press, 1979).

2 Robert Baldwin, *Beyond the Tokyo Round Negotiations*, Thames Essay, No. 22 (London: Trade Policy Research Centre, 1979), pp. 5–11. See also *The Times*, 5 September 1980, report of TUC debate on import penetration of paper and board products and their effects on unemployment.

3 See Bela Balassa, 'The new protectionism: an evaluation and proposals for reform', in R. C. Amacher, G. Haberler and T. D. Willett (eds), *Challenges to a Liberal International Economic Order* (American Enterprise Institute, Washington, D.C., 1979), and *The World Economic Crisis: Report of a Group of Experts* (London: Commonwealth Secretariat, 1980), pp. 34–8 and references cited therein. See also Robert E. Baldwin, 'Protectionist pressures in the United States', in Amacher *et al.*, op. cit., pp. 226–7.

4 I. M. D. Little, T. Scitovsky and M. F. Scott, *Industry and Trade in Some Developing Countries* (London: Oxford University Press, 1970); Anne Kreuger, *Liberalization Attempts and Consequences* (New York: National Bureau of Economic Research, 1978).

5   See Ian Little, 'The developing countries and the international order', in Amacher *et al.*, op. cit., p. 272.

6   J. Williamson, *The Failure of World Monetary Reform, 1971–74* (London: Nelson, 1977), p. 152.

7   Independent Commission of International Development Issues (Under the Chairmanship of Willy Brandt), *North-South: A Programme for Survival* (London: Pan, 1980), p. 234.

8   P. D. Henderson, 'Survival, development and the report of the Brandt Commission', *The World Economy*, vol. 3, no. 1 (June 1980), p. 111.

9   Williamson, op. cit., pp. 152–4.

10 Henderson, op. cit., p. 100.

11 J. Salop and E. Spitaller, 'Why does the current account matter?', *IMF Staff Papers*, vol. 27, no. 1 (March 1980), Section II. (Of OECD authorities) 'Their concern seems to reflect the view that adjustment is in order now; and that employment must be sacrificed to attain the desired improvement in the current account', (pp. 131–2).

12 For fuller expositions of the safeguards and adjustment issues see David Robertson, *Fail Safe Systems for Trade Liberalisation*, Thames Essay, No. 12 (London: Trade Policy Research Centre, 1977); A. I. MacBean, *A Positive Approach to the International Economic Order: Part I Trade and Structural Adjustment* (London: British–North American Committee, 1978), pp. 33–43; OECD Development Centre, *Adjustment for Trade: Studies in Industrial Adjustment Problems* (Paris: OECD 1975).

13 See MacBean, op. cit., pp. 34–6.

14 MacBean, op. cit., pp. 38–9 and OECD and UNCTAD studies referred to therein.

15 Goran Ohlin, 'Adjustment assistance in Sweden', in OECD Development Centre, op. cit., p. 208.

16 Caroline Miles, 'Introduction' to the OECD Development Centre, op. cit., makes this and a number of the other points included in this section.

17 The section 'Types of Assistance' and 'Some Policy Suggestions' are reproduced with permission of the British–North American Committee, from MacBean, op. cit., pp. 41–3.

18 G. R. Neumann, 'Assistance for trade. Displaced workers', in David B. H. Denoon (ed) *The New International Economic Order: A US Response* (London: Macmillan, 1980), pp. 125–32.

19 Robert Baldwin, *Beyond the Tokyo Round Negotiations*, Thames Essay, No. 22 (London: Trade Policy Research Centre, 1979), p. 18. See also Jan Tumlir, 'Can the international economic order be saved?', *The World Economy* (October 1977), p. 18.

20 ibid., pp. 19–20.

21 Quoted in Amacher *et al.*, op. cit., p. 43.

22 See D. Gale Johnson, *World Agriculture in Disarray* (London: Macmillan for the Trade Policy Research Centre, 1973).

BIBLIOGRAPHY

GENERAL

Bhagwati, Jagdish (ed), *International Trade: Selected Readings* (London, Penguin, 1969).

Cooper, R. N., *The Economics of Interdependence* (New York: McGraw-Hill, 1968).

Corden, W. M., *The Theory of Protection* (London: Oxford University Press, 1971).

Corden, W. M., *Trade Policy and Economic Welfare* (London: Oxford University Press, 1974).

Curzon, Gerard and Victoria, *Hidden Barriers to International Trade* (London: Trade Policy Research Centre, 1971).

de V. Graaf, J., *Theoretical Welfare Economics* (Cambridge: Cambridge University Press, 1957).

Kindleberger, C. P., and Lindert, P. H., *International Economics*, 6th edn (Homewood, Ill.: Irwin, 1978).

Little, I. M. D., *A Critique of Welfare Economics*, 2nd edn (London: Oxford University Press, 1957).

Little, I., Scitovsky, T., and Scott, M., *Industry and Trade In Some Developing Countries: A Comparative Study* (London: Oxford University Press, 1970).

INSTITUTIONS

Gardner, Richard N., *Sterling–Dollar Diplomacy*, 2nd edn (London: McGraw-Hill, 1969).

Harrod, R. F., *The Life of John Maynard Keynes* (London: Macmillan, 1966).

His Majesty's Government, *Proposal for an International Clearing Union*, Cmnd 6437 (London: HMSO, 1943).

IBRD, *World Bank Operations: Sectoral Programmes and Policies* (London: The Johns Hopkins University Press, 1972).

Lekachman, Robert, *The Age of Keynes* (London: Allen Lane, The Penguin Press, 1966).

van Meerhaeghe, M. A. G., *International Economic Institutions*, 2nd edn (London: Longman, 1971).

Richards, J. H., *International Economic Institutions* (London: Holt, Rinehart and Winston, 1970).

IMF

Aliber, Robert Z., *The International Money Game* (New York: Macmillan, 1973).

Crockett, Andrew, *International Money: Issues and Analysis* (Sunbury-on-Thames: Nelson, 1977).

Grubel, Herbert G. *International Monetary Reform: Plans and Issues* (Palo Alto, Calif.: Stanford University Press, 1963).

Grubel, H. G., *The International Monetary System* (Harmondsworth: Penguin, 1972).

Solomon, Robert, *The International Monetary System, 1945–1976: An Insider's View* (London: Harper & Row, 1977).

Swoboda, Alexander K., *The Euro-dollar Market: An Interpretation,* Essays in International Finance No. 64 (Princeton, N. J.: Princeton University Press, 1968).

Tew, Brian, *The Evolution of the International Monetary System 1945–77* (London: Hutchinson, 1977).

Triffin, Robert, *Gold and the Dollar Crisis* (New Haven, Conn.: Yale University Press, 1960).

Willett, Thomas D., *Floating Exchange Rates and International Monetary Reform* (Washington DC: American Enterprise Institute for Public Policy Research, 1977).

Williamson, John, *The Failure of World Monetary Reform 1971–74* (Sunbury-on-Thames: Nelson, 1977).

Yeager, Leland B., *International Monetary Relations: Theory, History and Policy*, 2nd edn (New York: Harper and Row, 1975).

GATT

Curzon, Gerard, *Multilateral Commercial Diplomacy The General Agreement on Tariffs and Trade and its Impact on National Commercial Policies and Techniques* (London: Michael Joseph, 1965).

Dam, K. W., *The GATT, Law and International Economic Organization* (London: University of Chicago Press, 1970).

Evan, J. W., *The Kennedy Round in American Trade Policy* (Cambridge, Mass.: Harvard University Press, 1971).

Golt, Sidney, *Developing Countries in the GATT System*, Thames Essay No. 18 (London: Trade Policy Research Centre, 1978).

Golt, S., *The Gatt Negotiations 1973–79: The Closing Stage* (London: British-North American Association, 1978)

Kock, Karin, *International Trade Policy and the GATT 1947–67* (Stockholm: Almquist and Wicksell, 1969).

Preeg, E. H., *Traders and Diplomats, An Analysis of the Kennedy Round of Negotiations under the General Agreement on Tariffs and Trade* (Washington, DC: The Brookings Institution, 1970).

UNCTAD

Amacher, R. C., Haberler, G., and Willett, T. D., *Challenges to a Liberal International Economic Order* (Washington, DC: American Enterprise Institute for Public Policy Research, 1979).

Balassa, Bela, *The Structure of Protection in Developing Countries* (Baltimore, Md.: Johns Hopkins University Press, 1971).

Baldwin, Robert, *Beyond the Tokyo Round Negotiations*, Thames Essay No. 22 (London: Trade Policy Research Centre, 1979).

Brown, C. P., *The Political and Social Economy of Commodity Control* (London: Macmillan, 1980).

Denoon, David B. H., *The New International Economic Order: A US Response* (London: Macmillan, 1979).

Independent Commission on International Development Issues (The Brandt Commission) *North-South: A Programme for Survival* (London: Pan, 1980).

Johnson, D. Gale, *World Agriculture in Disarray* (London, Macmillan for the Trade Policy Research Centre, 1973)

Johnson, H. G., *Economic Policies Toward Less Developed Countries* (London, Allen & Unwin, 1967)

Kreuger, Anne, *Liberalisation Attempts and Consequences* (Cambridge, Mass., National Bureau of Economic Research, Ballinger, 1978)

MacBean, Alasdair and Balasubramanyam, V. N., *A Positive Approach to the International Economic Order* (London: British–North American Committee, Part I, 1978, Part II, 1979).

MacBean, Alasdair, and Balasubramanyam, V. N., *Meeting the Third World Challenge*, 2nd edn (London: Macmillan, 1978).

Prebisch, Raul, *Towards a New Trade Policy for Development*, Report by the Secretary General of UNCTAD (New York: UN, 1964).

UNCTAD, *Proceedings of the United Nations Conference on Trade and Development*, Nairobi (New York: UN, 1978).

UNCTAD, *Report of the United Nations Conference on Trade and Development on its Fifth Session*, TD/268 (Geneva: UNCTAD, 1979).

INTERNATIONAL COMMODITY ARRANGEMENTS

Adams, F. G., and Klein, S. A. (eds), *Stabilising World Commodity Markets: Analysis, Practice and Policy* (Lexington, Mass: Lexington Books, 1978).

Arndt, H. W., *et al.*, *The World Economic Crisis; a Commonwealth Perspective*, Report by a Group of Experts (London: Commonwealth Secretariat, 1980).

Bauer, Peter, *The Rubber Industry* (Cambridge, Mass.: Harvard University Press, 1948).

Behrman, Jere R., *International Commodity Agreements: An evaluation of the UNCTAD integrated commodity programme* (Washington, DC: Overseas Development Council, 1977).

Brown, C. P., *Primary Commodity Control* (Kuala Lumpur: Oxford University Press, 1975).

Coppock, Joseph D., *International Trade Instability* (Westmead, Hants.: Saxon House, 1977).

Corbet, Hugh, *Raw Materials: Beyond the Rhetoric of Commodity Power* (London: Trade Policy Research Centre, 1975).

Davis, J. S., *International Commodity Agreements: Hope, Illusion or Menace* (New York: Committee on International Economics Policy, 1947).

Harris, Stuart, Salmon, M., and Smith, Ben, *Analysis of Commodity Markets for Policy Purposes* (London: Trade Policy Research Centre, 1978).

MacBean, Alasdair I., *Export Instability and Economic Development* (London: Allen & Unwin, 1966).

Radetzki, Marian, *International Commodity Market Arrangements* (London: Hurst, 1970).

Rangarajan, L. N., *Commodity Conflict* (London: Croom Helm, 1978).

Rowe, J. W. F., *Primary Commodities in International Trade* (Cambridge: Cambridge University Press, 1965).

Sengupta, Arjun (ed.) *Commodities, Finance and Trade* (London: Pinter, 1980).

Thoburn, J. T., *Primary Commodity Exports and Economic Development: Theory, Evidence and a Study of Malaysia* (London: Wiley, 1977).

Yates, P. Lamartine, *Commodity Control: A Study of Primary Products* (London: Jonathan Cape, 1943).

OECD

Aubrey, H. G., *Atlantic Economic Co-operation: The Case of the OECD* (New York: Praeger, 1967).

Camps, M., *'First World' Relationships: The Role of the OECD* (New York: Atlantic Institute for International Affairs, 1975).

ECONOMIC INTEGRATION (EEC, CMEA, ETC.)

Balassa, B., *The Theory of Economic Integration* (Homewood, Ill.: Irwin, 1961).

Balassa, B., *European Economic Integration* (Amsterdam: North-Holland; New York: American Elsevier, 1975).

Cairncross, A. K., *Economic Policy for the European Community* (Kiel University Inst. für Weltwirtschaft, 1974).

Curzon, V., *The Essentials of Economic Integration* (London: Macmillan, 1974).

El-Agraa, A. M. (ed), *The Economics of the European Community* (London: Philip Allan, 1980).

Hewett, E. A., *Foreign Trade Prices in the CMEA* (London and New York: Cambridge University Press, 1974).

Holzman, F. D., *Foreign Trade Under Central Planning* (Cambridge Mass.: Harvard University Press, 1974).

Holzman, F. D., *International Trade Under Communism: Politics and Economics* (London: Macmillan, 1976).

Kaser, M., *Comecon: Integration Problems of the Planned Economies* (London: Oxford University Press, 1967).

Krause, L. B., *European Economic Integration and the United States* (Washington, DC: The Brookings Institution, 1968).

Krause, M. B., (ed), *The Economics of Integration* (London: Allen & Unwin, 1973).

Lipsey, R. G., *The Theory of Customs Unions: A General Equilibrium Analysis* (London: Weidenfeld & Nicolson, 1970).

Macklup, F. (ed.), *Economic Integration: Worldwide, Regional, Sectoral* (London: Macmillan, 1976).

Robson, P., *Economic Integration in Africa* (London: Allen & Unwin; Evanston, Ill.: Northwestern University Press, 1968).

Robson, P. (ed.), *International Economic Integration* (Harmondsworth: Penguin, 1972).

Robson, P. (ed.), *The Economics of International Integration* (London: Allen & Unwin, 1980).

Scitovsky, T., *Economic Theory and Western European Integration* (London: Allen & Unwin; reprinted 1962).

Swann, D., *The Economics of the Common Market*, 4th ed (London: Penguin, 1978).

WORLD BANK

Hayter, Teresa, *Aid as Imperialism* (London: Pelican, 1971).

Mason, Edward H., and Asher, R. E., *The World Bank Since Bretton Woods* (Washington, DC: The Brookings Institution, 1973).

USEFUL JOURNALS

Finance and Development
Foreign Affairs
Journal of Common Market Studies
Journal of World Trade Law
OECD Observer
The World Economy

INDEX

253